Ethnicity and Ethnic Conflict in the Post-Communist World

Ethnicity and Ethnic Conflict in the Post-Communist World

Ben Fowkes
Honorary Visiting Professor
University of North London

First published 2002 by
PALGRAVE
Houndmills, Basingstoke, Hampshire RG21 6XS and
175 Fifth Avenue, New York, N. Y. 10010
Companies and representatives throughout the world

PALGRAVE is the new global academic imprint of
St. Martin's Press LLC Scholarly and Reference Division and
Palgrave Publishers Ltd (formerly Macmillan Press Ltd).

ISBN 0-333-79256-4

This book is printed on paper suitable for recycling and made from fully managed and sustained forest sources.

A catalogue record for this book is available from the British Library.

Library of Congress Cataloging-in-Publication Data
Fowkes, Ben.
    Ethnicity and ethnic conflict in the post-communist world / Ben Fowkes.
        p. cm.
    Includes bibliographical references and index.
    ISBN 0–333–79256–4
        1. Ethnicity–Europe, Eastern. 2. Ethnicity–Former Soviet republics.
    3. Europe, Eastern–Ethnic relations. 4. Former Soviet republics–Ethnic
    relations. 5. Europe, Eastern–Politics and government–1989– I. Title.
DJK26.F69 2002
305.8'00947–dc21   2001056128

10   9   8   7   6   5   4   3   2   1
11   10 09 08 07 06 05 04 03 02

Printed and bound in Great Britain by
Antony Rowe Ltd, Chippenham, Wiltshire

Contents

Preface

Ethnic conflict cannot be other than mysterious. Human beings all belong to the same species; if they are to be divided there are plenty of other ways of forming rival groups. Moreover, ethnically based divisions go against a major trend of modern times towards increasing contact between ethnic groups and growing ethnic mixture. There are many non-ethnic sources of conflict, arising, for instance, from class, religion, profession or region. Yet in most areas of the world they have been completely overshadowed since the early 1980s by ethnic conflict.

Since the beginning of the 1990s my main research interest has been the transition from Communism in Central and Eastern Europe and the lands of the former Soviet Union. When I started working in this field I assumed, in common with many other students of the subject, that ethnicity and nationalism were important, certainly, but that material questions and conflicts took precedence, and that if matters of ideology came to the fore this was usually in the form of a struggle between Communism and its opponents. How the ethnic groups lined up appeared to be of subordinate significance.

The course taken by events in the 1990s has gradually enforced a different view, making ethnicity and nationalism the central issues, if not everywhere, at least in very many areas. In my previous books on this subject I worked on a broad and inclusive canvas; here, in contrast, the theme is narrowed down to the area of ethnic conflict. I have endeavoured to deal with all relevant cases to make possible comparisons across countries. My concern has been, above all, to explain the presence or absence of ethnic conflict in particular situations – in other words to come closer to this mysterious problem, though hardly to solve it.

It might be appropriate at this point to give some indication of the general argument I hope to pursue in the course of this study. Nations, I claim, are not inventions of the twentieth century, at least not in Europe (Central Asia is another story, which will be taken up in the text). Nations are founded on pre-existing ethnic group solidarity, the nature and extent of which has to be a matter for concrete historical investigation rather than arbitrary assumptions driven by sociological theory. After outlining the background, I proceed to discuss the ethnic conflicts of the post-Communist era in detail. Ethnic conflict, I show, is not the inevitable result of the rise of ethnic awareness; it emerges under conditions determined by rivalry for material resources in which, precisely because of the existence of ethnic solidarity, the contending parties identify themselves as parts of an ethnic group. Ethnic conflicts often display common features, which are outlined in detail in Chapter 7, such as rival historical claims to the same territory, religious antagonisms, mutual fear, and the involvement of neighbouring states. Most of them are present in each case in varying and unique combinations.

This makes it hard to establish a firm typology. One may, however, tentatively identify three main types of post-Communist ethnic conflict: (i) very severe, likely to develop into civil war, between rival ethnic groups of similar size with overlapping claims to the same territory (most conflicts in former Yugoslavia fall into this category); (ii) moderately severe, but potentially military, between irredentist groups with aspirations to separate status and states holding their territory together (many former Soviet conflicts fall into this category, while their degree of severity has varied according to the readiness of outside forces, usually Russian, to intervene); and (iii) mild, fought out politically without the use of armed force, and soluble, arising from the claims of small ethnic groups to a degree of separate status (the Gagauzi in Moldova are a good example).

Because ethnicity is of historical origin, it is also transitory. So too is ethnic conflict. The outbreak of large-scale ethnic conflicts in the 1990s is a temporary setback to the processes of homogenization and integration which have been taking place ever since different peoples came into contact with each other, and are accelerated powerfully by the forces of globalization. The individual cases examined in this book all show a tendency in the direction of peaceful settlement, after much bloodshed. In a study which aims to be up to date, it is tempting to slide imperceptibly from evaluation of current situations to prediction of the future. Events will no doubt falsify a certain amount of what I say in dealing with the possibility of renewed ethnic conflict in places such as Kosovo and Macedonia, but that is unavoidable – as an option it is better than persistent fence-straddling.

There are certain terminological peculiarities in my book, above all a tendency to talk of 'ethnic groups' rather than 'nations'. The reason for this choice is simple. 'Ethnic group' (or *ethnie*) is a portmanteau term that allows one to side-step the distinction that used to be made between 'nations' and 'nationalities'. In the nineteenth century it was claimed that the former already had their own states, or could legitimately aspire to form them, while the latter had never possessed states and had a weaker practical claim to them, partly because they were too small or scattered, and partly because they were located in inconvenient places. The events of the late twentieth century have shown that any ethnic group with the will and power to do so can found its own state, provided that the international circumstances are favourable. Thus an ethnic group is a potential nation.

The nature of my theme means that I have dealt very briefly with areas where significant ethnic conflicts have not arisen (or are unlikely to arise). Conversely, and inevitably, the history of the former Yugoslavia bulks large. I have, however, refrained deliberately from any detailed consideration of war crimes and atrocities committed there during the 1990s. The International War Crimes Tribunal at The Hague is certainly doing a useful job, if one believes that criminals should be punished, but its deliberations have not helped us to establish what is really important: not 'What sort of crimes have been committed and who is responsible?' but 'How do people get into a position where they commit, or suffer, atrocities simply because they belong to a particular ethnic group?' I have tried to give some answers to the latter question.

I would like to thank my editors at Palgrave for their patience and their care, which has made it possible for me to avoid at least the most egregious errors and inconsistencies. I would also like to thank my former colleagues at the University of North London for allowing me generous quantities of sabbatical leave.

I dedicate this book to past students and present friends.

BEN FOWKES

List of Abbreviations

AO	*Avtonomnaia Oblast'* (Autonomous Region)
ARF	Armenian Revolutionary Federation
ASSR	Autonomous Soviet Socialist Republic
BBOstIS	*Berichte des Bundesinstituts für Ostwissenschaftliche und Internationale Studien*
CAM	*Central Asia Monitor*
CAS	*Central Asian Survey*
CEET	*Communist Economies and Economic Transformation*
CEMOTI	*Cahiers d'études sur la Meditérranée orientale et le monde turco-iranien*
CIS	Commonwealth of Independent States
CMRS	*Cahiers du monde Russe et Soviétique*
CPCS	*Communist and Post-Communist Studies: An International Interdisciplinary Journal*
DPS	Dvizhenie za Prava i Svobodi (Movement for Rights and Freedoms)
E-AS	*Europe-Asia Studies*
EEPS	*East European Politics and Societies*
EEQ	*East European Quarterly*
EI2	*The Encyclopaedia of Islam,* New Edition, Prepared by a Number of Leading Orientalists, 9 vols (Leiden: E. J. Brill, 1960–97)
EO	*Etnograficheskoe Obozrenie*
ERS	*Ethnic and Racial Studies*
FADURK	Fund for the Accelerated Development of the Less Developed Republics and Kosovo
FSN	Frontul Salvării Nationale (National Salvation Front)
FYROM	Former Yugoslav Republic of Macedonia
GASSR	Gorskaia Avtonomnaia Sotsialisticheskaia Sovetskaia Respublika (Mountain Autonomous Socialist Soviet Republic)
HDZ	Hrvatska Demokratska Zajednica (Croatian Democratic Union)

HHSH	Hayots Hamazgayin Sharzhum (Pan-Armenian National Movement)
HOS	Hrvatske Oružane Snage (Croatian Armed Forces)
HSD-SMS	Hnutí pro samozprávnou demokracii – Spolecnost pro Morava a Slezsko (Movement for Self-governing Democracy – Association for Moravia and Silesia)
HSP-1861	Hrvatska Stranka Prava – 1861 (Croatian Party of Right – 1861)
HVO	Hrvatsko Vijeće Obrane (Croatian Defence Council)
HZDS	Hnutí za demokratické Slovensko (Movement for a Democratic Slovakia)
JMH	*Journal of Modern History*
JNA	Jugoslovenska Narodna Armija (Yugoslav People's Army)
LCY	League of Communists of Yugoslavia
LDK	Lidhja Demokratike e Kosovës (Democratic League of Kosovo)
MBO	Muslimanska Bošnjačka Organizacija (Muslim Bosniak Organization)
MD	*Le Monde Diplomatique*
MDF	Magyar Demokrata Fórum (Hungarian Democratic Forum)
NKAO	Nagorno-Karabakhskaia Autonomnaia Oblast' (Nagornyi Karabagh Autonomous Region)
NP	*Nationalities Papers*
OE	*Osteuropa*
OSCE	Organization for Security and Cooperation in Europe
PDP (=PPD)	Partija za Demokratski Prosperitet (Party for Democratic Prosperity
PDSH (in Albania)	Partia Demokratike e Shqipërisë (Democratic Party of Albania)
PDSH (in Macedonia)	Partia Demokratike Shqiptare (Democratic Party of Albanians)
PPD (=PDP)	Partia e Prosperitet Demokratik (Party for Democratic Prosperity)
PMR	Pridnestrovskaia Moldavskaia Respublika (Trandniestr Moldavian Republic)

PRM	Partidul România Mare (Greater Romania Party)
P-SGE	*Post-Soviet Geography and Economics*
PSSH	Partia Socialiste e Shqipërisë (Socialist Party of Albania)
PUNR	Partidul Unităţii Naţionale Române (Party of Romanian National Unity)
RFE/RLRR	*Radio Free Europe/Radio Liberty Research Report*
RMMM	*Revue du Monde Muslime et de la Méditerranée*
RSFSR	Russian Soviet Federative Socialist Republic
SANU	Srpska Akademija Nauka i Umetnosti (Serbian Academy of Sciences and Arts)
SDA	Stranka Demokratske Akcije (Party of Democratic Action)
SDS	Săjuz na Demokratichnite Sili (Union of Democratic Forces) (Bulgaria)
SDS	Srpska Demokratska Stranka (Serbian Democratic Party)
SDSM	Socijaldemokratski Sojuz na Makedonija (Social Democratic Alliance of Macedonia)
SNS	Slovenská Národna Strana (Slovak National Party)
SOE	*Südosteuropa*
SR	*Slavic Review*
SSR	Soviet Socialist Republic
TTKB	*Türk Tarih Kurumu Belleten*
UÇK	Ushtria Çlirimtare e Kosovës (Kosovo Liberation Army)
UDMR	Uniunea Democrată Maghiară din România (Hungarian Democratic Union of Romania)
VMRO-DPMNE	Vnatreshna Makedonska Revolucionerna Organizacija-Demokratska Partija za Makedonsko Nacionalno Edinstvo (Internal Macedonian Revolutionary Organization – Democratic Party for Macedonian National Unity)
VPN	Verejnost proti násiliu (Public Against Violence)
ZRS	Združenie Robotníkov Slovenska (Association of Workers of Slovakia)

1
Introduction

On theories of Nationalism and Ethnicity

> No matter how many times a country has been conquered, subjugated and even destroyed by enemies, there is always a certain national core preserved in its character, and, before you are aware of it, a long-familiar popular phenomenon has emerged. (Goethe, 1998: 139)

> Nationalism is not the awakening of the nation to self-consciousness; it invents nations where they do not exist. (Gellner, 1964: 169)

The quotations above reflect two opposing views of the nation and nationalism. Their implications need to be examined. But before doing this, we must first introduce the concept of an ethnic group and examine its relationship to the nation. Ethnicity and nationhood, though closely related, are distinct. Ethnicity is a set of features characteristic of a given ethnic group. It has long been disputed whether they are inseparably part of the human character (this has been described as the 'primordialist' view), or constructed by elite groups for economic and political reasons (this has been described as the 'constructionist' view). Various views intermediate between these two extremes have also been put forward.

The 'primordialist' view is the intuitive one, as expressed by J. W. Von Goethe in the first epigraph to this chapter. 'Primordialists' think that some at least of the features of ethnicity are present objectively in the sense that they can be observed from outside.[1] The members of a primordial ethnic group, which Anthony Smith has described as an 'ethnic category', may not be aware of their own ethnic character and yet they may still remain part of the group (Smith, 1991:

20–1). In his seminal work, *Ethnic Origins of Nations*, published in 1986, Smith listed six necessary ethnic attributes. These can be summarized as: a collective name; a common myth of descent; a shared history; a distinctive shared culture, comprising language and/or religion and/or institutions and/or other cultural features; an association with a specific territory; and finally a sense of ethnic solidarity, in other words a recognition of each other as members of the same ethnic group. Smith's view in 1986 was that all these features had to be present to establish the existence of ethnicity (Smith, 1986: 15). Later on he abandoned this insistence, arguing instead that: 'the more [of these attributes] they have the more they approximate to the ideal type of an *ethnie*' (Smith, 1991: 21). But the individual's own subjective consciousness of belonging to an ethnic community, in other words the sense of ethnic solidarity referred to above, is the most important feature of all.

'Constructionists', in contrast, deny that any of these objective ethnic attributes is of any significance. In 1969, the Norwegian theorist, Fredrik Barth, rejected the traditional view of ethnicity, replacing it with an insistence on the 'critical question' of 'ethnic boundary maintenance'. For him, it was the 'ethnic boundary' that defined the group, and not the 'cultural stuff that it encloses' (Barth, 1969: 15). This view was developed further by Joanne Nagel, who claims that 'the individual carries a portfolio of ethnic identities' for 'various situations' to be played out before 'various audiences'. Ethnic identities are simply 'constructed out of the material of language, religion, culture, appearance or regionality', and the meanings of 'particular ethnic boundaries are continuously negotiated, revised or revitalised' (Nagel, 1994: 154). In one extreme version, ethnic identity does not exist, or at least should not be mentioned: 'It would be better, in dealing with modern societies, to speak of religious or linguistic communities, rather than *ethnies*' (Dunn, 1996: 55).

From a more moderate constructionist viewpoint, the elements in the ethnic 'portfolio' are never chosen at random, and the 'portfolio' itself is only present in cases of either pronounced ethnic mixture, or earlier in history – in other words at earlier stages of development when, it is assumed, ethnic identities are not yet fixed. 'Ethnic groups' says E. E. Roosens (1989: 156), 'are not merely a completely arbitrary construct: there is always a minimum of incontestable and non-interpretable facts' available: 'The reality is very elastic, but not totally arbitrary.' We shall deal in Chapter 2 with the process by which ethnic identities of this kind have become fixed in modern times in Eastern Europe and Eurasia.[2] We shall find that in the region under discussion,

Roosens' view dovetails far better with the observed historical facts than does the strictly constructionist approach. In contrast to ethnicity, which is arguably not dependent on conscious awareness, 'nationhood', or the sense of belonging to a particular nation, is always conscious. It presupposes ethnic consciousness but goes beyond it. Nationalism is one further stage beyond nationhood.[3] Essentially, it is a state of mind, the feeling that one's own nation is somehow more important than others and therefore deserves some kind of special, favoured treatment. This usually finds expression in agitation for the establishment of a nation-state, or, as Michael Hechter has put it, 'collective action designed to render the boundaries of the nation congruent with those of its governance unit' (Hechter, 2000: 7). In one view, nationalism is 'rooted in, and is an expression of, ethnic attachments' (Jenkins, 1995: 371). This last point has been energetically controverted by Eric Hobsbawm, who writes, 'nationalism and ethnicity are different, indeed, non-comparable, concepts. Nationalism is a recent political philosophy, while ethnicity expresses primordial group identity' (Hobsbawm, 1992: 4). Whether one can speak of a non-ethnically based nationalism is a doubtful question, at least in the modern European context.[4] Attempts made in the Communist world to create such an overarching nationalism on a territorial rather than an ethnic basis have generally foundered, and in any case the examples in question (Czechoslovak and Yugoslav) are still in a sense ethnically based, but on several ethnic groups rather than one. No doubt there were some Czechoslovaks and Yugoslavs who internalized the formal, territorially-based definition of the nation, but the majority view in both cases was ethnically skewed: Germans and Hungarians were not seen as part of the 'Czechoslovak nation', nor were Albanians or Hungarians seen as part of the 'Yugoslav nation'. The former was by definition the state of the Czechs and Slovaks, the latter the state of the South Slavs.

Conversely, where the ethnic basis for a nationalist movement has been absent, it has tended to fall at the first hurdle. This has been the modern fate of attempts to separate out Moravians from Czechs, or Ruthenes from Ukrainians. The heyday of Moravian territorial patriotism was the nineteenth century; it was soon superseded by Czech nationalism. There was a brief resurgence of Moravian autonomism in 1992, when it seemed to offer an alternative to the uncomfortable choice between retaining Czechoslovakia and setting up two separate states for Czechs and Slovaks. But it did not last. Similarly, the Ruthenian movement for separation from Ukraine was at its strongest in 1992 when the newly independent state was just taking its first steps, but little has been heard of it since then. In both cases the aspiring nationalist propagandists simply did not have enough material to work with.[5]

The distinction between 'ethnicity' and 'nationality' is also a distinction between disciplines. Anthropologists (or 'ethnologists') tend to talk about ethnicity, while political scientists and historians tend to talk about nations and nationality. This usually corresponds, though not always, to a difference in the magnitude (and the remoteness) of the object under investigation. The anthropologist's subject of study was traditionally the tribe, which was in practice a small ethnic group located in an undeveloped and remote part of the world. In recent times, however, anthropologists have interested themselves in developed, urbanized Western societies, and therefore in larger ethnic groups. Political scientists, in contrast, have always concerned themselves with the nation. It will be claimed here, as indicated above, that there are not just two disciplines but rather two different entities involved.

The ethnic group (or, if one prefers to use a single word, the Greek *ethnos*, or alternatively the French *ethnie*) is a constituent of the nation. A nation may consist of several closely related ethnic groups, each of which has decided tacitly to ignore the small differences that separate them ethnically (as was temporarily the case for the Czech–Slovak coalition that made up Czechoslovakia, or, equally temporarily, the Croat–Serb–Slovene coalition that made up Yugoslavia). It may cut across ethnic groups. In both these cases the resultant formation is likely to be unstable. In the area that concerns us in this study (an important reservation) a nation is more likely to be based on a single ethnic group: as Anthony Smith puts it 'nations require ethnic cores if they are to survive' (1986: 212). There is nothing permanent about these ethnic groups (though they sometimes last a very long time). *Ethnies* appear and disappear in the course of history, and one of the aims of the nation-state is to fix them semi-permanently. Once this has been done, other ethnic groups can be added to the core, either through conquest and absorption or through the integration of migrants. As a result, the modern nation often looks like 'an amalgam of historical communities which possessed a fairly clear sense of separate identity in the past but have now been brought together' (Birch, 1989: 8).

There are many theories of the nation and of ethnicity, often derived in different circumstances and on the basis of widely divergent examples, and it is not my intention to add to them. What I shall do instead is examine briefly the major theories, and estimate the extent to which they have been applied to the Central and Eastern European and Eurasian environments.

The theory of ethnicity that prevailed in the final decades of the Soviet Union, the most prominent advocate of which was Iulian V. Bromlei, saw the *ethnos* as a fixed and permanent entity determined by material and social factors and objectively present irrespective of the conscious wishes of the members of the ethnic group in question. As he and his collaborators wrote in 1975, 'the *ethnos* is a stable aggregate of persons, historically established on a given territory, possessing permanent characteristics of language and culture, recognising their unity and their divergence from other similar formations and expressing it by an ethnonym' (Bromlei *et al.* 1975: 11). This has aptly been described as a 'reification of the *ethnos*'. It has been seen as having had fateful consequences, because it allowed history to be rewritten in terms of permanently existing ethnic groups with fixed territories and boundaries (Berolowitch, 1998: 137).

In fact, the sequence of events was the reverse: Bromlei's theory reflected current Soviet practice, as well as the current Soviet situation, in which ethnic identity stubbornly continued to exist despite the initial expectation that ethnic differences would gradually decline with the growth of a Soviet nation (Banks, 1996: 22). However, one could well claim that what lies behind both Soviet practice and Bromlei's theory is Josef Stalin's (and also V. I. Lenin's) conception of nationality. There are unmistakable similarities between the definition of the *ethnos* given above by Bromlei, with its stress on the need to possess a territory, and to be marked out by permanent characteristics of language and culture, and the definition of a nation advanced by Stalin in 1913, in a pamphlet written at Lenin's request: 'a nation is a historically constituted, stable community of people, formed on the basis of a common language, territory, economic life, and psychological makeup manifested in a common culture' (Stalin, 1953: 307). The only difference between the respective formulations of Bromlei and Stalin is the latter's requirement that a nation possess a 'common economic life', which Bromlei and his collaborators no doubt excluded because the ethnic groups in question were now located on the territory of the Soviet Union, where economic differences between ethnic groups had allegedly vanished by the 1970s. The Soviet leader, Leonid Brezhnev, made the official view clear in 1972: 'the problem of equalising the levels of economic development of the national republics has been in the main solved' (Holubychny, 1973: 25).

The view taken of these matters in the West has been very different, particularly towards the end of the twentieth century. Here, ethnicity is treated as flexible, not at all fixed, and liable to vanish and return abruptly. The tendency in most recent Western anthropological work has been to see ethnicity (and nationality) as invented, or imagined, and historically contingent. Ernest Gellner's view, as indicated in the second epigraph to this chapter, is representative. A roughly similar line is taken by Benedict Anderson. For him, nations are 'imagined political communities', which are imagined as 'both inherently limited and sovereign'. But he differs from Gellner in recognizing these communities as genuine creations, rather than pure inventions with no real basis (Anderson, 1991: 6). Anderson's work is aimed at explaining in general historical terms how and why this 'creation of nations' came about. There are many fine insights in *Imagined Communities* into the factors that have stimulated national consciousness in recent times: the rise of 'print-capitalism'; the administrative use of the vernacular language; the restrictions placed on the promotion of indigenous civil servants from periphery to metropolis; the frequency of 'administrative pilgrimages' within colonial units, and the construction of census categories and maps.

All these points are developed in a worldwide context, and they are intended to apply universally. They are worked out in detail by Anderson for Latin America and South East Asia alone. Nevertheless, the closer look at Eastern Europe and Eurasia which follows confirms at least some of his insights. As we shall see in Chapter 4, census categories and maps defined previously fluid ethnic groups, while state-promoted language policies and the spread of vernacular newspapers promoted national consciousness.

Determinants of ethnicity

As noted earlier, there are many determinants of ethnicity, including language, culture, religion, dress, housing, and physical characteristics. In addition to this list, Stevan Harrell has suggested that we should also pay attention to 'kinds of behaviour that communicate meanings concerning ethnic group membership and relations', such as 'food, marriage patterns, rituals, and customs generally' (Harrell, 1995: 98). But it is above all language that has played the pre-eminent role in determining ethnic group membership in Europe, in contrast with Latin America, where 'language was never even an issue' for the early nationalist movements (Anderson, 1991: 47). Our present topic, namely the former Communist area, is constituted, geographically speaking, by Central and Eastern Europe and Eurasia. In Eurasia, language has perhaps been less important than culture and religion, but its importance has increased as the twentieth century progressed. But for Europe 'the existence of ethnic groups is almost exclusively marked by language distinctions' (Haarmann 1986: 40).

The members of a given ethnic group do not need to be fluent in the language they have adopted as a badge of identity: George De Vos (1995: 23) notes that 'ethnicity is frequently related more to the symbolism of a separate language than to its actual use'. If the converse also holds – that is to say, if language distinctions create ethnic groups – there is no bar in principle to ever-growing ethnic fragmentation. This thought was first expressed by K. W. Deutsch in the 1960s (1968: 605): 'The development of modern philology and modern education has made it possible to revive, modernise and utilise any ancient language ... At the same time, new ways of speech are formed through the changing and splitting up of all languages into new accents and idioms ... So far as the linguistic factor is concerned, the nationalistic disintegration of mankind may go on with hardly any limit.' He found the prospect distressing, though one could argue that a multiplicity of ethnic distinctions makes for cultural richness.

One of the most interesting insights of recent work on ethnicity has been the recognition that its determinants, including language, can be used very flexibly. The example of Québec has been quoted in this context. The national movement there was remarkable for its flexible deployment of the cultural bases of ethnicity. There was a shift in the mid-1950s from a religious definition of the Québécois to a linguistic definition in terms of the use of the French language; this also implied turning away from traditional nationalism with its glorification of rural life, conservative opposition to state intervention and stress on the spiritual, Catholic mission of the nation, to an approach which accepts and makes use of modernizing and industrializing trends (Guindon, 1988: 50–51).

The same point has been made for Eastern Europe by Gerlachus Duijzings (1997: 214–5): 'Ethnic identity,' he says, 'is not fixed ... but conjunctural and negotiated.' Katherine Verdery has introduced a further nuance by distinguishing between greater and lesser degrees of flexibility: 'Particular historical circumstances make group identities more or less malleable' (1996: 37). Identities, in Verdery's view, are more rigid in states with a long history of nation-building (she does not specify these: perhaps one should assume that the states of Western Europe are meant), and less so in the Middle East and South East Asia (the point clearly applies to Central Asia too), because in the former case the nation-state has a long period of existence to look back on, and nation-states *create* people who have a single fixed identity. In the Yugoslav case, the region contained people of different ethnicities before the new states existed (the implication here is that no history of nation-building preceded these new states); afterwards people were forced to choose a single identity even if they were of mixed origin. 'Ethnic cleansing,' adds Verdery (1996: 38), 'also means the extermination of alternative identity choices.' But she goes much further than this. She claims that ethnicity is a product of the state, and not its precursor: 'national identities do not develop from ethnic identities: rather the national identities create the frame within which ethnicity *qua* difference acquires social significance' (Verdery, 1996: 47).

This is a strong assertion, and a reversal of what has normally been assumed to be the order of events. It can only be justified if one considers that the absence of a fixed, inflexible ethnicity implies the absence of any ethnic identity whatever. But in fact, in the twentieth century, this absence was more often accompanied by the presence of multiple ethnic identities. Thus, to revert to the Yugoslav case, many Yugoslavs may well have had multiple identities (as being, simultaneously, for example, 'Yugoslavs' and 'Croats', 'Serbs', 'Slovenes' or 'Macedonians') but it does not follow from this that the new states of Croatia, Slovenia or Macedonia created Croat, Slovene or Macedonian ethnic identities that did not exist before.

The prehistory of ethnicity: continuities and discontinuities

Attempts to analyze the origins of ethnic groups (their 'ethnogenesis') are bedevilled by the continuous battle over ethnicity. This is hard fought on all sides. Many theoretical arguments are marshalled, and much specific evidence is deployed. On the one hand, there have been constant attempts on the part of historians and national propagandists to read back the existence of particular ethnic groups into the remote past; and on the other, there are repeated counter-attacks from sociologists of the school of thought associated with Ernest Gellner, who have a tendency to deny the existence of ethnicity altogether, or treat it as an invention of present-day 'print-capitalism' (to use the remarkable phrase coined by Benedict Anderson)[6] or a product of 'nationalist historiography' and the 'confusion between states and nations' (Kedourie, 1960: 73). It might be possible to gain a clearer view of these issues if we return to the contemporary documents to see how the people of the time viewed their own and others' ethnic and national characteristics. Some historians have indeed tried to do this.

But difficulties abound. The further back one goes, the more ambiguous and misleading are the references to ethnicity in the sources. Nationalist historians have 'corrected' these texts by reading them in a present-orientated fashion. This approach is mistaken, as it does violence to the historical evidence. Yet it is equally unsafe to assume that we are dealing here merely with external labels that served to conceal a humanity that was either universal or aspired to be so. One school of historical philologists inclines to the view that this universality did in fact exist in prehistoric times, when *Homo sapiens* first emerged. In this view, first launched by Clement Greenberg, the spread of the human species over the world led to differentiation. Different tribes emerged, and what was originally a single language (or perhaps three languages[7], or indeed fifteen, using an alternative classification (Greenberg, 1987: 337) became differentiated into thousands of mutually incomprehensible tongues.[8]

Of course, all this happened (assuming that it did happen in this way) long before the beginning of recorded time. The process of subdivision was already complete 5000 years ago. Humanity has been divided since then into *groups*, varying from small to large, and these groups have always been defined by a number of features, such as language, kinship, descent or imagined descent from a common ancestor, religious observance, and socioeconomic situation. Language was always an important component of this complex of distinguishing marks, because communication is impossible without mutual comprehension, which, above the most basic level, is only achieved through the use of words.

In classical antiquity, the formation of great empires, in particular the Roman Empire, in the second and first centuries BCE, had as one of its consequences the reduction of linguistic variety through the adoption of no more than two languages, Latin and Greek, as media of written communication in the Mediterranean world. A similar development took place further east with the formation of the Persian Empire. Within Western and Central Europe this situation lasted for roughly 1500 years. In Eastern and South Eastern Europe the arrival of the Slavs and the medieval development of Church Slavonic as a *lingua franca* added a third language.[9] Later on, at the close of the Middle Ages, the decline of the universal languages and the raising of local dialects to the level of languages used by sophisticated and educated people made them the touchstone of ethnicity, at least within Europe. Outside that continent, in the Middle East and Central Asia, the universal languages of Arabic, Persian, Ottoman Turkish and Chaghatai Turkic continued to be used for all written communications into and beyond the nineteenth century. This fact naturally hindered the growth of ethnic consciousness.

One distinction it is essential to make in trying to disentangle the historical evidence is that between the history of an ethnic group and the history of the territory which gave it its name. There are very few cases where ethnic groups have occupied a given territory continuously since their formation. Moreover, these cases are usually marked by an absence of ethnic conflict, which emerges from rival claims by ethnic groups to a particular territory, because it is claimed that one side or the other is not truly indigenous. Otherwise, and this is true most of the time, a region's ethnic past and its territorial past are completely different entities. But the temptation to identify the two is not always resisted when a particular territory is chosen as the subject of investigation.

The earlier history of Kosovo, or Kosova, is a case in point. Noel Malcolm, author of the recent book *Kosovo: A Short History*, inevitably regards his work as having a specific and defined subject, namely the history of 'Kosovo'. He is, however, forced to admit at the outset that his use of the term 'Kosovo' is arbitrary. Having noted the multiplicity of terms used to describe the area in the past, he adds: 'In order to hold some of these confusions at bay, a simple rule will be adopted in this book. The term "Kosovo" will refer to the entire geographical region' (Malcolm, 1998: 4).[10]

This is an elegant way of avoiding the problem. But it does not solve it.[11] The place-name 'Kosovo' does not occur historically before the famous battle of 1389, and even in 1389 it occurs only in the sense that a battle took place on the plain of Kosovo, or Kosovo Polje, a specific geographical location, not a political or administrative region. Moreover, after 1389 the word almost completely disappears from the sources. With one minor exception[12], none of Kosovo's successive rulers, whether they were Bulgarians, Byzantines, Serbs or Ottomans, recognized the region as a meaningful unit. In 1879, the Ottoman authorities finally set up a vilayet under the name of Kosovo, though this too did not correspond to the present-day province, being far larger in extent (it covered most of Macedonia as well).[13] The existence of an entity called 'Kosovo' was also ignored by the Albanian rebels of 1878 who set up the League of Prizren. Its main objective was to unite all four Albanian provinces (*vilayets*) into a single unit, which would then be granted autonomy by the Ottoman rulers.[14] In other words, for Albanians, Kosovo was simply the north-eastern part of Albania. For Serbs it was 'Old Serbia'.

Noel Malcolm's 'History of Kosovo' is in fact a version of the past, in the same sense as a 'History of Serbia' or a 'History of Albania' covering the same region would be.[15] Its purpose was clear: to provide scholarly ammunition to the opponents of Serbian control over the province. These comments are not intended to detract from Mr Malcolm's remarkable achievement in mastering the wide range of sources needed to write such a book, and in presenting them eloquently and clearly to the English-language reader. There is an interesting analogy to be found in recent studies of the ancient history of the Middle East: the upsurge of Palestinian revolt in Israel and the occupied territories had its effect in stimulating the rise of a school of ancient historians who saw the history of the region in terms not of a 'History of Israel' based on a reading of the Bible, but of a 'History of Palestine' based on ignoring the Bible in favour of the archaeological evidence (Whitelam, 1996).

This is not the only version of history in which a region's ethnic past has been identified with its territorial past. Noel Malcolm takes his place in a long series of historians who have engaged in the process of nation-building, particularly during the nineteenth century. The need to create a specific national history, which was felt so strongly by all the newly independent nations in the 1990s, has produced many fresh examples of this approach.[16] One, chosen at random, is a work produced in 1997 which includes the Greek settlements in the Crimea in the second century BCE as part of the history of Ukraine (Smolii, 1997: 15). We shall meet many more as we examine the roots of ethnic antagonism in the later part of this book.

It can be admitted that there is no single 'truth' about the past, but that does not give the historian *carte blanche*; the names of countries and territories are historically loaded, and to use them inappropriately is to distort the record. It is surely better to adopt a more inclusive view of history, in which the multiplicity of possible outcomes is recognized, than to see oneself as contributing to the creation of a national history (or a 'national myth') for any particular ethnic group, whether it be

Kosovo Albanian, Serbian, Ukrainian, or indeed Greek. Claims to exclusive national possession of particular areas of Eastern Europe have no historical foundation. No ethnic group can claim that it was 'there first'; not only does the mixture of conquest and reconquest stretch back to the beginning of recorded time, the 'purity' of each ethnic group has been to a greater or lesser degree diluted over time by intermarriage and by shifts in ethnic allegiance from one generation to the next.

Where groups with the objective characteristics of ethnicity did exist in pre-industrial times, the people concerned were not necessarily aware of this at a conscious level. There is some evidence that in Montenegro (Hrabak, 1987: 41–68) and in northern Albania (Bartl, 1978: 27–69) clan membership was more significant than ethnic group membership until the nineteenth century, or even, in the Albanian case, the early twentieth century.[17] Moreover, ethnic groups lived much of their lives under misleading names. After all, ethnonyms are usually first applied by outsiders; the members of the ethnic group in question, who referred to themselves until then in their own tongue as 'us', or 'human beings', or 'the people of the earth', or, more romantically, 'the sons of the eagle', have then to decide whether to accept the designation.

That curious minority, the Vlachs of the Balkans, for example, were on the face of it Romanians ('Wallachians') but in fact the name was also applied to Slavs who shared the same pastoral, nomadic life as the Romanian shepherds. The Orthodox refugees who settled on the border (*krajina*) between Habsburg and Ottoman territory, and who are in part the ancestors of the Krajina Serbs who lived in Croatia until driven out recently, were also described officially as Vlachs and given privileged military status under that name (the Habsburg ruler Ferdinand II issued a 'Statute of the Vlachs' for them in 1630). To apply the term Vlach to someone, therefore, was to say that they were either nomads or free peasant-soldiers. It did not imply a definitive conclusion about their ethnic group. Similarly, a 'Saxon' was a miner, and a 'Greek' was sometimes a merchant and sometimes an adherent of the Greek Orthodox Church, who could well have been ethnically a Serb (Sundhaussen 1993: 237).

While ethnicity seems to have existed in the pre-industrial past, nationhood did not. There are certainly cases where one is tempted to read back the modern nation into remote eras. Some modern nations have long written traditions. But in the absence of a continuous state existence (which is true of all the cases we have to deal with in this book) there are breaks in continuity which a nationally-inclined history can only deal with by passing hurriedly over awkward facts. These breaks in continuity have been stressed by R. G. Suny in his studies of Armenia and Georgia. Of ancient Armenia, he says: 'it should not be seen as approaching a nation-state in the modern sense' (1993: 8) In Georgia, too: 'the idea of a national and political collectivity had disappeared by the seventeenth century. The country was near extinction' (Suny, 1994: 51–3). These comments have a more general bearing. They tend to lessen the force of the classical nineteenth century distinction between nations 'with history' and nations 'without history', which has often worked to the disadvantage of the latter group. Rulers of states and leaders of political movements have tended to dismiss the claims of the nations 'without history', and privilege those of nations which can point to a continuous historical record. Much of Suny's work on Armenia and Georgia has been an attempt to even up the balance; there is a parallel in some recent work on Greek history, which has emphasized the lack of continuity between the Greek past and the Greek present, and the 'constructed' and 'modern' character of the Greek ethnic group. According to Michael Herzfeld, Greek cultural continuity across time was constructed by nineteenth century Greek scholars. Only after the Greek nation-state had already been established did the process of 'justifying the existence of Greek nationhood' begin (1982: 11–13).

Notwithstanding these cautionary observations, we must still admit that there are considerable differences between the respective historical trajectories of the nations that make up the twenty-first century world. For the present subject, which is the post-Communist landmass, there is a clear division between areas of Western, Christian tradition and those of Eastern, initially pagan, subsequently Buddhist or Muslim tradition. We can illustrate the point by taking an initial glance at the area to the south of the Caucasian ridge, located between the Black Sea and the Caspian Sea.[18] The Armenians and Georgians constitute 'historic nations', with an existence stretching back at least 1500 years, based on a number of elements we shall examine in detail later (in which religious traditions occupy a large place). Despite this, continuity is still an issue. For the Armenians, thanks to successive invasions and conquests which ended their independent state existence in the early Middle Ages, history up to the nineteenth century was, if we accept Suny's view, 'a broken trail' (1993: 5).

The long interval between ancient and modern Armenia, a gap which lasted from the eleventh century to the mid-nineteenth, had the result of almost breaking the continuity of language and of physical existence. The sheer physical survival of the group was frequently put in jeopardy by conquest and forced emigration. The long period of exile and the low social status of those Armenians who stayed on their historic lands combined to destroy much of the continuity between the Armenian past and the Armenian present. In the absence of any form of state after the fourteenth century, the job of preserving a separate national identity fell to the literate clerical elite, itself scattered to the four winds over the centuries. But the secular Armenian elite, which formed later, was deeply divided over clerical influence. The Armenian national movement of the nineteenth century contained a strongly anti-clerical faction, the members of which considered that the Armenian Church was now an obstacle to the growth of national identity, even though until the nineteenth century that Church was the second most important factor in holding Armenians together as an ethnic group (the first being the language itself).

Was Georgian history a 'broken trail' too? There are some grounds for thinking this. The medieval unity of the Georgian kingdom did not outlast the mid-fifteenth century, yet the survival of the Georgian nobility over the centuries, their continued hold on the land and the peasantry, and the inability – and unwillingness – of their neighbours to the East (the Persians) and the West (the Ottomans) to exert direct control over the area, meant that Georgian culture itself survived, although subject to strong Iranian and Ottoman influence.

The third major nation in South Caucasia,[19] the Azerbaijanis, hardly existed as an ethnic group, let alone a nation, before the twentieth century. The inhabitants of the territory now occupied by Azerbaijan defined themselves as Muslims, members of the Muslim *umma*; or as Turks, members of a language group spread over a vast area of Central Asia; or as Persians (the founder of Azerbaijani literature, Mirza Fath' Ali Akhundzadä, described himself as 'almost Persian'). 'Azerbaijani identity remained fluid and hybrid' comments R. G. Suny (1999–2000: 160). As late as 1900, the Azerbaijanis remained divided into six tribal groups – the Airumy, Karapapakh, Pavlari, Shakhsereny, Karadagtsy and Afshavy. The key period of the formation of the Azerbaijani nation lies between the 1905 revolution and the establishment of the independent People's Republic of Azerbaijan in 1918 (Altstadt, 1992: 95).

If we look further east, towards Central Asia (or 'Inner Asia'),[20] we find a similar situation. There the process of constructing national identity began as late as the 1920s. It is hardly complete even at the time of writing (Schoeberlein-Engel, 1996: 13). Looking specifically at the period before 1800, the main reason for the contrast between the early formation of ethnicity among Western and Central Europeans and its absence among Central Asians is that the former were spared the constantly shifting frontier that characterizes Central Asia. There, continuous nomadic invasions resulted in an ethnic brew in which the pot was constantly stirred, so that, one after another, Indo-European, Semitic, Turkic and Mongol identities occupied the foreground, but none ever attained exclusive dominance.

In Western and Central Europe the picture is entirely different. Here successive nomadic invasions only nibbled at the edges of solidly established societies. The last major alteration to the ethnic composition of Central Europe took place in the tenth century,[21] with the coming of the Magyars and their subsequent settlement on the lands they had conquered. Their absorption into the mainstream of European culture took place soon afterwards. The Mongol invasions of the thirteenth and fourteenth centuries, terrifying though they were to the local people, had no permanent impact outside Asia. Moreover, the Ottoman conquest of the fourteenth and fifteenth centuries affected only South East Europe, and even there it produced only superficial changes in the ethnic mix. Outside the eastern tip of the peninsula (now European Turkey), where Turkoman nomads were settled, the Ottoman Turks had a presence as administrators and soldiers, not as colonists or settlers.[22]

There are therefore clear historical reasons for a differential development of ethnicity in, on the one hand, the settled societies of Western and Central Europe, with their early state formations and rapid conversion to Christianity, combined with the absence of ethnic transformation through outside settlement, and, on the other hand, the originally nomadic societies of the East with their lack of any solid state formation, their repeated subjection to temporary empires and shortlived conquests, and their constantly changing ethnic kaleidoscope. There are also plenty of doubtful cases which cannot be placed definitively in either category. That is why there is no substitute for a historical treatment of each specific ethnic group, and this will be the task of the next two chapters.

2
The Formation of Ethnic Groups

I shall now try to put some flesh on the bare bones of this story by examining the most significant events in the formation of ethnicity in the region. Where the process was unproblematic I shall be brief; a more extended discussion will be needed in cases where there are doubts about the character and extent of particular ethnic groups and nations. The purpose here is to provide the elements of a historical explanation for the presence or absence of serious ethnic conflict in a given locality in recent times. Implicit in all this is the belief that some examination of the historical background is relevant, and that the history of each ethnic group or situation is not a purely arbitrary construction by national myth-makers. It would, however, be pointless to enter here into the many controversies over territorial priority which began in the mid-nineteenth century and show no sign of dying down at the start of the twenty-first century. The whole subject has been distorted by the deliberate use of the search for origins to bolster the territorial claims of one or the other ethnic group in the region.

East Central Europe[1]

The ethnic groups of modern times were formed relatively early in most of East Central Europe, which I define here as the area covered by Poland, Hungary, Slovakia and the Czech lands. They also developed rapidly into nations. For our purposes, there are only two categories to be considered: large ethnic groups which already formed the core of long-lasting states in medieval times (the Poles, Hungarians, Czechs); and smaller ethnic groups which had no state (the Slovaks). For the former group, the existence of a state meant also a developed social structure, with a nobility and a peasantry, a developed national cultural tradition (including a national literary language), and a strong national consciousness, at least in the negative sense that a clear line of demarcation was drawn between 'ourselves' and 'the others'. Thus, by the fourteenth century, the Czechs saw themselves as a nation distinct from, and antagonistic to, the Germans and the Poles (Graus, 1965: 62). The subsequent, post-medieval, loss of the state entailed a threat to some features of Czech national existence, but nowhere did the Czechs die out or disappear.

The same points apply to the Hungarians and Poles. There were already kingdoms of Hungary and Poland in the early Middle Ages. They both subsequently enjoyed centuries of continuous existence. It is true that both states eventually disappeared (independent Hungary lasted until 1526, while the Polish state survived until 1795), but in both cases the long period of state existence allowed the formation and development of a uniform written literary language, a culture, and a numerically large upper class, the gentry. By the nineteenth century, all these features of national identity were too well entrenched to be undermined by a relatively short period of foreign subjection (or, in the Hungarian case, semi-subjection). After 1918, the independent Hungarian and Polish states were restored, this time on an ethnic rather than, as before, a territorial basis. The new states clearly possessed a strong historical tradition. Ethnic problems and conflicts certainly arose, but they were related to minorities and never called Hungarian or Polish national identity into question.

The fate of the Slovaks was different. They were prevented from developing a state of their own by the Hungarian conquest of the tenth century. There had been, it is true, the Great Moravian Empire in the ninth century, which is sometimes described as the first Slav state, and Slovak historians have claimed it as Slovak, but, even granting this possibility, the break in continuity (lasting ten centuries) was too long for Moravian imperial memories to have any real significance. The absence of a state in the Slovak case meant also that there was no developed Slovak social structure, no Slovak cultural tradition and no Slovak literary language. All these vital elements of national existence had to be constructed laboriously in modern times.

South East Europe

The category 'South East Europe' is not simply geographical. It also delineates a cultural region.[2] The lands covered by this term have much in common. They share a political background of centuries of control by outsiders, in the shape of, first, the Byzantines, and then the Ottoman Turks. These external restraints held back the development of the kind of ethnic consciousness that grew up to the north of the Danube and the Alps in the pre-modern era. Economically, the lands of South East Europe have long had in common the relative backwardness of the region,[3] which, given the links between industrialization, urbanization and literacy on the one hand, and ethnic consciousness on the other, was another reason why the latter did not develop. They also shared a history of considerable ethnic mixture, resulting from centuries of conquest and long-term migration – the 'metanastasic movements' seen by the Yugoslav geographer Jovan Cvijić as decisive in the formation of the ethnic makeup of the area (1918: 112).

There were many reasons for migration. One was the Ottoman conquest, although we must guard against assuming that this led to a great exodus of the Christian population (it is more likely that what happened was a gradual process of conversion from Christianity to Islam stretching over a century or more). Another reason for migration was the institution of the blood feud, still predominant as late as the twentieth century among Montenegrin and Albanian clans. If one member of a family committed a murder, all its members were potentially subject to revenge attacks by members of the victim's family. This was clearly an inducement to flee for anyone who did not wish to live in constant fear. There were also plenty of less dramatic inducements for moving from one place to another, above all the prospect of self-improvement for the individual and the individual's family.

As a result, the inhabitants of South Eastern Europe had much in common. According to one widely-held view this led to the development of a 'cultural community' among them (Ivanova, 1999: 82).[4] It would, however, be equally possible to stress the many features that produced fragmentation. Religion, language and customs all differed. By the end of the Middle Ages the ethnic physiognomy of South Eastern Europe had assumed roughly[5] its modern form, or, to be more precise, its early-twentieth century form, before the immense simplifications produced during the following years of the twentieth century by migration, voluntary or involuntary, and killing, accidental or deliberate.

To say this is to imply a particular view about the nature of ethnicity, namely that it can exist as an objective characteristic, of which the people concerned may or may not be conscious. A shared language is the leading, though not the only, mark of ethnicity. Religious and cultural features may also play a part. At the time of the Ottoman conquest of the Balkans, in the late fourteenth and early fifteenth centuries, ethnic groups had already taken shape. They lacked any 'common ethno-political consciousness' or 'awareness of their past' (Karpat, 1997: 334–5). But the ethnic substratum was present. How far this was modified by Ottoman rule is a controversial matter. In particular, there is considerable disagreement about the contribution of, respectively, converted indigenes and outside settlers to the growth of Muslim ethnic groups. Conversion seems the most likely explanation.[6] The next stage after the development of ethnicity was the growth of ethnic consciousness, followed by the development of nationalist demands for autonomy, leading eventually to calls for independence. In South Eastern Europe this did not take place until the nineteenth century. We shall examine each stage of this process in turn.

Let us start with the Albanians, who have long occupied the area of present-day Albania with a northern extension into what is now Kosovo, and parts of Montenegro, Serbia and Macedonia. They spoke a language unrelated to that of the surrounding Slavs and Greeks, though there were borrowings in the lexicon, especially from Latin and Greek, and certain structural similarities with other Balkan languages.[7] The Albanian language is first mentioned in the sources as early as 1285, when it is recorded as being spoken in the hills behind Dubrovnik: 'I heard a voice shouting on the mountainside in the Albanian tongue' (Hammond, 1976: 57). But it was very slow to assume a written form, and in fact there were two powerful institutions which deliberately opposed the growth of an Albanian literary language – the Greek Orthodox Church, and the Ottoman rulers of the area. The Orthodox Church, which was the church of most of the Christian population of the south of the country, wanted the Albanians to learn Greek instead.

The Ottomans brought their own Turkish language with them for official use, and under the *millet* system they defined the Albanians purely in religious terms. They saw them simply as Muslims (or, where appropriate, Orthodox Christians), and therefore regarded the development of an Albanian language as unnecessarily divisive. Until the nineteenth century, they forbade education, reading and writing in Albanian. Even then, while allowing Albanian to be written, they tried to enforce the use of the Arabic rather than the Latin script. For these reasons, the development of a written form of this very old language was long delayed. But if cultural development was slow, Albanian political development was non-existent before the mid-nineteenth century: in the north, the Ottoman period had the result of destroying medieval political structures and 'revivifying archaic social phenomena, namely clan organisation and customary rules of law belonging to an epoch when no state existed' (Schmaus, 1973: 296–7). In the south, meanwhile, the establishment of Ottoman (or indigenous Muslim) landowners meant that the ruling elite was tied to the maintenance of alien rule and took no part in the national risings of the nineteenth century.

In Romania, at the other end of the Balkans (or, as some would say, outside the Balkans altogether),[8] there was, in contrast, an early development towards political homogeneity and unity. This appears at first to be surprising, since, in Transylvania, the main region inhabited by Romanians and the successor of Roman Dacia, the Hungarian conquest of the tenth century produced a social and political system dominated by the Magyar nobility, associated later with their subordinates the Széklers and the Saxons (Germans). The Romanians were 'excluded from all possible participation in political life' (Sugar, 1977: 147). The incorporation of Transylvania into the Habsburg Empire by the Treaty of Karlowitz (1699) did not change this situation.

So Romanian national development started not in Transylvania but further east, where two Romanian principalities emancipated themselves from Hungarian overlordship towards the end of the Middle Ages (Wallachia in 1338, Moldavia in 1365). The Ottoman conquest, which followed shortly afterwards, had a less decisive effect than elsewhere in South East Europe, because the local principalities retained considerable autonomy. The people were not converted to Islam, and the native nobility (the boyars) were not dispossessed (Dinić 1966: 565). Even the replacement after 1715 of elected local rulers by Phanariot Greeks from Constantinople did not affect the principalities' special status. The continued existence of distinctively Romanian state formations and institutions meant that the main constituents of Romanian ethnicity were already present at the dawn of modern times. But the language used for ecclesiastical and administrative purposes in Wallachia and Moldavia was Church Slavonic.

The Romanian language was therefore very late to appear in written form (1521). It took even longer before it possessed a literary standard (the translation of the Bible into Romanian in 1688 is the key date here). Despite this, the language had a unitary character by the seventeenth century, with very few differences between the dialects, and those mainly in vocabulary (Du Nay, 1977: 112). Moreover, cultural differences within the Romanian ethnic group were not very pronounced. The religious division introduced in Transylvania in the seventeenth century by the introduction of the Uniate (Greek Catholic) Church there (for reasons of Habsburg policy) did not give rise to any ethnic division.

Rather the reverse, in fact. After the formal conclusion of the union between the Orthodox Church and Rome at a general synod held in 1700, this half-way house between Catholicism and Orthodoxy provided the formative milieu for Romanian nationalism. It would prove to be an ideal foundation for a specifically Romanian national consciousness, in a country which was half in and half out of the Balkans. A Uniate bishop (Ion Clain) was the first spokesman for Romanian national rights, and most of the leading figures of the Romanian cultural revival of the late eighteenth century (Gheorghe Şincai, Petru Maior, Ion Budai-Deleanu and Samuel Clain) were educated as Uniates (Hitchins, 1969: 62–103). This did not mean that they took a narrow confessional attitude towards Romanian culture; in fact, they devoted their efforts to bridging the religious divide between the Greek Catholic and Greek Orthodox faiths. They resisted attempts to Latinize their church ritual because they felt this would alienate them irrevocably from their Orthodox brethren, and members of both the Greek Catholic and Orthodox Churches collaborated in the petitions of 1790–2 to the Habsburg emperor which are regarded as the first real expression of Romanian nationalism (Hitchins, 1969: 60–1, 134).

The Romanian national renaissance, at least in its early stages, was thus located in subject Transylvania rather than semi-independent Moldavia and Wallachia. But it was slow to make the transition from cultural development to political demands, because it faced strong competition from the emerging nationalism of the Hungarians. A sense of weakness prevented the Romanian nationalists in Transylvania from pressing for more than autonomy within the Habsburg monarchy. It was instead the principalities of Moldavia and Wallachia, culturally less developed, but socially and politically stronger, which made the running, achieving first autonomy (1859), and later independence (1880).

Bulgaria too possessed a state in medieval times, though only intermittently. In the year 864, Khan Boris of Bulgaria, who had toyed previously with the idea of a Roman connection, decided instead to place his people under Constantinople's ecclesiastical jurisdiction, thus establishing Orthodoxy as a basic feature of the Bulgarian ethnic background. His son Simeon (Tsar of Bulgaria from 893 to 927) established an empire that stretched from the Adriatic to the Black Sea and promoted a vigorous cultural life, as a result of which the Old Bulgarian literary language developed. In the tenth century (temporarily in 972, definitively in 1018) Bulgaria came under the direct control of Byzantium, but recovered its independence in 1197 after a long struggle. The Bulgarian ruler at the time, Kalojan, set the seal on this victory in 1204 by having himself crowned King of Bulgaria by a papal envoy. The second Bulgarian state thus inaugurated lasted until the Ottoman conquest, which took place in 1393. After that, the country ceased to exist as a separate entity until the nineteenth century. Unlike Romania, it was placed under direct Ottoman rule. The relatively independent position of the Orthodox Church, however, despite its subordination from 1394 to the Patriarchate in Constantinople, meant that Bulgarian ethnic identity was preserved, through the use of Church Slavonic rather than Greek in the liturgy. Whatever Bulgarian culture survived through the period of Ottoman rule did so 'behind the protective walls of monasteries' (Sugar, 1977: 265).

In what later became Yugoslavia, there emerged a clear distinction between the south-eastern half, conquered and held by the Ottoman Turks for four centuries, and the north west, which successfully resisted the Turks, coming instead under Habsburg rule. Before the fifteenth century, all the peoples of Yugoslavia were roughly speaking on the same cultural level. All had their moments of imperial greatness, all displayed signs of incipient cultural progress. Serbia was perhaps the most dominant Balkan state in the fourteenth century, under Stephen Dušan (1331–55). Late medieval Serbia was strong enough to rival the Byzantine Empire and self-confident enough to make the attempt (Dinić 1966: 537–40). Everything changed after the Ottoman conquest, which was a gradual process rather than a sudden event. The conquest started with the Battle of Kosovo in 1389 (after which the defeated Prince of Serbia was forced to become a Turkish vassal), and ended with the seizure of the last Serbian position, the fortress of Smederevo, in 1459, and the extinction of the Serbian state. After their definitive victory, the Ottoman Turks 'destroyed every document concerning Serbian national life', and as a result 'creative literary work among the Serbs ceased in 1459', not to be revived until the eighteenth century; even then, the earliest Serb writers were exiles in Hungary, Vojvodina, Venice and Dalmatia (Barac, 1976: 21). Moreover, most of them were under the shadow of the Orthodox Church and wrote, not in the Serbian language, but in a mixture of Serbian and Church Slavonic which was known as 'Slaveno-Serbian' (Hopf, 1997: 283).

On the western side of the peninsula, meanwhile, settled by Croats and Slovenes rather than Serbs, two kinds of political institution emerged in the Middle Ages: the state of Croatia, and the semi-independent towns of the Dalmatian coast. The latter were 'classic areas of voluntary ethnic symbiosis' between the incoming Slavs and the settled Romans (or the Romanized indigenous population of Illyria). This process gradually resulted in the predominance of the Slav element (Grothusen, 1974: 80). The former arose as an independent state in the ninth century, and by the eleventh century had wrested control of Slavonia to the north-east and the coastal strip of Dalmatia in the south from the Byzantine Empire. In 1089, however, King Zvonimir of Croatia died without an heir, and the land passed to the King of Hungary, Ladislaus I. But Hungarian rule did not alter the position of the Croat nobility, who were fully autonomous in domestic affairs. Thus the two elements that later went to make up Croatia were in place by the later Middle Ages.

Soon after that, however, came the severe setback of the Ottoman conquest. This resulted in the temporary loss of Slavonia, which remained under Ottoman control for the next two centuries. Croatia proper only saved itself by voluntary subjection to the Habsburgs in 1527, though the Croat gentry survived as a class,[9] and the Croatian state kept a large measure of autonomy. Until the late eighteenth century the Croats regarded themselves as equal partners rather than subjects of the Hungarians. Meanwhile, the Italian city-state of Venice was extending its sway over the Slav towns of the eastern coast of the Adriatic Sea. Further south, another Slav city-state, Dubrovnik (also known by its Italian name Ragusa) made its own form of accommodation to the new situation: it began to pay 'an insignificant tribute of twelve thousand five hundreds ducats a year' (Dinić 1966: 559) to the Ottoman Turks in return for autonomy and the right to trade throughout the empire. This turned out to be the road to prosperity and success. Dubrovnik enjoyed 'full independence for all practical purposes' until 1808 (Sugar, 1977: 175). During the sixteenth and seventeenth centuries, the wealthy bourgeois patrons of the city encouraged many writers, in particular the poet Ivan Gundulić (1588–1638) and Abbot Mauro Orbini (d. 1614), the first historian of the Slav peoples in the Balkans (Hösch, 1972: 100).

The Slovenes, who settled to the north of the Croats in the sixth century, had meanwhile undergone a different historical experience. They became subject to German rule almost immediately (in the eighth century) and did not emerge from this status until the twentieth century. They never possessed a state of their own, yet in one sense they benefited from their continuous subjection: they did not suffer from invasion and insecurity. It is indeed remarkable that this over-whelmingly peasant people, without state traditions or a developed class structure, were able to develop a literary culture not inferior to that of the Croats living further south. But it is not unique: the same can be said of the Estonians and Latvians, as we shall see.

A stark contrast emerged between these Slovenian and Croatian areas of the north west, characterized in early modern times by a flourishing literary culture and (with the exception of Dubrovnik) continuing political subjection, and the Serbian lands of the south east, culturally undeveloped and at first subject to the Ottomans, but ultimately quicker to attain full political independence.

Bosnia-Hercegovina occupied an intermediate position, conquered certainly (in 1463),[10] but possessing a local elite converted gradually to Islam in the sixteenth century, which was able to achieve a consider-able degree of autonomy when the Ottoman administration began to break down at the end of the eighteenth century. In the period of Ottoman decline, 'the local lords ran the province as they pleased' (Sugar, 1977: 236).[11] This refers, of course, to the Muslim elite. The Muslim peasants, who constituted two-thirds of the population by the early seventeenth century, were not much better off than the Christians, who made up a third. However, the growth of towns in the next two centuries tended to create a town–country division between ordinary Muslims and Christians: Muslims left the countryside and moved into the towns, and formerly Christian town-dwellers con-verted to Islam.

It is doubtful whether there was any sense of conscious national self-identification among the Muslims of Bosnia up to the twentieth century; Muslim peasants were as suspicious as Christian peasants of the predominantly Muslim inhabitants of the towns, regarding them as 'a clique which exploited them economically and ruled them politi-cally'. In the countryside, too, a sense of Muslim solidarity was absent: 'social boundaries between aristocrat and peasant were as sharp as between any two ethnic groups' (Lockwood, 1978: 213–4). According to Francine Friedman, 'there are few convincing data to indicate that the Bosnian Muslims under the Ottoman Empire can be correctly identified as a distinct national entity' (1996: 47). They were by no means without culture; but their cultural achievements were supra-national, and belonged to a broad Islamic, rather than a narrow local, tradition. Their literature was written in Turkish, Arabic or Persian (Malcolm, 1994: 102).

The Christians of the area were in turn divided into Roman Catholics (who can be seen as Croats) and Orthodox (who can be seen as Serbs). The Croat aristocracy of Bosnia-Hercegovina was destroyed by the Ottomans, and the ordinary people fell back on the Roman Catholic Church. Nevertheless, they retained a sense of community and an ethnic awareness, despite the long period of Ottoman rule, during which their religion was not recognized (the Roman Catholics were subordinated to the Orthodox *millet* under the system established by Mehmet II in 1453) (Sugar, 1977: 49). One particular religious order, the Franciscans, played a vital part in preserving Croat individuality in Bosnia (Moacanin, 1992–4: 135–8).

The origins of the third major element in the ethnic make-up of Bosnia-Hercegovina, the Serbs, are doubtful. It is possible that they were immigrants who came into the area in the sixteenth century, encouraged to do so by the Turks as a replacement for Catholics who had fled into the Habsburg lands, leaving the territory relatively empty. There is some evidence that many who became Serbs were originally Vlachs: a sixteenth-century traveller in the region referred to 'Serbs, who call themselves Vlachs' and come from 'Smederevo and Belgrade' (Curipeschitz, 1910: 34–5), and there is much other evidence of a Vlach presence. Noel Malcolm concludes his discussion of this point by saying that modern Bosnian Serbs have 'a large element of non-Slav ancestry' (in other words, they are descended from Vlach, or Romanian, settlers of the sixteenth century) but that in any case 'the concept of a Serb' is a 'nineteenth and twentieth century construct' (Malcolm, 1994: 81). It is not at all clear why he singles out the Serbs in this way: either all ethno-national concepts are nineteenth-century constructs (which would be a perfectly tenable 'constructionist' view), or they have deeper roots. In the latter case there is no reason to ignore the large number of cases where travellers coming from outside the region, as well as the Serbs themselves, used the ethnonym 'Serb' before the nineteenth century.

Just as the Catholic Church preserved the individuality of the Croats, the Orthodox Church did the same for the Serbs. The memory of the medieval Serbian state was preserved by the Orthodox Church, especially after the restoration of the Archbishopric of Peć (Ipek) in 1557, with jurisdiction over the whole of the formerly Serbian lands. Also in the sixteenth century, Serbs (or were they really Vlachs?)[12] were invited by the Habsburg rulers to leave Ottoman territory and take up land on the border with the Ottoman Empire, in return for which they would serve as soldiers, and be free to practise their Orthodox religion. This was the origin of the Military Border (*vojna krajina*).[13] But these particular Serbs did not contribute much to the growth of Serbian national identity, which was a product rather of the autonomous position achieved by the Serbian state after the revolutions of 1804 and 1815 against Ottoman rule.

We should, finally, mention one part of the Balkans that recovered its independence very early: Montenegro (Crna Gora), which became a vassal state of the Ottoman Empire in the fifteenth century, under the Crnojević dynasty, but become of its isolated geographical position was able from 1697 in practice to 'opt out of the Ottoman Empire'. The original ruling dynasty was replaced, roughly at the same time, by the family of the Bishops of Montenegro, the Njegoši, who then became the state's hereditary rulers (Hösch, 1972: 116). Montenegro was a tribal society which made a seamless transition to full independence in the mid-nineteenth century, to be included in Yugoslavia after the First World War.

We have now to examine the area to the east of the Habsburg and Ottoman lands, an area originally so diverse that no single descriptive phrase could encompass it, but brought together in modern times by the common experience of subjection to the Russian Empire and subsequently the Soviet Union. We look first at the Baltic states, moving further south and east by stages.

The Baltic area

Despite having much in common, the three small nations on the eastern edge of the Baltic did not all undergo the same course of development. The Lithuanian tribes were far in advance of the other two. They had already developed an ethnic awareness by the twelfth century (Bojtár, 1997: 190). A century later, the Lithuanians were not just an ethnic group but the bearers of a state (Vardys and Sedaitis, 1997: 7). By 1246, Grand Duke Mindaugas had united the Lithuanian tribes together under his aegis (Kiaupa *et al.*, 2000: 54). Although the Grand Duchy of Lithuania entered into a personal union with neighbouring Poland in 1385, it at first retained its separate status, and was not incorporated definitively into the Polish Commonwealth. This meant that a separate Lithuanian nation had time to form, with a 'common Lithuanian consciousness' (Kiaupa *et al.*, 2000: 92). Biblical texts and prayers began to be printed in Lithuanian in the sixteenth century.

Incorporation into Poland in 1569 resulted in the gradual polonization of the Lithuanian nobility. Naturally, this retarded Lithuanian cultural evolution. The University of Vilnius, previously a centre of
Lithuanian publishing, began to publish more Polish than Lithuanian
books. From 1697, the state language of the Grand Duchy was Polish.
'Being Lithuanian' was no longer counterposed to 'being Polish'. The
situation of the Lithuanians at the time was summed up neatly in the
Latin phrase *gente Lituanus, natione Polonus* (Lithuanian by race, Polish
by nationality) (Milosz, 1995: 250). Among the peasantry, however,
knowledge of the Lithuanian language and Lithuanian culture survived
(Kiaupa *et al.*, 2000: 303), and eventually, in the eighteenth century, a
cultural revival began, not in Poland, but in East Prussia, part of which
lay in previously Lithuanian territory, thanks to the efforts of the poet
and Protestant minister Kristijonas Donelajtis (1714–64). For the first
time, a secular Lithuanian literature emerged.

The development of the Latvians and Estonians from tribe to ethnic
group, and later into nation, was held back by alien conquest, rather
than, as in the Lithuanian case, by a voluntary merger with an allied
cultural group. German invaders from the west entered the Baltic in
the early thirteenth century, with the joint objectives of setting up
colonies and converting the locals to Christianity. They were unable to
make any headway in Lithuania, but by 1230 Livonia (which com-
prises much of present-day Latvia) had been conquered by one of the
German religious-military orders, the Knights of the Sword. To the
south, in Courland, an area which later became divided between Latvia
and Lithuania, the task of conquest and colonization was undertaken
by another order, the Teutonic Knights. During the many subsequent
centuries of German rule, various Baltic tribes in the area of southern
Livonia and Courland – the most important being the Kurs,
Semigallians and Latgallians – gradually merged together to form the
Latvian ethnic group; it was a slow and obscure process.[14] The name
'Latvian' does not appear in the sources until 1648.

The Estonians, a group of independent (and allegedly warlike and
predatory) tribes, inhabited northern Livonia and Estonia. They were
subdued gradually at the end of the twelfth century by the Danes. In
1219, Waldemar II of Denmark succeeded in pacifying Estonia, and
bringing its inhabitants into subjection. The Estonians originally
lacked an ethnonym, referring to themselves only as 'people of the
Earth' (Bojtár, 1997: 105). As time went on, though, they gradually
adopted the name 'Estonian', which was given to them by their conquerors. In 1346 Estonia was sold by Denmark to the Teutonic Knights,

subsequently passing (in 1561) into the hands of the Swedish Empire. Livonia was added in the 1620s, after a period of Polish rule. Eventually, in 1721, the whole area passed into the hands of the Russian Empire. At no time during this long period did either the Estonians or the Latvians enjoy any vestige of independence.

The absence of any form of state among the Latvians and Estonians, and the lack of any social class other than the peasantry (a situation which reflects 500 years of German social and political domination), are sufficient explanations for their slower development as ethnic groups in comparison with the Lithuanians. Yet cultural development was not held back by political subjection or the absence of a developed social structure. In fact, the first surviving Estonian text (1535) pre-dates the first Lithuanian text (1547). The first Latvian text dates from 1585. Books began to be printed in Estonian in the seventeenth century, and elementary education was being conducted in that language in the late seventeenth century. The explanation for this paradox is simple: the period of Swedish control.

Before Sweden took over, 'the Estonians were on the verge of losing their identity as a people' (Piirimäe, 1993: 368). The Swedes changed all this by encouraging the use of the Estonian language in education, publishing, Church services, and even official communications. A solid cultural foundation was laid. The Russian conquest brought only a temporary setback. Educational expansion continued in the eighteenth and early nineteenth centuries, resulting in an astoundingly high level of literacy. By 1850, 90 per cent of the Estonian population could read (Raun, 1987: 55). There was, however, one drawback: until the 1840s, all endeavours to promote Estonian culture remained in the hands of German 'Estophils' rather than the indigenous population.[15]

The eastern Slav lands

The Russians were the people of state, the backbone, of the Tsarist Empire (and subsequently of the Soviet Union). This possibly explains their rather weak sense of nationality; they tended to identify themselves, not with a particular nation, but with either the state, the head of the state (the tsar) or the Orthodox Church. As an ethnic group, however, they had existed since the Middle Ages, and a distinctive Russian literature and culture developed early. As in the case of other imperial peoples (such as the Turks and the Austrians) they found no reason to make the move to fully-fledged nationalism until they had lost their empire. We shall therefore reserve our discussion of this topic to a later chapter.

There were two other major Slavic groups on the territory of the Russian Empire: the Belarusans and the Ukrainians. The Ukrainians have to share much of their earlier history with the Russians, since the first Ukrainian state, Kiev Rus', was also the first Russian state.[16] Culturally, it belonged to both groups, or more precisely to the East Slavs in general. It was only after the decline of Kiev and under the impact of the Mongol invasion of the thirteenth century that three East Slavic nations emerged: the Ukrainians, the Belarusans and the Russians. Ukrainian separateness from Russians was further increased in the fourteenth and subsequent centuries by the divergent paths followed by the two: while the Russians were gradually unified under the independent rule of Moscow, the Ukrainians were included in the Lithuanian, then the Polish-Lithuanian state.[17] Hence, when Ukraine itself came under the rule of the Russian tsars, with the partitions of Poland at the end of the eighteenth century, it was inhabited by a Ukrainian ethnic group with a distinct language and culture which proved to be resistant to assimilation to Russia, even though the tsars made the attempt.

One of the paradoxes of Belarusan nationalism is that the Belarusan language itself had a longer pedigree than the languages of more successful ethnic groups. State business in the Grand Duchy of Lithuania was conducted until the mid-sixteenth century in Old Belarusan[18] rather than Lithuanian; hence a distinctive Belarusan culture emerged on Lithuanian territory at this time. However, the union of Lithuania with Poland in 1569 meant that the language lost its independent position. Initially it was replaced by Latin,and later by Polish. When the area was absorbed by Russia following the late eighteenth century partitions of Poland, the use and publication of works in Belarusan was banned. The Belarusans and their language seemed to have disappeared from history.

The south Caucasus: the three 'historic nations'

In the closing decades of the Roman Empire there were already three established state formations in the area to the south of the Caucasian Mountains: Armenia, Georgia and Albania. Each of them converted to Christianity in the fourth century, and each adopted a script and began to create a written literature. But the state of the Caucasian

Albanians was unfortunately placed. It lay beside the Caspian Sea, on an invasion route, and it was unable to survive the constant pressure exerted in turn or together by Alans and Khazars from the north, Byzantines from the west, Arabs from the south, and Persians from the east. Caucasian Albania (or 'Arran' as it is described in Arab sources) was destroyed by the Arab conquests of the seventh century; the Albanian language and culture survived for a short period, to be extinguished, it is thought, by the next great invasion, that of the Saljuq Turks in the tenth century (Golden, 1996: 67). No text in Caucasian Albanian has survived.[19] Hence any attempt to link ancient Albania with modern Azerbaijan must remain pure speculation, though these speculations played an important part in the Azerbaijani nation-building process from the 1960s onwards.[20]

In fact, in medieval times the name 'Azerbaijan' was applied not to the area of present independent Azerbaijan but to the lands to the south of the Araxes river, now part of Iran. The lands to the north west of the Araxes were known as Albania; the lands to the north east, the heart of present-day post-Soviet Azerbaijan, were known as Sharvan (or Shirwan) and Derbend. It is probable that by the twelfth century most of the inhabitants of the area were descended either from Turkic invaders from the north or indigenes who had by then adopted Turkish culture and language in its Azerbaijani form. But much is speculation here. In the case of Armenia and Georgia, in contrast, there are firmer grounds for asserting continuity between past and present.

The Armenians are thought to have existed as a people since the sixth century BCE, when the King of Persia recorded that he had conquered them, with difficulty. By the time that they were converted to Christianity (in 314 CE) their ethnic identity had become firmly fixed. In other words, they were an ethnic community sharing a name, a myth of descent, a culture, a language, and finally a distinctive religion (Armenian monophysite Christianity, an independent faith attached neither to Rome nor Constantinople). These features counterbalanced the weakness of their state, in which the monarch was rarely able to overcome the feuding of the leading noble families (Thomson, 1996: 26).

Like the rest of the Caucasus, Armenia was subjected to waves of invasion and conquest throughout its history. Its position on the borderline of successive great empires meant that it was fought over constantly. First came the long contest between the Byzantines and the Persians; this is not seen by historians in an entirely negative light. In fact, the renowned Caucasian specialist, Professor Cyril Toumanoff, asserted that it was precisely the equilibrium between the 'cultural and political influences of Byzantium and Iran that fostered the individuality and autonomy of Caucasia and ensured their survival' (Toumanoff, 1959: 3). The Byzantine and Persian Empires were still locked in conflict when the Arabs invaded in the seventh century; conquest by the Arabs helped to strengthen Armenian individuality by 'protecting the country from the gravitational pull of the Byzantine Empire'. The subsequent period saw the first great expansion of Armenian literature (Nichanian, 1989: 181).

Then came the disasters of the eleventh century: the reincorporation of Armenia in Byzantium in 1045, followed by the invasion of the Saljuq Turks in 1064 and the first wave of mass emigration. Invasions and conquests succeeded each other throughout the next four centuries: first the Mongols (1236); then Tamurlane and the Aq-Qoyunlu Turks (late fourteenth century), then the Safavid rulers of Persia (1502), whose continuous conflict over the next two centuries with the Ottoman Turks can be viewed as a form of repetition of the earlier Byzantine–Persian conflict.

Not surprisingly, the culture and language of the Armenians came under substantial Persian (Iranian) and Turkish (Ottoman) influence throughout this period, though without changing its fundamental character. In the course of these years of devastation and invasion, most Armenians left their ancestral lands. Emigration (and forced deportation) began in the sixth century CE and continued until the nineteenth century. Paradoxically, those who stayed behind were less likely to preserve their Armenianness than those who left; it was in diaspora that the language and Armenian culture were preserved.

There were two main reasons for this. First, the determination of the Armenian Church to remain distinctive. It refused steadfastly to identify itself with either Roman Catholicism or Greek Orthodoxy. Second, the continued existence of an Armenian state-in-exile. This was the kingdom of Cilicia, which lasted from 1189 to 1375 under the protection of the Crusaders, and provided a favourable environment for the growth of a literary language, Middle Armenian, which was closer to the speech of the people than *grabar*. But in 1375 the Cilician kingdom of Armenia finally succumbed to the Egyptian Mamluks.

The next three centuries were the darkest time for the Armenians and their language. This now split into two parts: *grabar*, a literary and ecclesiastical language, used for writing by a few monks and priests; and *ashkharhabar*, the language of the people, which had by that time disintegrated into a number of mutually incomprehensible dialects (Nichanian, 1989: 240). Most rural Armenians in the Ottoman Empire began to speak Turkish; even in the cities the language came under strong Turkish influence; only in the eastern part of the Caucasus, particularly in the remote region of Karabagh, was Armenian preserved in a relatively pure form (Nichanian, 1989: 244). However, continuity was provided by the autocephalous Armenian Church and by the ancient scriptures, written in *grabar*.

Ordinary Armenians respected, but could no longer comprehend these ancient writings. Little by little, the language of the people had moved away from Classical Armenian, with the result that eventually the two diverged almost completely (Nichanian, 1989: 177). To restore the link between speech and writing it was necessary to establish a literary standard based on spoken Armenian; though here too there were substantial differences between the western version of the language, spoken in diaspora, and the eastern version local to Armenia itself.

When the revival of Armenian national literature started, in the late seventeenth century, it was, somewhat paradoxically, the work of a Catholic order, the Mekhitarist monks, located first in Venice and then also in Vienna. They revived Armenian learning over the next century by reprinting the works of the early Armenian historians; their aim in doing this was to bring the Armenian Gregorian Christians back to the true faith. Meanwhile, Armenia itself remained in subjection, although the Armenians themselves prospered under Turkish rule until the massacres of the late nineteenth century. The Ottoman rulers tended to persecute the Armenian Catholics and favour the Gregorians, the majority, who were more easily controlled through their patriarch, and were regarded as a particularly loyal group (Deny, 1960: 640–1). At the beginning of the nineteenth century, eastern Armenia exchanged rulers: the Russian conquest meant the replacement of a Muslim master with an Orthodox one. In the 1840s Armenian nationalism began to emerge in the Russian Empire, among intellectuals who rejected the quietist traditions of the Church, as well as its retrograde insistence on preserving the ancient form of the language. The Armenian national movement fought its first battles against the Armenian Church, not alongside it, and in defence of the right to publish in *ashkharhabar*, the common tongue, rather than in *grabar*, the language of the Church (Suny, 1993: 23).

Like the Armenians, the Georgians had a continuous history stretching back several centuries before the Christian era. They too were converted to Christianity in the fourth century CE, and they too adopted a distinctive alphabet, which was perhaps invented by the Armenian monk, Mesrop Mashtots.[21] The main differences were that the

Georgians did not retain their separate Church, returning instead to the fold of Orthodoxy, that the Georgian nobility lived in the countryside rather than the towns, and that for many centuries they were unable to weld their separate principalities into a single state. This did not happen until 1008, when Bagrat III established a unified kingdom, which was at first under heavy Armenian cultural influence. Georgian kings often conducted their correspondence with foreign monarchs in Armenian, and the province of Dzavakheti was completely Armenian in character until the mid-tenth century (Toumanoff, 1952: 257–8).[22] The twelfth century, however, saw a strengthening of Georgian power and self-confidence, culminating during the reign of Queen Tamar (1184–1212). This is when 'a distinctive Georgian Christian culture and civilisation' emerged, with the establishment of a literary standard. Georgia's greatest medieval poet, Shot'a of Rust'avi, who composed the epic poem 'The Knight in the Panther's Skin', is regarded as the prime mover in this respect (Suny, 1994: 38).

Despite these promising beginnings, the medieval state of Georgia rested on an unstable foundation. It comprised a number of fissiparous elements. Disintegration was a constant threat. United Georgia collapsed under the impact of three Mongol invasions following each other in quick succession during the thirteenth century (1220, 1222 and 1236). The country again became divided into a number of principalities. An opportunity for recovery appeared in the fifteenth century, after Alexander I (1412–42) restored political unity, but his ineffectual successors failed to seize it, partly because their hands were tied by a system of joint kingship which promoted internecine conflict (Suny, 1994: 45–6; Allen, 1932: 132–8; Toumanoff, 1966: 628). After the defeat of Giorgi VIII at the battle of Chikhori in 1463 the country dissolved into eight sections: Svaneti, Abkhazeti, Samegrelo, Guria, Samtskhe, Imereti, Kakheti and Kartli.

In the sixteenth century, the eastern half of Georgia came under Persian control, while the west entered increasingly into the Ottoman orbit. Over the next two centuries all parts of Georgia were fought over and changed hands repeatedly. Despite occasional temporary reunifications of parts of Georgia, a complete and lasting unity was never achieved (Suny, 1994: 46). This rendered impossible any effective defence of the country against the two rival empires struggling continuously for control at this time. Yet the principalities still 'retained a precarious autonomy or independence' as late as the mid-eighteenth century (Suny, 1994: 55). Eventually despairing of any other way out, the last Georgian kings appealed for Russian aid, which eventually came in the shape of the annexation of the country to the Russian Empire in 1800.

Most of the principalities that went to make up medieval Georgia were recognizably Georgian in culture and religion. There were exceptions, though. The Mingrelians spoke a language related to Georgian, but the two languages were not mutually intelligible (Aves, 1996: 48). The Ajarians in the south west were separated from Georgia not by language but by religion. The local aristocracy of Ajaria retained control of the land even after the Ottoman conquest of the fifteenth century by converting to Islam. The subject population held on to Christianity for a hundred years but finally followed the nobility's example (Dartchiachvili, 1999: 265).

To the north west lived the Abkhazians: they were linguistically, if not culturally, distinct from the Georgians. A separate Abkhazian kingdom existed until 978, and then again during the fifteenth century. Subsequently, Abkhazia, unlike eastern Georgia, came under Ottoman rule, another point of difference, because it was followed by gradual conversion to Islam. In 1810, Abkhazia was incorporated into Russia as a separate principality. In 1864, the principality of Abkhazia was renamed the Sukhumi Military Department. The failure of the rising of 1866 led to an initial wave of emigration towards Turkey; and there was another mass exodus after the war between the Russian and Ottoman Empires in 1877–8.

These population movements had a decisive effect on the ethnic composition of the region, because Russians and Georgians moved in to fill the empty lands. From then, the Abkhazians were in a minority in their own country. The majority of them were also no longer Muslims; many Muslims emigrated to Turkey, while others converted to Christianity. Hence the vast majority of Abkhazians who remained were, by the end of the nineteenth century, Orthodox Christians (the proportion was roughly 80 per cent) (Wixman, 1980: 103, n.3). The Abkhazian nobility and clergy spoke and wrote in Georgian; it was the peasants who spoke Abkhazian. Hence the language continued to lack a written version (Chervonnaya, 1994: 190, n.19).

Georgian ethnicity survived the long interval between the twelfth and nineteenth centuries because of the continued existence of Georgian state formations and ruling elites. The Church also played a part in nurturing language and culture, though its contribution was not as great as in the Armenian case. In the late eighteenth century, when the national revival started, 85 per cent of the books printed were religious texts. Secular literature circulated in manuscript

(Vateishvili, 1973: 46). It would be an exaggeration to say that Georgian culture died out during the period of Persian and Turkish rule, but it was at a low ebb. Even after more than half a century of national revival, the Georgian language remained divided into many different dialects, and in 1897 the Russian census-takers felt the need to distinguish between Georgians properly so-called (numbering 813 413 in Transcaucasia), Imeretians (272 217), Mingrelians (239 252) and Svans (15 720) (Bauer *et al.*, 1991: 220–1). Even so, all these groups would soon be regarded (and counted) as part of the Georgian nation.

As hinted earlier, the history of Azerbaijan and of the growth of an Azerbaijani *ethnie* is more problematic than the other two cases. The lack of a clear way of differentiating between the various Turkic languages spoken and written in medieval and early modern times is one of the difficulties. Another is the absence until the twentieth century of an Azerbaijani state. Attempts have been made to solve these difficulties, but not very convincingly. It has been suggested that the Safavid rulers of sixteenth-century Persia were Azerbaijanis, on the basis that the poet Khatai, who also ruled Persia as Shah Ismail ɪ (1501–25) wrote in Turkish rather than Farsi, and that 'everything in the Safavid empire was in the hands of Turks'. It was true that Safavid Iran was initially Turkish in character (although later it took on the colour of its Persian surroundings) (Frye, 1975: 230), but what is the relationship between Turks and Azerbaijanis? The modern Azerbaijani view of this problem is as follows: the conquest of Azerbaijan by Turkish-speaking tribes did not alter the anthropological makeup of the Azerbaijanis, as they remained a part of the 'Greater Europeoid race' despite adopting a Turkic language (Sumbatzade, 1990: 275).

The North Caucasus: a society of clans

Further north, on the other side of the Caucasus Mountains, there was a large number of ethnic groups, often of obscure origin. They lacked a literature of their own until the twentieth century, although they certainly possessed distinctive languages and customs. Here (as in the examples of Albania and Montenegro in South East Europe) the main point of identification was not the *ethnie* but either the clan, in the narrower context, or the community of mountain dwellers (in Russian: *gortsy*), in the broader context. Each ethnic group was divided into numerous clans, but all ethnic groups were united by common cultural and economic practices, so that until the 1920s the inhabitants of the North Caucasus constituted a 'huge ethnic society of North Caucasian mountaineers' (Volkova and Lavrov, 1968: 330). They were strongly resistant to outside influence, so change came very slowly. In religion they were a curious mixture of pagan, Christian and Muslim. Eventually the North Caucasus became a stronghold of Islam, but only very gradually, as the mountainous heartland of the area 'long resisted Islamization' (Bosworth, 1978: 350). When Islam did finally triumph, it was less through foreign conquest than through the conversion of individuals by travelling merchants and Sufi holy men.

Central Asia

The peoples of Central Asia did not develop individual national identities until the twentieth century. Before that they were conscious of their character as Muslims, members of the *umma*, or community of Muslims everywhere, and as members of local communities or clans, with local loyalties. Ethnicity was extremely fluid, partly because of the succession of invasions and conquests suffered by the area up to the sixteenth century. Questions of ethnogenesis in Central Asia are extremely complex, and diametrically opposed views can be found in the literature. We shall attempt to summarize the view taken by most modern scholars, though it should be said that this runs counter to what is accepted and taught in the schools and universities of the region itself.

Uzbek ethnogenesis is most problematic of all. There were at least three elements present in what later became Uzbekistan: the Sarts, who were a settled indigenous population, of either Iranian or Turkic origin; the Turkic nomads who conquered Central Asia in the early Middle Ages; and the Qipchaks, who arrived in the fifteenth century and conquered Turkestan. The Qipchaks, who were also called Uzbeks, founded three states. The first Uzbek leader to emerge was Abulkhayr (1412–68), founder of the Abulkhayr Shaybanid dynasty, who established a state in Transoxania (Western Turkestan), which later became the khanate of Bukhara. Another group of Uzbeks, the Yadigarid Shaybanids, seized control of the region of Khwarazm in the early sixteenth century, eventually establishing the khanate of Khiva. A third group of Uzbeks, the Ming, set up the khanate of Khoqand in the eighteenth century. These three Uzbek principalities were ruled by elites whose culture was a mixture of Persian and Turkic elements; the literary language that emerged there, Chaghatay, was also a mixture of the two. They ruled over subject populations with no clear ethnic identity, though some of these 'ended up by calling themselves Uzbeks' (Roy, 2000: 16). But ethnic group membership was not yet a significant fact. Other forms of identity (religious, local, political) were far more important.[23] In any case, throughout the nineteenth century at least four terms of ethnic identification were in use in addition to 'Uzbek': Sart (discussed below), Muslim, Turk and Chaghatay. After the Bolshevik Revolution these terms were abandoned successively, leaving only 'Uzbek' (Baldauf, 1991: 89).

The second major group we need to consider are the Kazakhs. The Turkic word 'Qazaq' means 'free, independent man', and was applied to an Uzbek tribal confederacy which threw off Uzbek ascendancy and migrated north-eastwards in the seventeenth century (Barthold and Hazai, 1978: 848). The Kazakhs were a nomadic people, culturally homogeneous, but lacking political unity in pre-modern times. Certain rulers were able to assert themselves at intervals, but they were never able to supplant the authority of tribal leaders.

By the early eighteenth century the Kazakh tribes had coalesced into three hordes (the Greater, Middle and Lesser Hordes). A fourth (the Bükey Horde) emerged in the early nineteenth century. In 1730, under the pressure of attack from Dzhungarian nomads, the Khan of the Lesser Horde, Abilay, decided to place his people under Russian rule (Sarkisyanz, 1961: 318–21). The tsar accepted his offer, and this began a gradual process of Russian expansion (accompanied by a creeping colonization of the north of the country by Slav peasants). This was not a voluntary process; in fact, there was considerable resistance from the Kazakhs, but the inexorable Russian advance culminated in 1848 with the suppression of the last of the hordes (the Greater Horde) and the establishment of direct Russian rule over most of Kazakh territory (Soucek, 2000: 195–7).

There were two further major groups of Turkic origin in Central Asia: the Kyrgyz, who settled in what is now Kyrgyzstan, and the Turkmen, who spent much time raiding the Persians to the south, and eventually settled to the east of the Caspian Sea. Their nomadic way of life prevented them from coalescing into *ethnies*, and they remained divided into tribes until the twentieth century.

The Central Asian picture can finally be completed with a reference to the Tajiks, Persian-speaking Muslims who differed from the Turkic tribes both in language and in their more settled and urban way of life. The Tajiks were described as 'Sarts' from the fourteenth to the sixteenth century. Then they started to be described as Tajiks, while the term 'Sart' began to be applied to the settled populations of the towns of Central Asia who spoke Turkic languages (Soucek, 2000: 32–3). The Tajiks played a considerable part in the life of the Uzbek-ruled khanates which dominated Turkestan before the Russian conquest, but they never established a political formation of their own.[24]

3
Ethnic Groups into Nations

The processes by which ethnic groups became nations varied substantially within the region; certain common factors can, however, be picked out. The first, in order of external prominence if not necessarily of importance, is the development and imposition of a national language. This process was often completed surprisingly late in national development, but its initial stages always coincided with the first stirrings of national consciousness.

In many cases, the written, standardized language differed markedly from the existing dialects of the spoken language. This was sometimes a matter of deliberate archaism: the nationally-inclined men of learning who took the lead in establishing a written standard looked back to a 'golden age' when the language allegedly existed in pure, classical form. In Czechoslovakia, for example, the Czech written language imposed by the nationalists was out of date by two centuries, divorced from any spoken dialect, and unnecessarily different grammatically from ordinary speech. This was because Josef Dobrovský (1753–1829), the father of modern literary Czech, took a grammar written in 1571 as his starting point (Millet, 1983: 504).

The makers of the national revivals in the nineteenth century fixed more than simply language; they tended to enforce, or at least to encourage, ethnic choices. Étienne Haumant put this point many years ago, in the course of a discussion of rival Italian and Slav claims to the nineteenth-century population of Dalmatia:

> These differences (in the figures for Italian and Slav inhabitants) can be explained partly by bias on the part of statisticians, but also by a certain national indecision, among both the unawakened masses and the ruling classes. For them the choice between two languages

and two peoples was not posed precisely at the start; first there had to be propaganda work, often inspired from outside. (Haumant, 1930: 497)

East Central Europe after 1800: a rapid growth of nationhood

The Poles were certainly a nation by 1918, the year of the restoration of Polish independence. Polish national identity, at first limited to the upper classes, seeped down gradually to the Polish masses in the course of the national struggles and the economic advances of the nineteenth century. But their country, Poland, was by no means ethnically homogeneous (according to the census of 1921, only 69.2 per cent of the population was ethnically Polish). This was because the Polish state was restored in 1918 in (roughly speaking) its historical rather than its ethnic boundaries. In particular, the new Poland possessed a large Ukrainian minority (14.3 per cent of the total population in 1921) located mainly in the eastern part of the country. Other, smaller minorities were Belarusan (4.1 per cent in 1921), Jewish (7.8 per cent), and German (3.9 per cent).[1] The official Polish response to diversity was not acceptance, but a determined effort at nation-building, or, as Chris Hann has put it, 'a strategy of exclusion and assimilation', which lasted through the 1920s and 1930s (Hann, 1998: 843).[2]

The process of assimilation had flourished under the first Polish state, given the strong magnetic pull of Polish culture, and it even continued during the nineteenth century, when Poland was no longer independent; now, however, things were different. The ethnic minorities proved highly recalcitrant. When in 1939 the short interwar period of Polish independence came to an end, as a result of the joint German and Soviet invasion of the country, the minorities were still there, more embittered and aggrieved than ever.

But the minorities problem found a 'solution' of a kind by the complete remodelling of the ethnic map which resulted from the tragic events of the Second World War and its aftermath. As is well known, Poland lost most of its Jews during the war through the Nazi extermination programme; between 1945 and 1947 it also lost most of its Germans (by expulsion), and its Ukrainians and Belarusans (by their inclusion in the Soviet Union). The result was that Poland went from being one of the most heterogeneous to one of the most homogeneous nation-states in Eastern Europe (95 per cent of the inhabitants were ethnic Poles after 1947) (Bugajski, 1994: 363). This did not prevent the ruling Communist party from mounting an anti-Semitic campaign in 1968, as a result of which most of the remaining Jews left the country. But, that apart, the material for ethnic conflict was simply not present in Poland, so that even after 1989 there was little likelihood of its recrudescence. According to the 1992 census, 98 per cent of the population were ethnic Poles. Nevertheless, there is still a 100 000-strong Ukrainian minority in the country, who are, it is claimed, prevented from expressing themselves nationally by the overwhelming dominance of Polish culture (Hann 1998: 863).

Like the Poles, the Hungarians recovered their independence in 1918. Unlike the Poles, they did not particularly welcome the events of 1918--19 because they saw them as a painful defeat, involving the separation of three million Hungarians from their homeland (this situation was given international legal force by the Treaty of Trianon in 1920). The presence of so many Hungarians outside their borders gave rise to ethnic tension and conflict in three neighbouring states (Yugoslavia, Romania and Czechoslovakia). But it also meant that there were no substantial ethnic minorities within the country itself. Trianon Hungary was ethnically 90 per cent Hungarian, and, despite the upheavals of the Second World War, the proportion remained the same after 1945.

The Czechoslovak story is split in two until the early twentieth century. Before that there were two separate ethnic groups, the Czechs and the Slovaks, closely allied but differing in historical experience and also to some extent in culture. The Czechs had, as we saw earlier, a history of medieval statehood; they also had a tradition of written literature. All the national revivalists of the early nineteenth century had to do was reach back to the past and select the appropriate aspects of an old-established, although buried, culture. This was, as noted earlier, the work of Josef Dobrovský, who fixed the Czech language in the form it has subsequently retained, despite the quarrels in the twentieth century over purism and language reform (Auty, 1980: 175).

For the Slovaks it was different. Slovak nationalists could claim that the Great Moravian Empire of the ninth century was the first Slovak state, but it was destroyed within a hundred years by the Magyar invasion, and there was no later revival of Slovak statehood until the twentieth century.[3] Right up to the end of the eighteenth century, and even beyond, the Slovaks did not use their own language for official and literary purposes. Instead, they used Czech, alongside Latin (Bartoš and Gagnaire, 1972: 7–8). With the coming of the Reformation, a religious division arose between the Lutherans and the Roman Catholics in Slovakia. This had an impact on their attitudes towards their neighbours. The Lutheran minority of Slovaks continued to make no distinction between Czech and Slovak, but the Catholic majority moved towards establishing a separate Slovak literary language. In the seventeenth and eighteenth centuries, the Catholic University of Trnava played an important part in promoting Slovak culture. This reached a finished form in the mid-nineteenth century thanks to the efforts of two scholars, Anton Bernalák (1762–1813) and Ludovit Štúr (1815–1856). Bernalák created the first Slovak literary language in 1787, but it was accepted only by the Catholic majority, the Slovak Protestants continued to use Czech. In the nineteenth century, a debate developed about the most desirable form for the Slovak literary language; this debate was resolved in 1844 in favour of Štúr's version, the central Slovak dialect, which was further away from Czech than the version used earlier by Bernalák. A further step had thus been taken towards Slovak linguistic separation from Czech.

Despite this promising start, the development of Slovak literature was held back for half a century by restrictions imposed by the Hungarian authorities, who ruled the country until 1918. Moreover, Hungarian rule, with its accompanying Magyarization, also meant that a Slovak elite was practically non-existent. Even at the primary level, education was conducted in Magyar rather than Slovak at this time: only 276 out of the 3520 schools in Slovakia in 1917/18 did their teaching in Slovak; 30 000 school pupils were taught in Slovak, and 200 000 in Magyar (Hoensch, 2000: 8). As late as 1918, the total number of 'educated and politically conscious Slovaks' was estimated at between 750 and 1000 (Seton-Watson, 1931: 30).

The evident lack of any firm basis for a Slovak national movement led many Slovak opponents of Hungarian rule towards the idea of calling on the aid of their far more developed brother nation to the west. The political project of 'Czechoslovakism' was born. The increase in the popularity of this strategy after 1900 was a result of the work of the group of Slovak intellectuals and political activists who gathered around the journal *Hlas*, and who took their lead from the founder of Czechoslovakia, T. G. Masaryk (Leff, 1988: 34). The inclusion of Slovakia alongside Bohemia and Moravia in the new Czechoslovak state in 1918 can be regarded as their work. It was not the outgrowth of a popular movement among Slovaks themselves. They generally took a passive attitude politically during the First World War (Hoensch, 2000: 77). Census takers sent to Slovakia in 1919 found that the villagers replied to their questions as follows: 'Slovak or Hungarian? What difference does it make? If the Hungarians are doing well I want to be a Hungarian, if the Czechs are doing well I want to be a Slovak.' They met this reply so often that they described it as 'a general feature of Eastern Slovakia' (Peroutka, 1991: 135).

The 'Czechoslovakism' of Masaryk and his political allies had a further fateful implication: it required the rejection of the national claims advanced by the large ethnically German minority who resided in the Czech provinces of Bohemia, Moravia and Silesia, and who were subsequently described, somewhat inaccurately, as the 'Sudeten Germans'. Their nationalism was 'particularly vehement and intense' (Rothschild, 1974: 126). In December 1918 these people were included forcibly in the new Czechoslovak state. They were a constant irritant to successive Czechoslovak governments, and their majority support for Nazism in the 1930s was the reason both for the destruction of the first Czechoslovakia in 1938–9 and for their own dispossession and expulsion after 1945, which solved the problem in a brutal, but it would seem definitive, manner.[4]

With the foundation of Czechoslovakia, most Czechs and some Slovaks considered it pointless to spend energy on developing a separate Slovak literary language. The official language of Czechoslovakia was declared to be the 'Czechoslovak language represented by two literary forms'. The language law of 29 February 1920, which has been described as 'a threat to the Slovak language', was part of a general policy of fusion between the two nations pursued 'relentlessly' by the Czechs and their Slovak allies in the inter-war years (Kirschbaum, 1995: 169). Czechoslovak censuses taken in the inter-war years did not distinguish between Czechs and Slovaks. President Thomas G. Masaryk himself proclaimed in 1928 that Czechs and Slovaks were 'one nation with one language' (Masaryk, 1928: 13). And here is J. S. Roucek's sharp formulation: 'Slovak is the name given to the easternmost division of the Czech-speaking people' (1946: 353).

This was a view held much more firmly by Czech than by Slovak intellectuals, although it would be wrong to ignore the many Slovaks who favoured 'Czechoslovakism': in the interwar years, 10 per cent of Slovaks voted regularly for the Czechoslovak Social Democrats, who intended to solve the Slovak problem through 'strict centralism and a complete cultural and national assimilation of the Slovaks into the Czech people' (Hoensch, 2000: 117, n.15). It must be admitted that there were considerable differences between the two in language, and in cultural and historical background. The Czechs were an urban and industrial people. The Slovaks' occupations were predominantly agricultural (the 1921 proportion was 61 per cent), and very few Slovaks lived in towns: in 1921, 89 per cent of them were country-dwellers, and the proportion was still 86 per cent in 1931 (Rothschild, 1974: 91). Instead of recognizing the deep divisions in the nation, Czechs caused resentment by assuming that Slovaks were simply somewhat backward brethren who spoke a rather inferior, nonliterary dialect. Albert Pražák's assertion that 'literary Slovak is non-existent' was characteristic of this viewpoint (1929: 130). Most Slovak intellectuals rejected this point of view because they considered that Slovak was an independent language, not a mere dialect (Millet, 1983: 455).

Meanwhile, in the political sphere, the nationalistically-inclined Slovak People's Party, led by Andrej Hlinka, accused the Czechs of going back on the Pittsburgh Agreement of 20 May 1918, which contained a promise that Slovakia would have its own 'courts, administration and assembly' in the future Czechoslovakia (Leff, 1988: 152). T. G. Masaryk (later President of Czechoslovakia) signed this agreement, but ten years after this he described the document as 'forged', using the specious argument that his Slovak partners in the agreement were not a properly constituted political party. In any case, he claimed, the Slovaks had had autonomy since 1918, so they had no grounds for complaint.[5] This statement was clearly false; there was no local autonomy until 1928, and even after that date the competence of the local representative organs (not entirely representative, since a third of their members were nominated) was 'very limited' (Bartoš and Trapl, 1994: 16).

The Slovak nationalists did their best to force Prague to put the Pittsburgh Agreement into effect, while the Czechs resisted, on the grounds that, as Beneš remarked in 1933 (Kirschbaum, 1995: 170), 'separatism or political autonomy would simply be a new and major artificial political obstacle to the normal and inevitable biological and sociological evolution of our nation' (in the direction of fusion of its two parts, of course).

This lack of sympathy for Slovak aspirations on the part of the Czech majority was one reason why Slovak nationalism evolved in a more radical direction in the 1930s (there were other reasons too, such as the impact of the Great Depression). The Slovak People's Party moved away from its original demand for cultural and national autonomy within Czechoslovakia towards a separatist approach. Slovak separatism went hand in hand with a growing reliance on German assistance in the international arena. The well-known Munich Agreement, which deprived Czechoslovakia of its Sudeten German areas, was followed rapidly in October 1938 by the Žilina Accord, which converted the country into a hyphenated state – 'Czecho-Slovakia' – and established full autonomy for the Slovak half.

This was followed rapidly, in March 1939, by the complete destruction of Czecho-Slovakia at the hands of the Nazis, which opened the way for the setting up of an 'independent' Slovak republic with the formal attributes of sovereignty, such as a diplomatic service and an army, although in reality it was a German puppet state with room for manoeuvre, which continued to shrink as the Second World War continued. After the defeat of the Nazis in 1945 the Slovak republic naturally also disappeared, although in the restored Czechoslovakia the notion of a Slovak nation and a Slovak language was retained, with at least formally federal arrangements. After the Communist takeover in 1948, Slovak autonomy was reduced progressively . Slovak resentment about this was one of the driving forces of the Prague Spring of 1968, and the sole reform of 1968 that survived the Soviet invasion was Slovak autonomy: it come into force with the federal constitution of 1969.

The nations of South East Europe after 1800: a complex and tortuous creation process

Five, or perhaps six, nations come into consideration here. We shall say little about the Greeks, because their path diverged from that of the others after 1945, and they no longer belong to our story. That leaves the Romanians, the Bulgarians, the Albanians, and assorted Yugoslavs, including the Macedonians. We shall deal with them in the above order, after noting that the one thing they all have in common, in contrast with the peoples of Central Europe, is a delayed development of nationhood. One possible explanation for this is that the Ottoman Empire moved from indirect to direct rule far later than empires in other parts of Europe. Nationhood developed in the early and mid-nineteenth century in Serbia, Greece and Bulgaria in reaction to the first Ottoman attempts to impose political centralization on local notables who previously had enjoyed considerable autonomy (Hechter, 2000: 74–5).

Religion in general, and the Greek Orthodox Church in particular, also contributed to holding back national movements in the Balkans. While on the one hand the Church contributed to the preservation of each ethnic group's collective identity through the recognition of separateness accorded by the *millet* system under the Ottoman Empire, on the other hand it worked against the growth of nations because religious identity had no national content, and both Islam and Orthodoxy were self-consciously ecumenical in character. Thus the development of separate Greek, Serbian, Romanian and Bulgarian nations in the nineteenth century was assisted powerfully by the successive establishment of separate Greek (1833), Romanian (1865), Bulgarian (1870) and Serbian (1879) Churches, within the umbrella of Orthodoxy; but all this was achieved in the teeth of fierce opposition from the patriarch, the head of the Greek Orthodox Church in Constantinople (Kitromilides, 1989: 178–81).

In Romania, the transition to nationalism came in the 1790s, and it was, as usual, partly a reaction to attacks from outside, and partly a development internal to the community itself. Attacks from outside came both from the Habsburg rulers, with their centralizing reforms, and the Hungarians, with their insistence on controlling the whole of 'the lands of the crown of St. Stephen', including Transylvania. The main internal cultural development was the rise of Romanian feeling among the Uniate clergy, who were given a privileged position by the Habsburgs, and whose Latin-based education made it an obvious step, given the Latinate nature of the Romanian language, to claim that Romanians were descended from the Romans who ruled the area in the first few centuries of the Common Era (Verdery 1983: 119).

These developments all took place in Transylvania, the part of Romania controlled by the Habsburgs. Further east, in the semi-independent principalities of Moldavia and Wallachia (known collectively as the 'Danubian principalities') Romanian national feeling was directed initially more against the Phanariotes, Greeks who administered the land on behalf of the Ottomans, than against Ottoman domination itself. After 1829, Ottoman control was replaced by a Russian protectorate, although the Ottomans retained a theoretical suzerainty. The tsar's position as the guardian of the two Danubian principalities was confirmed by the Treaty of Adrianople. The principalities were also guaranteed full internal autonomy. This also meant that indigenous princes, rather than Phanariot Greeks, were elected to govern them.

However, there was still no Romanian national movement in existence. This did not develop until the 1840s, and then not on the spot but among Romanian exiles in Paris, who took their inspiration from the ideals of the French Revolution (Jelavich and Jelavich, 1977: 94). As elsewhere, the revolutions of 1848 were an attempt to put these ideals into practice, suppressed after a year or so by the restored powers of the old order. The Ottoman sovereign of the two principalities collaborated with their Russian protector, Nicholas I, to suppress a movement aimed at joining them together to form a Romanian state.

A decade later, the Romanians tried again, and this time they succeeded. In 1857, both Divans (Assemblies) demanded the unification of the two principalities; but opposition from several Great Powers and from the Ottomans resulted in the calling of the Paris Conference of 1858 to decide the issue. This imposed a compromise. The principalities were each given a constitution that excluded political union, though a federal association was set up with various joint institutions. It was the Romanian people (or, more accurately, the Romanian boyar elite, since most Romanians were still serfs) rather than outside powers who brought the idea of unity to fruition with the election in January 1859 of Alexander Cuza as *hospodar* of both principalities, thereby creating a personal union between Moldavia and Wallachia. The decision by the local Romanian elite was accepted by the Great Powers in 1862 and confirmed by the election in May 1866 of a king of united Romania. The person chosen was a minor German princeling, related to the Prussian royal house, Carol of Hohenzollern-Sigmaringen. Support for Romanian unity was not at first entirely unanimous. Some Moldavians did not want to give up their separate status, but their violent demonstrations against unification were suppressed by the army. Romania was given a constitution which provided for a single and indivisible state, with a single parliament. Full independence was not achieved, however, until 1878, when the Treaty of Berlin brought Ottoman suzerainty to an end.

The Bulgarians were a long-established ethnic group whose transition to nationhood was delayed by their centuries of subjection to the Ottoman Empire, and by their inability to establish even an autonomous position within it until the nineteenth century. Exactly how belated the Bulgarian nation was is a subject of dispute. Anastasia Karakasidou, in the course of a detailed attempt to justify her view that ethnicity was a late invention in the Balkans, maintains that 'American missionaries invented the Bulgarian nation' in the 1850s 'by creating the first Bulgarian script and basing the national language on the dialects of Thrace and Eastern Macedonia' (1997: 83).

This statement is questionable on several counts. It is true that there were some American missionaries in Bulgaria, but it is clear from Thomas Meininger's study that the American missionaries played a rather minor part in educating the Bulgarian nationalist intellectuals of the mid-nineteenth century in comparison with the contribution of

Greeks, Russians and native Bulgarians (Meininger, 1987: 229–30). Moreover, Karakasidou's dating of the invention of a Bulgarian script and the establishment of a national language in the mid-nineteenth century appears to be way off the mark. Bulgarian literary historians all agree that the founder of modern literary Bulgarian was Stojko Vladislavov (Sofronij Vračanski), who in 1806 produced *Nedelnik*, a volume of sermons, 'the first book to be printed in the modern Bulgarian language' (Moser, 1972: 44), and an autobiography, which was 'the first work in good modern literary Bulgarian' (Sugar, 1977: 266). A standard literary language developed soon afterwards. However, Bulgarian books could not be published within Bulgaria itself until Greek cultural predominance had been overthrown, and a prerequisite for this was an independent Bulgarian Church.

So the Bulgarian national struggle of the mid-nineteenth century had two goals: to destroy Ottoman political hegemony and to escape Greek ecclesiastical domination. The latter goal was attained in 1870, when an independent Bulgarian Church was established under its own exarch, in defiance of the Greek patriarch in Constantinople, who denounced the Bulgarian move as an example of 'chauvinism' (Kitromilides, 1989: 181). The political struggle took longer to win. It started in the 1860s, and culminated in the rising of 1876, which was on the face of it a heroic failure, but opened the way to victory by inducing the Russian Empire to intervene (Jelavich and Jelavich, 1977: ch.9). Two years later, having been defeated on the battlefield by the Russians, the Ottomans were forced to concede *de facto* Bulgarian independence.

The Albanians remained an ethnic group rather than a nation through much of the nineteenth century. The development of Albanian literary culture was held back not just by extreme economic backwardness but by deliberate obstruction from the Turkish side. The reformers who took charge of the Ottoman Empire in 1908, the Young Turks, made Turkish (written in the Arabic script) compulsory in all schools (Byron, 1976: 34–9). In the same year, however, a group of Albanian patriots reached agreement on a consistent way of writing their language, adopting the Latin script for the purpose. Their efforts were encouraged by the Roman Catholic Church, which had a certain following in the north of the country, and favoured the development of the vernacular. The Albanians enjoyed one great advantage, which balanced their cultural disadvantages: a complete absence of *diglossia*. In other words, there was no competition from traditional scholarly or ecclesiastical ways of writing the language of the kind that caused so many problems for the Greeks, the Bulgarians, the Serbs and, further east, the Armenians (Drettas, 1989: 171). This did not solve the problem of which form of Albanian to choose as a basis. As is the case with any unwritten language, there were considerable differences in dialect. The main, but not the only, distinction was between the speech of the Gegs, who lived in the north of the country, and that of the Tosks in the south. The dialects were, however, mutually comprehensible. A remarkable fact about the Albanians is that, despite this contrast in language, and other contrasts in social structure (by modern times clans existed only in the north, among the Gegs, and aristocratic landownership existed only in the south, among the Tosks) culture (music in the north was characteristically monophonic, in the south polyphonic), and religion (70 per cent of the Albanians were Muslims, but there was a Greek Orthodox minority of 20 per cent in the south and a Catholic minority of 10 per cent in the north) (Vickers, 1995: 178), they had a sense of unity that grew throughout the nineteenth century. This was not achieved without effort: the representatives of the Albanian cultural revival spent much time calling on their compatriots to forget religious divisions and forge a new 'Albanian' identity (Duijzings, 2000: 161).

In 1923, the authorities in the new Albanian state (independent since December 1912, with a wartime interval of dismemberment and occupation by Greeks, Italians, Serbians, Montenegrins, Austrians and French, after which independence was regained) chose one of the northern, Geg, dialects as the language standard, rather than the Tosk spoken by southerners, and a unified literature arose on that basis, although the low level of literacy and the lack of communication between different parts of the country meant that linguistic unification was still incomplete.

After the victory of the Communists in 1944 and the setting up of the Albanian People's Republic, a fresh start was made, but this time they took Tosk as the basis. There were several reasons for this change of standard. Most of the top Communist leaders (20 out of 27) were Tosks; the Geg-speaking areas of the north were a Catholic stronghold and therefore suspected of disloyalty to the new regime; and Tosk was the original language of the Albanian cultural revival of the late nineteenth century. In 1952, the Albanian Writers' Union resolved that Tosk alone would be used in publications (Byron, 1976: 61–5). It might be thought that this would prove divisive, but the outcome was quite the reverse. Some Geg elements were introduced into standard Albanian, and the language became a 'composite of the two dialects' (Byron, 1976: 65). The result of the subsequent forty-five years of Communist rule was the creation of a homogeneous nation. The north–south contrasts of earlier years were lessened considerably by the expropriation of Muslim landowners in the south and the prohibition of the blood feud in the north. As a result, post-Communist Albania, to use Andrew Baruch Wachtel's succinct phrase, is 'uniethnic and uninational,' though it remains 'multicultural' (Wachtel, 1998: 234). The result of this policy of unification was that there was no basis for ethnic conflict within the country. There has, in fact, been so little that the president at the time of writing, Rexhep Maidani, was able recently to offer his country as an example to others: 'Albania,' he said, 'can play a major role in stabilizing the Balkans and reducing nationalism. Borders will have less impact once the whole region becomes part of the united states of Europe.'[6]

We shall conclude this section by taking up the case of the formation of Yugoslavia. Here, the main issue was not the creation of a nation out of a pre-existing ethnic group, but the unification of 'the three tribes' of the area (Serbs, Croats and Slovenes) into a single nation. This was a long-drawn-out process, covering over two centuries. Ultimately, we can say with hindsight, it was unsuccessful. There were three attempts to achieve a political movement towards unification before 1918, all of them located in Croatia. It could well be claimed, with only a little exaggeration, that the idea of a democratic and voluntary union of the south Slav peoples is a Croatian invention.

The first attempt at unification was the Illyrianism of the 1830s and 1840s which developed around the figure of Ljudevit Gaj. This failed partly because of political repression (the Habsburgs suppressed the movement in 1843), partly because it disregarded the fact that a separate, independent Serbian state already existed. But Gaj had at least succeeded in placing the question of Yugoslav unity on the agenda. The second attempt was made in the 1860s, when a movement for 'Yugoslavism' was led by Bishop Josip Juraj Strossmayer and Canon Franjo Rački. This failed in part because it met strong resistance within Croatia itself from the Party of Right, which was set up in 1861 by Ante Starčević with the aim of achieving Croatian independence.

The third attempt was the most successful one: in 1905, two former supporters of the Party of Right who hailed from Dalmatia, Frano Supilo and Ante Trumbić, set up the Croato-Serb (or Serbo-Croat) Coalition, which was the majority party in Croatia right up to 1918, and also co-operated closely with the Slovenes. The aim of the Coalition was a federal Yugoslavia; its supporters therefore saw the establishment of a unitary kingdom of Serbs, Croats and Slovenes on 1 December 1918 under the Serbian royal house as both a victory and a disappointment.[7]

The key to success or failure in unifying Yugoslavia was, as Wachtel argues, the degree of cultural unification that could be achieved. Political unity alone was insufficient, although the two processes ran parallel. Cultural unification involved both unity of language and unity of literature (unity of language is not an absolute prerequisite for a united culture, but most nation-builders think and act as if it is). Several attempts were made during the nineteenth century to create a single Yugoslav literary language. This was difficult not only for the usual reason – namely, the existence of a plurality of different dialects, one of which would have to be chosen over the others, thereby creating resentment among the losers – but also because several centuries of divergent development had produced both a Croat and a Serb literature.

The Serbian language reformer Vuk Stefanović Karadžić (1787–1864) took the *ijekavski* dialect of the *štokavski* branch of the language as a basis, rather than the *ekavski* dialect spoken in Serbia and Vojvodina, because it 'can unite us with our brethren of the Roman law,' that is, the Croats (Franolić, 1983: 86). But Karadžić's Yugoslavism looked very much like Serbianism. It was based on the view that all *štokavski* speakers were in fact Serbs, even if they claimed to be Croats (Lampe, 1996: 61). 'Clever Serbs,' he wrote in 1836, 'both Orthodox and Roman Catholic, admit they are one nation.' The Croats 'do not know they are Serbs but in time will become Serbs' (Tanner, 1997: 53–4). Attempts were also made to unify the vocabulary (an example is the *Dictionary of the Croatian or Serbian Language* produced by the Serbian linguist Djura Daničić, which started to appear in 1880) and to set up a canon of 'Yugoslav' literature, based on the folk poetry of the south Slavs.

All these efforts to achieve cultural and political unification faced an insuperable obstacle: they came too late. Separate nations already existed, with either separate states (Serbia, Montenegro) or aspirations to separate statehood (Croatia), or a separate language and culture (Slovenia). Separate literary standards and separate literary traditions already existed, or were in the process of emerging, for the three south Slav nations, Slovenes, Croats and Serbs.[8]

The Mountain Wreath, published in 1847 by the prince-bishop of Montenegro, Petar II Petrović Njegoš (1812–51), was the greatest and most renowned epic of the south Slavs, but Njegos saw himself specifically as a Serbian writer. Moreover, the hero of the poem, Bishop Danilo, is depicted as a bloodthirsty man, intolerant towards Muslims in general and Muslim Slavs in particular: 'May God strike you, loathsome degenerates/Why do we need the Turk's faith among us?' he exclaims at one point (Wachtel, 1998: 46). Even so, *The Mountain Wreath* was also open to a more inclusive, Yugoslavist interpretation. The Turks of the story are occasionally given good lines: 'Though this country is a bit too narrow/Two faiths can live together side by side/Just as two soups can be cooked in one pot.'[9] The ambiguities of Njegoš's message made it possible for him to be treated as the 'posthumous prophet of Yugoslavdom'. The more offensive passages from his work could simply be ignored.

Somewhat later (in the early twentieth century) a multicultural Yugoslavism was propagated by several writers and artists, the most prominent of whom was the Dalmatian sculptor, Ivan Meštrović. Meštrović received commissions from King Aleksandar of Yugoslavia both to design a mausoleum for Njegoš's relics and to build a monument to Serbia's victory in the First World War (which was at the time considered to be Yugoslavia's victory). It must be stressed, however, that this endeavour to construct a multicultural Yugoslavism was the work of a minority, and it remained limited to the literary and cultural field. Even in literary circles, Meštrović's work was criticized by the left-wing Croatian writer Miroslav Krleža as being too Catholic, and too Croatian, and having 'nothing in common with the Byzantine foundation of the [Yugoslav] people's character' (Wachtel, 1998: 112).

The historians were another matter. They showed no interest at all in Yugoslavism. The authors of the pre-1914 historical textbooks recently analyzed by Charles Jelavich took as their main theme the conflict between the soon-to-be Yugoslav nations rather than their co-operation, and both the Serbian and the Croatian material examined was aimed at inculcating respect for the glorious past of the separate nations, particularly their medieval past, rather than any concept of a common Yugoslav heritage. Jelavich concludes unambiguously: 'None of the books – Serbian, Croatian or Slovenian – even remotely conveyed the type of information and enthusiasm about Slav unity that was being expounded by intellectuals ... before the war' (1990: 272). The sole example of a Serbian textbook that recognized that the Croats had made a certain independent contribution to south Slav history was the sixth edition of Milenko M. Vukičević's *History of the Serbian Nation for Secondary Schools*, published in 1914. Vukičević's book marks 'the first significant departure from Serbianism to Yugoslavism' (Jelavich,

1988: 109). However, because it was an isolated (and late) example, it exerted very little influence on popular opinion, which remained firmly nationalist, in the narrow sense.

This situation did not change materially after the First World War. Political victory was achieved in 1918 with the setting up of a Yugoslav state, but there was still no Yugoslav nation. The creation of a nation, in this as in other cases, was a cultural as well as a political task. There were two possible models for the creation of a unified Yugoslav culture: the existing culture of Serbia, which had grown up within the independent kingdom of Serbia during the nineteenth century; or a new culture combining elements of existing cultures, Serb, Croat and Slovene. The first model, though it had its supporters, such as the writers around the *Srpski Književni Glasnik* (Serbian Literary Gazette), based in Belgrade, who published only in Cyrillic and ignored Croat writers and artists, was clearly too divisive.

The second model was associated with the journal *Nova Evropa*, based in Zagreb, which propagated the idea of a 'unified, synthetic Yugoslav culture' throughout the 1920s and 1930s. This had a chance of acceptance by Serbs and Croats provided both sides accepted the essential unity of the language (Serbo-Croatian). But it was bound to meet with opposition from the third component of the Yugoslav nation, the Slovenes. Their language was too far apart from the other two to make unification a practical proposition, except on the basis of self-abnegation. *Nova Evropa*'s invitation to the Slovenes to give up their language met with a definite rejection in 1932 (Wachtel, 1998: 89).

The proponents of cultural, and in particular linguistic, unification considered that once this had been achieved, a united Yugoslav nation could be created. There are, however, other dimensions to ethnicity than simply language. Religion is one. It is clear that religion, or rather community membership as defined by religion (an expression which allows the inclusion of non-believers in specific religious camps), was vital in the Yugoslav case. There were marginal cases. Eugene Hammel refers to 'Catholic Serbs in Dubrovnik who celebrate the *slava* (an Orthodox feast)' (Hammel, 1993: 7).[10] These do not invalidate the main point. Religion is a strong marker of ethnicity, and membership of ethnic communities, particularly in Yugoslavia, was related closely to religious belief.

Another problem to be faced in achieving Yugoslav unity was the existence of large groups of people who could not be brought within the rubric of the 'three tribes.' This applied to Hungarians, other minorities in Vojvodina, to Albanians in Kosovo, to Macedonians, and to the Muslims of Bosnia. In Vojvodina and Kosovo it was tempting to solve the problem by encouraging Serbian immigration. In Vojvodina, ethnic Serbs constituted only a third of the population in 1918; by 1941 there was a Serb majority there (Bebler, 1993: 73). So partial success was achieved.

The situation in Kosovo was, and is, serious enough to warrant a more detailed discussion. As we saw earlier, the Albanians were an ethnic group rather than a nation in the nineteenth century. Naturally, this applied to the Kosovo Albanians as well. Serbian writers tended to downplay the existence of Albanian ethnicity. Cvijić describes the Albanians of Kosovo as 'mutated Serbs,' who had become used to 'mimicking' the real Albanians in order to improve their situation under Ottoman rule: their nationality and their religious affiliation, he thought, was only skin-deep (Cvijić, 1918: 587). The solution was simple: 'the expulsion of all Moslems and the reconstruction of the great Serbian Empire' (Durham, 1985: 263).

But in 1878 a movement for Albanian independence had begun, with the setting up of the League of Prizren, located in Kosovo. This movement made no distinction between Kosovo and the rest of Albania; Albanian revolts took place both in Kosovo (in 1885) and outside it (in 1893). Edith Durham, travelling through the area in 1908, found clear evidence of Albanian ethnic consciousness in Kosovo: 'The average Albanian believed that the land was his rightly for all time. The Serb conquered him, held him for a few passing centuries, was swept out and shall never return again' (Durham, 1985: 294). The claim of the Albanians to Kosovo was not recognized by the Great Powers of Europe. The borders of independent Albania, as established at the London Conference of 1912–13, were based on the 'historic rights' of Serbs, Montenegrins and Greeks rather than on ethnicity. Kosovo was assigned to Serbia. More than half of the ethnic Albanians were left outside Albania by this decision, which turned out to be permanent. Some Albanian tribes, such as the Hoti and the Gruda, became split by international borders (Qosja, 1995: 281).

In September 1913, the Kosovo Albanians rose in revolt. Their rising was cruelly suppressed, Muslims were pushed out to Turkey where possible, and a policy of Serbian settlement was instituted. The Albanians' situation improved temporarily during the First World War when the Serbian army was defeated (1915) and part of Kosovo was occupied briefly by Austria-Hungary (1916 to 1918). But at the end of the war the returning Serbs took a fearsome revenge, after which the province was integrated into the new Serb-dominated kingdom of Serbs, Croats and Slovenes (Vickers, 1998: 92–5).

A systematic attempt was now made to convert the area into Serb territory, using the two methods of Serb immigration and forced Albanian emigration. This sparked off resistance to Serbian rule, led by Azem Bejta and his *kaçaks* (outlaws), who used the neighbouring territory of independent Albania as a safe haven. This situation was eventually brought to an end by the decision of the prime minister (and later king) of Albania, Ahmet Bej Zogu, to hunt the *kaçaks* down when they crossed the border. [11] Serbian land confiscations and police harassment of Albanians were a feature of the subsequent period. There was also a considerable amount of emigration from Kosovo by Albanians and other Muslims. Estimates vary between 77 000 and 240 000 (Malcolm, 1998: 286). Even so, the attempt to make Kosovo Serb territory was largely unsuccessful. The proportion of Albanians fell, but only very slightly. In 1921, it was 64 per cent, and in 1931, 63 per cent, according to the Yugoslav census figures. A second attempt at Serb colonization and Albanian expulsion was planned in the late 1930s but lack of funds and then the coming of war probably prevented this (Vickers, 1998: 103–20).

Given the history of Kosovo over the previous thirty years, it was not surprising that the Axis occupation of Yugoslavia in 1941 was seen as a liberation by local Albanians, because it meant the inclusion of most of Kosovo in Albania. The Italian occupation authorities introduced the Albanian language for purposes of education and administration, and allowed the Albanian flag to fly. About 50 000 Serbs and Montenegrins who had settled in Kosovo in the interwar years now fled back to their original homes.

The Kosovo Albanians naturally rejected the attempts of the Communist partisans to persuade them to join in the fight for the liberation of Yugoslavia. According to a British agent who travelled in the area in 1944, the majority of Albanians in Kosovo would have nothing to do with the Communists and Tito: 'He appears to them as simply another manifestation of the Serb–Montenegrin menace' (Vickers, 1998: 134). Hence the victory of the partisans and the re-establishment of Yugoslavia in 1945 looked to the Albanians like another foreign conquest. Kosovo became a province of the Serbian republic, although a further six months of fighting were needed before local Albanian resistance was overcome.

Macedonia was another 'debatable land',[12] a third of which was destined to form part of Yugoslavia. No one seemed to want to admit that the Macedonians existed. They were regarded by Serb nationalists simply as Serbs. The Serbian view was that there was no such thing as a Macedonian language or people. Bulgarian nationalists preferred to see Macedonians as Bulgarians 'speaking a degenerate dialect' (Friedman, 2000: 182). The Macedonian dialects were at various points on the continuum of south Slav speech between Serbian and Bulgarian, and the language standard adopted in 1944 was roughly in the middle (Friedman, 2000: 175).

Greek nationalists, and foreign journalists influenced by them, regarded the existence of pockets of Slav speech in their part of Macedonia as a primitive survival which would disappear with the progress of education: 'Yes, I admit, there are many Greeks in Macedonia who are Slavonic in speech, that is to say Greeks who speak Slavo-Macedonian.' The French journalist Michel Paillarès then explains why: 'Greek is a learned language. Only educated people can write and speak it. But in Macedonia the flux and reflux of Bulgarian and Serbian invasion has deposited an alluvium of Slavonic words that has become the Slavo-Macedonian dialect. This is a patois the very restricted vocabulary of which can be handled by people of the lowest intelligence' (Paillarès, 1907: 401). This was not an isolated comment; Loring Danforth gives a number of examples, dating from as late as the 1950s: 'It is an idiomatic form of Bulgarian with a very scanty vocabulary of about a thousand words ... without syntax, without grammatical components and without spelling' (Danforth, 1995: 33–4). In point of fact, a Macedonian literary language had already emerged by 1903 (Friedman, 1986: 297).

Ownership of the territory of Macedonia was disputed during the nineteenth century between four rivals – the occupying imperial power of the Ottomans, and the kingdoms of Bulgaria, Greece and Serbia. Partition was one alternative; another was the establishment of a single Macedonian state. This was the dream of one faction of the Internal Macedonian Revolutionary Organization (VMRO) established secretly in Thessaloniki in 1893. Krste Misirkov called in 1903 for the 'recognition of Slavs in Macedonia as a separate nationality: Macedonian'. There were intellectuals and revolutionaries who proudly proclaimed themselves Macedonian. Temko Popov wrote in 1888: 'the national spirit in Macedonia today has reached such a degree that if Jesus Christ himself came down from heaven he could not persuade a Macedonian that he is a Bulgarian or a Serb' (Koneski, 1980: 59). This was something of an exaggeration. As one outside observer wrote, the largely illiterate peasants of the area had no sense of national identity: 'they could just as easily be turned into Serbians as Bulgarians' for 'they had no *patria*, and the propagandists failed to move them' (Durham, 1905: 61–2).

Moreover, there was a competitor for their allegiance: the other faction of VMRO, the Supreme Committee based in Sofia from 1895. This group aimed at annexing Macedonia to Bulgaria. The Ilinden uprising of 1903, the aim of which was to set up an autonomous Macedonia, was suppressed by the Ottoman authorities, and the local VMRO leaders were killed. This failure meant that the eventual solution (so far) to the Macedonian problem came from outside. In the last three months of 1912, during the First Balkan War, the three rival claimants to Macedonia – Serbia, Bulgaria and Greece – overthrew Ottoman power in the region, and divided the country into three parts: Serbian, Bulgarian and Greek Macedonia. Slight readjustments, to Bulgaria's disadvantage, took place after the Second Balkan War, and were confirmed by the Treaty of Bucharest, made in August 1913, but the essence of the territorial carve-up of Macedonia was not altered, either at that time or subsequently.

The Serbian part of the country (Vardar Macedonia) was described officially as 'New Serbia,' and 90 000 troops were deployed there in 1913 to put down resistance. After 1918, the use of the Bulgarian or Macedonian language was prohibited; Bulgarian schools and churches were closed; nearly 2000 people were killed in a reign of terror; Serbs were encouraged to immigrate to raise the level of this 'backward territory,' and the emigration of non-Serbs, particularly Turks and Albanians, was encouraged strongly (Banac, 1984: 317, n.25). But the problems could not be solved in this way (Boeckh, 1996: 154–5). Few Serbs responded to their government's call to move to Macedonia, and over the next twenty years a sense of separate Macedonian identity emerged gradually in the region, partly as a result of the continued efforts of VMRO, which led the resistance to Serbianization during the 1920s and 1930s despite being split between autonomist and pro-Bulgarian wings (Wilkinson, 1951: 299–300).

There was also a strong Communist movement in the area, and its attitude towards the Macedonians was therefore of some importance. The Yugoslav Communists' position on the national question went through a number of twists and turns during the interwar period, passing all the way from extreme centralism to demanding the dissolution of the country into its separate national units. A period of Yugoslav centralism was followed by, first, a recognition that there were three separate nations within the country with the right of self-determination, and then, under pressure from the Comintern, which in 1924 demanded agitation for 'the separation of Croatia, Slovenia and Macedonia from Yugoslavia and their establishment as independent republics,' the Yugoslav party proclaimed the right of Macedonia to independence and to unification with Pirin and Aegean Macedonia in a single state (Djilas, 1991: 85). This extreme position met with some opposition within the party, on the grounds that it meant attaching excessive importance to the national question and 'thrusting socio-economic and class interests into a secondary place' (Carr, 1964: 228–9). But the dissidents were condemned and expelled, and the party continued to advocate independence for Macedonia, alongside Croatia, Slovenia and Montenegro.

The turn towards the Popular Front tactic led in 1934 to a modification of this line, but not a complete reversal of it: the Comintern now ruled that the Macedonians were a separate nation, with the right of self-determination, but that this right could also be exercised within the Yugoslav context. The Yugoslav Communists took steps to put this into practice by adopting a policy of preserving the country from dissolution, but turning it into a federation. Separate Croatian and Slovene Communist parties were formed in 1937, and preparations were made to set up a Macedonian party; this happened eventually in 1943.

After the Communists' victory in the Second World War they set about implementing the Macedonian policies that had been formulated ten years earlier by the Comintern. On 2 August 1944, at the first meeting of the Anti-Fascist Assembly of Macedonia, they proclaimed a Macedonian republic, with Macedonian as its official language. Thereby, for the first time in history, Macedonian cultural institutions received state support (Troebst, 1992: 423–42). The very late development of a Macedonian identity does not mean it can be dismissed as 'imaginary,' argues Loring Danforth, since many apparently more deeply-rooted identities have also been constructed recently, despite appearances (1993: 7).[13]

The part of Macedonia included in Bulgaria after 1913, generally called Pirin Macedonia, was similarly subjected to forced assimilation. Throughout the inter-war years Bulgarian intellectuals and politicians 'unanimously' (Drezov, 1999: 47) denied the existence of a separate Macedonian nation and language, as did the majority faction of VMRO (a minority faction continued to call for a separate Macedonian state). When the Communists came to power in Bulgaria after 1945 they recognized Macedonian as a minority language, in line with the policy being pursued next door by Tito and the Yugoslav Communists

(Friedman, 1986: 298). Between 1945 and 1965 the party promoted Macedonianism; in other words, it adopted the position that the inhabitants of Pirin Macedonia were not Bulgarians but Macedonians, a separate nationality. Macedonian was recognized as a minority language in which books and newspapers could be published, and the Pirin Macedonians had schools where teaching was conducted in Macedonian (Friedman, 1986: 297–8). In 1956, the majority of the population of Pirin Macedonia was put down in the census as 'Macedonian' (179 000 Macedonians were recorded and, 94 000 Bulgarians).

This policy changed after 1965. It was decided that there were no Macedonians in Pirin Macedonia, nor had there ever been. The Pirin Macedonians were now described simply as 'Bulgarians' (Angelov, 1996: 105–6). This was clearly part of a move to construct a homogeneous Bulgarian nation, and it was in fact accomplished with little difficulty, since the cultural and linguistic differences between Macedonians and Bulgarians were not great. The failure of a Macedonian question to surface again in Bulgaria after 1989 was perhaps an indication that Pirin Macedonia had been absorbed successfully.

Assimilation to the dominant nation was also the rule in the part of Macedonia that fell to Greece (sometimes called Aegean Macedonia). Greek governments and politicians denied that there was a Macedonian nation. Slav speakers in the area were Hellenized in the manner described by Anastasia Karakasidou in her remarkable local study of a Macedonian town: 'Priests, teachers and powerful local families' changed the cultural fabric and formed a Greek national consciousness that had not existed before (Karakasidou, 1997: 111).

This policy, combined with the massive population exchange between Greece and Turkey after the First World War, converted a Greek minority of 42.6 per cent (1912) into an overwhelming majority of 88.8 per cent (1926). By 1930, 90 per cent of the Greek refugees from Turkey had been concentrated in Macedonia and western Thrace (Karakasidou, 1997: 145). The events of the Greek Civil War of 1946–9 removed the remaining consciously Slav element. The Greek Communists came out in support of Macedonian autonomy in 1946, partly to win over the Macedonians to their side. Accordingly, many Slav Macedonians allied with them. The result of the Communists' defeat in September 1949 was the flight of a further 35 000 Macedonians from the country. The Greek author, Evangelos Kofos, describes this as a 'beneficial side-effect of the Civil War' (1964: 186). A minority of 20 000 to 50 000 Slav speakers remain in Greece, but they tend to identify themselves as Greeks rather than Macedonians (Karakasidou, 1997: 22). The issue is hardly central to Greek politics any more, though emotions still run high over it; in general, one may conclude that the combination of assimilation and immigration practised in Greek Macedonia has succeeded.

Interwar Yugoslavia had yet another ethnic problem, in the shape of the Bosnian Muslims. The Serbian view was that these people were 'Islamicized Serbs' (Cvijić, 1918: 353), descendants of the old upper class of Bosnia who lived in the towns and adopted Islam in the course of the fifteenth and sixteenth centuries. The Croatian view was similar, except that they saw them as 'Islamicized Croats.' Whatever their presumed origins, the Bosnian Muslims were already a separate ethnic group by the mid-nineteenth century, differentiated not just by their Muslim faith, but by a tendency to live in the towns (32 per cent of the total population of Bosnia-Hercegovina was Muslim, but the proportion increased to 50 per cent in urban areas) (Friedman, 1996: 62) and by a strong land-owning element. In 1878 there were 7000 Muslim land-owners in Bosnia exploiting 85 000 servile peasants (*kmets*), 65 000 of whom were Orthodox, 23 000 Catholic, and 2000 Muslim. The 77 000 families of free peasants were overwhelmingly Muslim in religious affiliation (Stavrianos, 1958: 462).

Despite all these advantages, the Bosnian Muslims lacked a sense of national identity. The shift from ethnic group to nation was slow. One reason for this was the absence of nationalism among the intelligentsia. 'The Muslim intelligentsia,' writes S. M. Džaja, 'had first of all to set in motion their own national identification process, i.e. discover their own national identity' before they went over to promoting the national idea among their co-nationals (1994: 216). This did not occur until the early twentieth century.

The growth of a Bosnian Muslim identity was further delayed by the policy of the Austro-Hungarian authorities, who ruled Bosnia-Hercegovina from 1878 to 1918. Benjamin Kállay, joint finance minister of Austria-Hungary, who was in charge of Bosnia-Hercegovina under the peculiar constitutional arrangement invented by the imperial government in order to avoid including the territory in either Austria or Hungary, 'attempted to introduce an official Bosnian nationality, to which all the religious groups of the province would belong, and which would separate them from the Serbs,' who were the monarchy's great bugbears (Pinson, 1994: 103). In the 1890s, the Habsburg government also subsidized a newspaper, *Bošnjak* (The Bosnian), which had two tasks: to defend Muslims against those who would merge them into either the Croat or the Serb nation, and to promote a common Bosnian ethnicity (*bošnjaštvo*) for all Bosnians, irrespective of religious affiliation. The Habsburgs succeeded in the former aim, but not the latter. Perhaps this was one of the great missed opportunities of Balkan policy: to overcome the confessional divide and build a nation on a purely territorial basis.[14] But the campaign for *bošnjaštvo* hardly even got off the ground. The Orthodox and Catholic communities in Bosnia showed no sign of being won over to a Bosnian identity at this time (Friedman, 1996: 64) and the Muslims of Bosnia evolved towards self-identification as *Muslimani* instead of adopting a secular, all-inclusive Bosnian outlook.

After Kállay's death in 1903, the Austrian government abandoned his policy and instead allowed specifically Muslim organizations to form. In December 1906, a group of Muslim leaders met at the town of Slavonski Brod (just outside Bosnia) and set up the Muslim National Organization. By then, Serbian and Croat elites were already locked in conflict over the future ownership of the region, as well as over the question of whether the Muslims should be seen as Serbs or Croats (Banac, 1984: 361). Jadranka Grbić sees this pre-war period as the time of the 'final institutionalized division' of Bosnia-Hercegovina into 'three basic national communities': the Bosnian Serbs, the Bosnian Croats, and the Bosnian Muslims (1997: 15–16).

By the time the state of Yugoslavia emerged there were three separate national groups within Bosnia, with their own institutions and organizations. The Yugoslav Muslim Organization (JMO),[15] set up in 1919, succeeded in preserving a Bosnian entity for a decade, thanks to the efforts of its leader, Mehmed Spaho. Under the Vidovdan Constitution, adopted in 1921, the existing administrative unit of Bosnia-Hercegovina was retained. But in 1929 the region was subdivided into several different districts, and it was not reunited until after the victory of the Communist partisans in the Second World War.

The emergence of the three small Baltic nations

We now move to the territories further east, which belonged in the nineteenth century to the Russian Empire, and later on either became independent or formed part of the Soviet Union. We look first at the lands to the east of the Baltic Sea. We shall not examine the Finnish case, because Finland did not subsequently pass through the Communist experience and therefore moves out of range of our story. Three states are left: Estonia, Latvia and Lithuania. They all achieved independence after the First World War, confirmed by treaties with Soviet Russia in 1920, then enjoyed a brief period of statehood in the next twenty years. This was followed by the upheavals of the Second World War, and after that they reverted to Russian control (formally speaking, Soviet control).

In Estonia, the process of national awakening began in the late 1850s. It was spurred on partly by the reform discussions initiated under Tsar Alexander II, and it was facilitated by the relaxation of press censorship at that time. The expansion of Estonian literature under Alexander II can be shown by comparing the frequencies of book publication. Between 1848 and 1855, thirty-two books a year were published in Estonian; while between 1856 and 1863, the figure was forty-eight a year (Kruus, 1935: 139). The first Estonian language weekly newspaper, J. W. Jannsen's *Pärnu Postimees* (The Pärnu Postman) began to appear in 1857. By 1881, there were eight. The first Estonian daily followed in 1891. A literary standard was established for the language in the course of 1870s, based on the dialect spoken in the north east. In 1878, K. R. Jakobson founded the journal *Sakala*, which had a programme of strengthening Estonian national individuality, emancipating Estonian culture from German influence, and freeing the Estonian peasantry from the grip of the local Baltic German landowners (Hroch, 1985: 76–7). Although Jakobson's *Sakala* only survived for four years, its agitation was successful. By the 1890s, Estonian intellectuals were no longer communicating in German but in their own language (Raun, 1987: 77).

At roughly the same period a national programme began to take shape. In 1881 a petition was sent to Tsar Alexander III calling for equality with the Baltic Germans and for the establishment of two administrative units, one for Estonians, the other for Latvians, in place of the existing historically-based division into Estland (inhabited by Estonians but only covering part of the Estonian area), Livland (inhabited by both Estonians and Latvians), and Courland (inhabited by Latvians and Lithuanians).

Economic and social changes strengthened the position of the Estonians in the late nineteenth century. Urbanization and industrialization brought an influx of Estonians to the cities, reducing the Baltic Germans to a minority (there was also an influx of Russians, but not in such great numbers). By 1897, 67.8 per cent of the urban population in the future Estonia was ethnically Estonian. Estonian national claims were at this stage moderate, given that the country was small, and that a future independence could not be envisaged. The most any Estonian expected until 1917 was the transformation of the Russian Empire into a federal state, with autonomy for its peoples, including the Estonians. The First World War and the resultant collapse of the Tsarist empire changed this situation. The first call for an independent Estonia was made in December 1917, partly as a way of preventing the German occupation which was clearly impending (Kruus, 1935: 244). By January 1918, all Estonian parties except the Bolsheviks had associated themselves with it. On 25 February 1918 a Committee of Elders of the Provincial Estonian Assembly (*Maapäev*) declared independence and set up a provisional government. The entry of German troops into the country a day later rendered this a short-lived initiative. However, once the war had ended (November 1918) the Estonian provisional government re-emerged, and in February 1920 the period of uncertainty as to whether Estonia would be Bolshevik or not was ended by the decision of Soviet Russia to sign a peace treaty and recognize Estonian independence. The period of Estonian history which began then was important, because it meant that the Estonians had a period of independent statehood to look back on when they were again under Russian occupation (in 1940–1 and in 1944–91).

Events in Latvia approximately mirrored those in Estonia. First came the movement of cultural revival, centred around the 'Young Latvians' of the 1850s. Then came the formation of patriotic associations, the first signs of the emergence of a genuinely national literature, and the publication of newspapers in the national language (the first one was published in 1878). Social changes ran alongside these intellectual developments. There was an influx of Latvian peasants into the towns (by 1881, 37 per cent of the inhabitants of the chief city, Riga, were Latvians). This gave rise rapidly to a Latvian working class and the elements of a middle class. In the revolutionary years after 1905, the Latvians, like the Estonians, hoped to gain their aims through an alliance with Russian democrats and social democrats, and did not expect to achieve independence. The turn towards independence was a by-product of wartime events. Latvia's declaration of independence was even later than Estonia's, coming as it did in November 1918. Like Estonia, the country then experienced twenty years of independent statehood, initially under a democratic system.

The Lithuanian national movement of the nineteenth century had very different priorities from those of Latvia and Estonia. Whereas German influence, both culturally and socially, was the main obstacle to Latvian and Estonian national development, and Russification was of secondary importance, as it began very late, when the national movement had already developed, the first task for the Lithuanians was to emancipate themselves from Polish influence. There were no German landowners in Lithuania, and the problem for Lithuanian patriots was rather to develop a separate, non-Polish national identity.

There was, however, no unanimity on this point. For some Lithuanians the Poles were fellow Catholics and traditional allies against Tsarism. Thus many Lithuanians took part in the Polish revolt of 1863 with the aim of restoring the Polish state within its 1772 boundaries, including the whole of Lithuania. The Lithuanians also faced other obstacles in developing their own national movement, such as the fragmentation of ethnically Lithuanian territory into two states (the Russian and German Empires) and four administrative units (Kaunas, Vilnius, Suvalki, and East Prussia); the Russian prohibition on printing books in Latin characters, and indeed on Lithuanian-language publication in general; the relative retardation of economic growth (there was no influx of Lithuanian peasants into the towns comparable with what was happening further north); and finally the ambivalent position of the Roman Catholic Church, which had served as an instrument of Polonization in earlier years, and continued to have no interest in promoting the Lithuanian national cause (Loit, 1985: 59–77). In the course of time, all these problems were overcome, and a Lithuanian national council proclaimed independence in February 1918, which became a reality in November with the military collapse of the German occupiers. Twenty-two years of independent statehood followed.

Infirmities of empire: the eastern Slavs divide

It is possible to make a distinction between Russian ethnic identity and the broader claims of the Russian territorial empire. The language itself provides for this: the ethnic Russian's homeland is *Rus'*; the Russian empire is *Rossiia*. Geoffrey Hosking's recent book is built around this distinction. His central theme, he writes, is 'how the building of a *rossiiskii* (Russian) empire impeded the formation of a *russkii* (Russian) nation' (1998: xix). In 1832, Nicholas I's future education minister, Count S. S. Uvarov, formulated the triple slogan 'orthodoxy, autocracy and nationality.' Superficially, this looked like nation-building. But it was clear from the context that Uvarov's 'nationality' referred to 'allegiance to the Russian empire' rather than to a Russian nation

(Riasanovsky 1959: 137–8). In any case, his slogan went out of fashion under Nicholas I's liberal successor Alexander II; and it was left to Alexander III to attempt a policy of 'Russia for the Russians' in the 1880s (Dixon, 1996: 53). This was unsuccessful. It strengthened the nationalism of the non-Russians, by reaction, and it did not leave much impression on the attitude of the Russians themselves.

There is a good explanation for the weakness of pre-revolutionary Russian nationalism: the continuing strength of social divisions. The division of Russian society into estates, and the predominance of the nobility, meant that the latter class alone came into question as bearers of nationalism. This was far too narrow a basis for national feeling, and it collapsed with the expropriation and deracination of the Russian nobility in 1917 and the years that followed.

With the collapse of the Russian Empire, the other two Slavic nations had the opportunity to put their national demands into effect, in so far as they had any. National movements developed in the late nineteenth and early twentieth centuries among both the Belarusans and the Ukrainians.

The Belarusan linguistic and national revival came very late. It started in the mid-nineteenth century, but was not able to secure a foothold in the Russian Empire until 1905, when the ban on the publication of works in Belorussian was lifted. Not until 1918 was a modern literary standard set, when Branislaŭ Turaškevič published his *Belorussian Grammar for Schools* (Mayo, 1993: 888). The concept of Belarusan nationality was also late to emerge. In the 1890s, Francišak Bahuševič posed the question 'What is Belorussia?' for the first time. But ethnic awareness among Belarusans hardly existed at that time. They were an overwhelmingly peasant people as late as the census of 1897 (97.1 per cent of them were classified as rural inhabitants); 85 per cent of them were illiterate; and a mere 0.2 per cent were members of the professional classes. As late as 1919 they were 'still gripped in a medieval condition of national inertia' (Hroch 1985: 207). The only Belarusan newspaper of the early twentieth century, *Naša Niva*, pursued cultural rather than political objectives (Vakar, 1956: 87). So when, in 1906, the Belarusan Socialist Association called for the conversion of the Russian Empire into a 'federation of free peoples' in which Belarus would enjoy autonomy, it lacked the mass support to make this a popular slogan among the Belarusans themselves.

Independence finally came on 25 March 1918. But it was a gift of the conquering Germans and lasted only as long as German bayonets were there to uphold it. Nevertheless, an important first step had been taken towards the creation of a Belarusan national tradition. After 1921, Belarus fell into two halves. The western half of the ethnically Belarusan area was incorporated into Poland, a country where Belarusan cultural institutions were barely tolerated and Belarusan political aspirations ruthlessly crushed. Hence Belarusan nationalists tended to look more favourably on the Soviet Union, where the other half of the Belarusan nation was then located, and where, as we shall see later, an energetic programme of Belarusan cultural development was put in hand, at least during the 1920s (Rothschild, 1974: 42).

The Ukrainian national movement of the nineteenth century had rather deeper roots, but it too was somewhat fragile. There were many obstacles to overcome, in particular the division of what we now know as Ukraine among the Austrian and Russian Empires, and the relentless hostility of the Russian government to the idea of a separate Ukrainian nation. For the nineteenth-century rulers of Russia, Ukrainians were simply Russians who spoke a strange dialect. The Tsarist reaction to the mid-nineteenth century Ukrainian cultural revival associated with the name of Taras Shevchenko was to prohibit the publication of Ukrainian books and newspapers, and the use of the Ukrainian language in education. These prohibitions lasted until the revolution of 1905.

The Habsburgs, in contrast, allowed a Ukrainian press to develop in Galicia, partly as a way of holding the Polish nationalists in check. But on both sides of the border there was very little in the way of a social basis for a Ukrainian national movement. Few Ukrainians were literate (14 per cent in the Russian Empire in 1897), the vast majority were country-dwellers (94 per cent in the Russian Empire in 1897), and even among the tiny group of intellectuals of Ukrainian origin the majority preferred to assimilate into the larger Russian whole. The Ukrainian peasants had a 'poorly developed sense of national identity'. The peasant 'wore his ancestors' clothes and spoke his ancestors' tongue but was hardly aware that the language he used in his daily life was Ukrainian' (Krawchenko, 1985: 28). Nevertheless, the Ukrainian nationalist movement had time and opportunity to develop after 1905, and by 1917 'the identification between peasant aspirations and the programme of the Ukrainian national parties was quite close' (Guthier, 1979: 46).[16] The events of the revolution and the Russian Civil War strengthened this sense of Ukrainian nationhood, so that when the Bolsheviks overran the area for the third and last time in December 1919, it made a lot of sense to adopt a policy of political autonomy and cultural development.

The western part of Ukraine, comprising roughly four million Ukrainians (mixed with Poles), was incorporated into Poland after 1918. In the long run, they were better off, but initially they had several reasons to be dissatisfied with their situation. Although they constituted a very large minority – 14.3 per cent of the population in 1921 – an attempt was made to Polonize them. Ukrainian cultural institutions were frowned on by the Polish state and never given official status. As with the Belarusans, it looked in the 1920s as if unification with their brethren in the Soviet Union (where Ukrainian culture was flourishing) was a better option. It was, of course, an illusion, which did not survive the news that leaked out in the 1930s of the terrible famine that had followed agricultural collectivization in Soviet Ukraine, but the Poles did not take even this opportunity to win back the Ukrainians' allegiance by making concessions in the cultural sphere: on the contrary, they saw the situation as 'a licence to ignore the Ukrainians' aspirations' (Rothschild, 1974: 43).

The Caucasus after 1800

The nineteenth century witnessed a national revival among the two Christian peoples of South Caucasus; this is the point at which ethnicity developed into nationhood for the Armenians and the Georgians. The first phase of the process was cultural nationalism: the rediscovery of the language by a handful of intellectuals and an endeavour to establish a uniform literary language which could then be transferred to the mass of the people. This was the task accomplished in Armenia in the 1850s by the secular nationalists, people such as Mihayl Nalbandian and Stepanos Nazariants, and in Georgia in the 1860s by Ilia Chavchavadze.

Once this had been done, it was relatively easy for a whole series of separate national cultural institutions and political parties to develop. By the end of the century, the whole political and social spectrum was present among both the Armenians and the Georgians. There were certain differences in the relative weights of social and political groups: in Armenia, liberalism, nationalism and the middle class predominated; and in Georgia, socialism, the working class and the peasantry. But there was no doubt in either case about the attributes of nationhood, though for the Georgians there were a number of countervailing forces, such as competition from other ethnic groups and the absence for most of the time of an urban middle class (Suny, 1996: 251).

In the case of the third major ethnic group of South Caucasus, the Azerbaijanis, the path towards nationhood was strewn with obstacles. First, there was uncertainty about Azerbaijani ethnic identity, which was a result of the influence of Azerbaijan's many and varied pre-Russian conquerors, starting with the Arabs in the mid-seventh century and continuing with the Saljuq Turks, the Mongols, the Ottoman Turks and the Iranians. Hence the relatively small local intelligentsia wavered between Iranian, Ottoman, Islamic, and pan-Turkic orientations. Only a minority supported a specifically Azerbaijani identity, as advocated most prominently by Färidun bäy Köchärli.

Second, there was the simultaneous presence in Azerbaijan of a socialist movement, *Himmät*, which was based on the ethnically mixed working class of the oilfields of Baku. *Himmät* saw the future of Azerbaijan not in ethnically based nationalism but in a union of all the many national groups that inhabited the area under the aegis of a democratic revolution over the whole of the Russian Empire (Swietochowski, 1996: 218–23). The third obstacle was the retention by the mass of the people of what Swietochowski calls 'a universalistic *umma* consciousness'; in other words, the sense of belonging to the broader Muslim community as opposed to a narrower national group within it (1985: 193).

It was not surprising, therefore, that the growth of an Azerbaijani nation took place after, and not before, the gaining of independence (1918). Even then, the nationalist Musavat party was in power for too short a time (two years) to allow it to achieve much in the way of Azerbaijani nation-building. The Bolshevik reconquest in 1920 meant that an Azerbaijani nation would continue to be built, but in an entirely different manner.

What we have said of Azerbaijan is even more applicable to the Muslims of Central Asia. As late as 1917 they lacked any sense of national identity. The political and cultural movements that developed in reaction to the activities of the Russian conquerors embraced the whole area on a Muslim traditionalist, Muslim reform (*jadid*) or pan-Turkic basis. Even in 1917 only one Central Asian nationalist party was visible: the Kazakh party *Alash Orda*. All the other Central Asian political movements of the year of revolution were pan-Turkic, pan-Islamic, or socialist and internationalist (Roy, 2000: 43). When the Bolsheviks reconquered the area after the Civil War the strongest resistance they met came from the *Basmachi*, a movement led by Muslim traditionalists. The creation of ethnic groups in Central Asia, and their subsequent growth into nations, was the work of the Bolsheviks themselves, as we shall see in Chapter 4, and the raw material for this operation was provided not so much by the Central Asians themselves as by the efforts of nineteenth century Russian educationalists, geographers, scholars and census-takers.

Issues of continuity and discontinuity

It is clear from the evidence presented in this chapter that most of the ethnic groups discussed here had made the transition to nationhood by the time the Communists came to power (Central Asia is an exception); all the issues that were to plague the region subsequently were already in place. But before we examine the way the Communists reacted to these problems, we must examine the issue of continuity. Was there continuity or discontinuity between the pre-modern *ethnie* and the post-nineteenth century nation? The question of national continuity has long been disputed, and the argument still continues. In 1972, the Hungarian theorist, Jenö Szúcs, launched the idea that the pre-modern nations were limited to the nobility and therefore there was no continuity with the modern nation, which was plebeian in character. The Polish historian, Benedykt Zientari, took the opposite view: for him, the pre-modern nation had a meaning wider than the narrow circle of the nobility, hence there were genuine elements of continuity between past and present (Třeštík, 1995: 167).

More recently, R. G. Suny has argued strongly for discontinuity even in the Armenian, Georgian and Jewish cases, despite the fact that most writers on the subject have seen them as possessing a continuous, unbroken historical tradition. These were classic cases of 'nations before nationalism,' to use John Armstrong's phrase (1982: title page). Suny, in contrast to this, asserts that 'a discontinuous and varied history has been simplified into the story of a relatively fixed "nation" moving continuously through time, struggling to realize itself in full nationhood and eventually independent statehood' (Suny, 1999–2000: 146).

We are inclined to think that this is an underestimate of the element of continuity from ancient times. To take the Armenians and Georgians first, their languages certainly changed over time, but they retained specific features that distinguished them from others; there was a demonstrable continuity of religious institutions and belief; there was also a continuity in the ethnic substratum (though clearly there was also intermarriage and the absorption of new elements from outside). If we turn now to the Jews, we find that Maxime Rodinson, on whom Suny relies for his treatment of this case, is far less insistent on discontinuity than the latter implies: thus he states that 'the Jewish *ethnos* ... continued to exist' as 'an ethnic nucleus' throughout classical times, and that during the Middle Ages Judaism was 'a religion having certain characteristics of an ethnic group'. Moreover, although Judaism 'was on the road to complete liquidation' through assimilation in modern times, it was 'preserved by the constant influx of Jews from Eastern Europe or the Muslim world, where medieval conditions had often persisted'. Thus even Rodinson comes down by and large in favour of continuity (Rodinson, 1983: 93–110).

Continuity, however, does not signify ethnic 'purity.' Throughout history, ethnic groups have been revivified and altered by admixtures from outside. And continuity often hangs by a thin thread, which is easily broken. We have seen this when examining specific cases in the course of this chapter.

4
Ethnicity and Nationhood under Communism

The period of Communist control, starting roughly in 1917 in the case of the Soviet lands and around 1945 in the case of Central and Eastern Europe, used to be seen as a time when the differences between nations were suppressed and a determined effort was made to eradicate nationalism. In this view, the course of history was diverted for a half century or more, only to revert to 'normality' after 1989 or, in the Soviet case, 1991. But, in fact, as Rogers Brubaker has noted, 'far from ruthlessly suppressing nationhood, the Soviet regime pervasively institutionalized it' (1996: 17). That comment was made specifically about the Soviet Union, but one can say the same of Communist Central and Eastern Europe. We shall examine direct measures to promote nationhood in the course of this chapter.

But, in addition to this, the Communist system also stimulated nationalism in an indirect way. It was an 'economy of shortage' or, to use Katherine Verdery's expression, 'a system of organized shortage' (1993a), and in conditions of scarcity, informal economies develop on ethnic lines: where unofficial, personal connections are vital, people tend to turn first to members of their own ethnic group (Chazan, 1986: 142–3). Admittedly, Ladislav Holy (1996: 7) excludes the 'economy of shortage' as a factor in the Czechoslovak case, but this was a country where ethnic conflict and the use of ethnicity by the rulers was far less pronounced than in South East Europe. The only reform to survive the Soviet invasion of Czechoslovakia in 1968, for example, was a concession to the Slovaks: the establishment of a federal system, replacing the Prague-based centralism of the 1950s and early 1960s.

So the Communists contributed both directly and indirectly to the creation and strengthening of ethnic and national consciousness. To show this in detail, we shall examine in succession the situation in the Soviet Union, Central Europe and Eastern Europe.

The USSR: a communal apartment for the nationalities

The territorial settlement in and after the victory of the Bolsheviks in the Civil War predetermined in some ways the course of future ethnic and national conflicts. We shall examine the origins of the most serious cases of conflict later in this section. But first, some general comments should be made about the nature of Bolshevik policy.

The nation-building process was accelerated powerfully everywhere in the Soviet Union by the decision of the Bolsheviks to set up the USSR as, in Yuri Slezkine's words a 'communal apartment' (Slezkine, 1994) in which all the ethnic and national groups could live side by side under conditions of autonomy and the free development of their cultural aspirations. The establishment of federations on the former territory of the Russian Empire (the RSFSR in 1918, and the USSR in 1922) reflected a complete change in Lenin's attitude. Before 1917 he had polemicized frequently against the federal principle, saying that, under the principle of self-determination, each national group had a choice of either seceding and setting up its own state or becoming part of the new international socialist state, which would be organized on a unitary basis. There could be no third way. But after 1917 he changed his mind: there was a third way – federation. He now thought that a federation was 'the most suitable form of organization for a multiethnic state' (Smith, 1996: 5). This policy was carried through with rigorous logic. In the newly formed RSFSR and USSR, what T. D. Martin (1996) has described as an 'affirmative action' policy was pursued during the 1920s and part of the 1930s, thereby anchoring and fixing certain ethnic and national identities which until 1917 were fluid and uncertain, especially in the Asian parts of the Soviet Union. This was the epoch of indigenization (*korenizatsiia*), a period when every single one of the 192 languages identified in the census of 1926 was made official at some level, a task which in many cases involved arriving at a common literary standard, coining many new words and even creating written forms for hitherto purely oral dialects. Indigenization continued even after the 'Great Change' of 1929. It was made more systematic, in fact, by the requirement that even small national minorities within existing national republics should have their own cultural autonomy (Slezkine, 1994: 430–9).

It would take us too far afield to examine each individual example of this process.[1] We shall simply pick out some of the more significant cases. Belarus is one. The Soviet authorities set up a Belarusan SSR in 1919, and they pursued a policy of 'Belarusanization' between 1924 and 1930, promoting the Belarusan language and creating a Belarusan intelligentsia and a group of Belarusan party cadres. The Russian language virtually disappeared from offices, schools and universities. Stalin himself publicly looked forward to a time when the cities, as yet predominantly Russian, would be purely Belarusan in ethnic character (Slezkine, 1994: 423). These policies undoubtedly strengthened Belarusan nationhood. Indeed, Jeremy Smith's verdict is that 'Belarus would not exist as a recognized political entity in any form, let alone as a nation state, had the Bolsheviks not chosen to promote the Belorussian nation in the way they did' (Smith, 1999: 242).

The situation was very different in the part of Belarus which fell to Poland after 1921. There no vestige of autonomy was permitted and a determined campaign was mounted against the Belarusan ethnic group, including the closing down of Belarusan schools and universities. The number of Belarusans in Poland, which David Marples estimates as initially three million, fell to 1 060 000 people (according to the Polish census of 1921), and then to 990 000 (according to the 1931 census). This was not so much a result of the suppression of Belarusan institutions (it happened too quickly for that) as of systematic undercounting. All Belarusan Catholics were classified as Poles, and a category of 'locals' was introduced, which covered 707 000 people in 1931, who were probably all Belarusans (Marples, 1999: 7–8; Rothschild, 1974: 36).

Against this background, the situation of the Belarusans in the USSR looked favourable. But the Soviet honeymoon did not last longer than a decade. A campaign against 'national deviationism' started in 1930. Belarusans were removed from important state positions and replaced by outsiders. The intellectuals who benefited from indigenization in the 1920s found themselves in jail by the end of the 1930s.

The decision of the Soviet authorities to base their nationality policy on ethnic categories meant that territorial units formed on any other than a purely ethnic basis were not encouraged. This line of approach has been subjected subsequently to severe criticism, but one must be clear about one thing: the adoption of an ethnic basis for the construction of national entities, whether in the west or in the south Caucasus, was entirely in accordance with the traditions and the existing ethnic consciousness of those areas. Soviet nationality policy of the 1920s recognized existing divisions rather than creating new ones. Any other policy, either of subdivision or of association in a larger regional unit on a geographical or economic basis, would have been subjected to even fiercer criticism. It was not the policy itself that was wrong, but rather the artificial and unreal character of the autonomy granted to component units of the Soviet Union. But this was inevitable, given the centralization of the instruments of power in a Communist system.

One reservation must be made, however. There is a distinction between the more easterly parts of the Soviet Union, where ethnic divisions were as yet unknown, and the west and south (Ukraine, Belarus, the Baltic lands,[2] Armenia and Georgia) where, by the 1920s, fully-fledged ethnically-based national movements existed and had already struck deep roots in popular consciousness. In Central Asia and the culturally closely allied region of the North Caucasus, a unity which still existed in the early 1920s, expressing itself in the joint participation of many ethnic groups in resistance and rebellion against first Russian and then Soviet power, was, no doubt partly for that very reason, dismantled.

The Caucasian 'mountaineers' originally had their own 'Mountain Autonomous Socialist Soviet Republic' (GASSR), set up in January 1921. It did not last more than a few months in that form; it was divided and redivided during the next few years, and the new, smaller units then formed a basis for the development of national, or at least ethnic, identity on a smaller scale. The top local Bolsheviks would have preferred to stay together in a single republic (Wixman, 1980: 136). But from the beginning there was, it seems, strong support from below for ethnic subdivision.[3] Stalin, who was in charge of these matters, commented on one application: 'if the workers of Kabardia want to separate, so be it' (Daudov 1997: 171). In line with this policy, separate ethnically-based administrative units were set up for most North Caucasian *ethnies*: Kabards, Cherkess, Karachai, Balkars, Chechens, Ingush, North Ossetians and Adygeians. A little later, the Karachai were combined with the Cherkessians, and the Kabardinians with the Balkars, in both cases in defiance of ethno-linguistic principles (the Cherkessians and Kabardinians were practically the same nation, as were the Karachai and the Balkars, yet they were deliberately separated).[4]

So the ethnic principle was not always strictly applied; indeed, it could not be applied at all in the case of Dagestan, where the complexity of the ethnic picture made it impracticable. The Dagestan ASSR, first set up alongside the Mountain ASSR in 1921, continued to exist throughout the Soviet period. This was an exceptional arrangement; everywhere else in the Russian Soviet Federative Socialist Republic (RSFSR)[5] the application of the ethnic principle led to the establishment of numerous small administrative units which were incapable of exercising any real autonomy. The whole arrangement of autonomous republics within Russia has been criticized severely over the years by most Western authors, as well as Soviet dissident writers.[6] Russian writers, both Soviet and post-Soviet, have tended to justify it on grounds of necessity.[7]

A similar policy of ethnic subdivision was adopted in Central Asia, after some hesitation. Initially, in 1921, an ASSR of Turkestan was set up, a multi-ethnic republic covering what later became Kyrgyz, Turkmen, Uzbek, Karakalpak and Tajik areas. In 1924 it was decided to divide Turkestan into separate national units, by the process known as 'national delimitation' (*natsional'noe razmezhevanie*), also against the wishes of local Communist leaders, who would have preferred to retain the unity of the region (Soucek, 2000: 220).[8]

In the South Caucasus, in contrast, a policy of unification was followed initially. Armenia, Azerbaijan and Georgia were thrown together in December 1922 to form a Transcaucasian Socialist Federative Soviet Republic (TSFSR), even though all three had enjoyed a period of separate statehood just after the First World War. This solution did not last, however. In 1936, the TSFSR was dissolved into its three component parts, which have since 1991 become the three independent states of Armenia, Azerbaijan and Georgia.

After the mid-1930s the policy of indigenization was abandoned with regards to national minorities. It was replaced, not by Russification, but by 'concentration on a few full-fledged and fully equipped nations'; in other words, the titular nations of the republics and autonomies. 'The Soviet communal apartment,' as Slezkine wittily puts it, 'was to have fewer rooms but the ones that remained would be lavishly decorated' (1994: 445). In fact, this remark needs to be supplemented: the lavish decorations were now in traditional Russian style, because of the universal abandonment after 1938 of the use of Latin characters and the introduction of Cyrillic for writing the languages of almost all the non-Russian nations.[9]

Moreover, the RSFSR was by far the largest republic of the Soviet Union, its titular nation being the Russian nation itself. Until 1932, non-Russians within the RSFSR benefited from a policy of 'ethnic proliferation', which involved promoting all national cultures equally, whether they were in the minority or the majority. After 1932, this changed. One sign of what was to come was the abolition on 15 December that year of all Ukrainian institutions in the RSFSR. This was a serious matter, given that the Ukrainian minority consisted of roughly four million people at the time. From then onwards, Russian culture alone was promoted in the Russian Republic. There was, however, a partial exception to this rule: where indigenous non-Russian nations already possessed ASSRs (Autonomous Soviet Socialist Republics) within the RSFSR, their cultural institutions continued to be recognized (Martin, 1998b: 111).

This was not all that Stalin did in the 1930s to worsen the situation for non-Russians. Titular nations in the union republics retained their formal privileges, but in practice their elites suffered considerable blood-letting in the purges of the late 1930s. In some cases, this amounted to a considerable setback for the nation in question. In the Belorussian SSR (Belarus), for example, the national elite formed in the 1920s was destroyed in the purges; the local Communist party lost 40 per cent of its members (Zaprudnik, 1999: 87).

The national minorities, having lost their cultural autonomy, suffered still worse treatment. Some of them were already being deported to Central Asia and Siberia in the late 1930s. The main reason for this seems to have been that they were likely to have had ties with non-Soviet citizens, since most of them already had their own nation-states outside the USSR: this applied to Poles, Germans, Finns, Estonians, Latvians, Chinese and Iranians. But Kurds were also deported (Martin, 1998a: 813–61). A fresh wave of deportations, which also affected a number of titular nations, and was more severe in numerical terms, took place towards the end of the Second World War. In 1944, a number of North Caucasian nations were selected on a strictly ethnic basis for deportation to Central Asia. Units of the NKVD were instructed to round up every single member of the relevant ethnic group, although in the case of the North Ossetians a distinction was made between the majority group (known as the Iron Ossetians), who were not deported, probably because they were Orthodox Christians, traditionally loyal to Russia, and the 20–30 per cent Muslim minority (the Digor Ossetians), who did suffer this fate (Leeper, 1995: 180).

All the deported nations were non-Christian in religious background (either Muslim or Buddhist). They were all located in or very close to zones held briefly by the Nazis in 1942–3, and the official reason given for deportation was that they had collaborated with the Nazi invaders. There were indeed many instances of collaboration, primarily among the Cossacks (who were not deported), the Crimean Tatars, the

Kalmyks, the Karachai and the Balkars (Simon, 1991: 197). It has, however, been pointed out that, first, the Chechens (for example) were in no position to collaborate with the Germans, since their territory remained in Soviet hands throughout the war, and, second, there were plenty of potential collaborators among those nations spared from deportation.

Why, for example, were the Kabardinians spared? They were after all very troublesome to the Russians in the nineteenth century. Semyon Lipkin's moving novel *Dekada*, set in the wartime Kabardino-Balkar ASSR, depicts the decision to deport the (Turkic) Balkars and not the (Caucasian) Kabardinians as entirely arbitrary: Stalin had, as we saw earlier, sent his greetings back in 1921 to a Congress of Soviet Kabards, while saying nothing about the Balkars (Lipkin, 1983: 26–7). It seems that the idea of deporting the Balkars came from Beria, who wrote to Stalin in February 1944 suggesting this. The deportation took place a month later (Knight, 1993: 126–7). The Balkars may have been picked out because they were a Turkic people, and therefore suspected of Pan-Turkism. The simultaneous deportation in 1944 of the (Turkic) Karachai rather than the (Caucasian) Cherkess is a point in favour of this explanation. Or perhaps Beria was simply currying favour with Stalin by demonstrating his extreme vigilance.

Whether arbitrary or not, the deportations had important results. Being singled out for a common fate on an ethnic basis strengthened the national self-consciousness of the deportees, particularly the Chechens, with the result that when they were allowed to return home in the 1960s they were very aware of what separated them from both the Russians and the other Caucasian national groups. This had important consequences for the future.

After the death of Stalin, Soviet nationality policy changed once again. There began what Gerhard Simon has described as a 'silent process of indigenization', whereby more and more members of the non-Russian nations gained representation in their local party and state leaderships, especially in the Baltic states and the Caucasus. Local elites were able to entrench themselves, in the union republics if not in the ASSRs.[10] By the 1960s 'locals held virtually all top positions in propaganda and culture' (Simon, 1991: 276).

The general rule was for the titular nation to be represented in the local elite in proportion to its share of the population. In fact, a comparison of 1979 census figures with the proportion represented in leading posts in party and state institutions shows a slight over-representation in most republics: the figures for the three Baltic republics are 68.0 per cent of the population and 72.3 per cent representation; for the three Transaucasian republics, 77.3 per cent of the population and 81.9 per cent representation; and for Kazakhstan, 36.0 per cent of the population and 44.9 per cent representation. For Ukraine, representation was exactly in line with population – 73.6 per cent of the population, 73.4 per cent representation. For the four Central Asian republics it was slightly below – 64.3 per cent of the population, and 58.2 per cent representation (Houle, 1997: 347–66).

Only in the SSRs of Moldavia and Belorussia did representation fall seriously below entitlement on an ethnic basis (the figures for Moldavia were 65.4 per cent of the population and 37.2 per cent of leading posts; for Belorussia, 81.1 per cent of the population and 63.1 per cent of leading posts) (Hodnett, 1978: 103).[11] The well-nigh permanent boss of the Belorussian republic, Pyotr Masherau (head of the party from 1965 to 1980) was allegedly 'dedicated to Belarusan interests,' and he is known to have spoken the national language 'at some official functions' (Marples, 1999: 20). He nevertheless presided over a continuous deterioration in the position of ethnic Belarusans in education, literature and urban life in general (Guthier, 1977: 275).

The post-Stalin method of administering the non-Russian components of the Soviet Union had fateful results for the future. Each republic was treated increasingly as a national polity which 'belonged' to its titular nation and to no other. There developed what Gregory Gleason has called a 'bureaucratized nationalism' (Gleason, 1991: 5) based on the republican elites of the respective titular nations. Hence, after the collapse of the Soviet Union and the achievement of independence by the union republics, the temptation to continue in the same way was irresistible.[12] There are also comparisons to be made with the situation in Czechoslovakia and Yugoslavia, where similar structures allowed a similar consolidation and entrenchment of ethnic elites at the republican level (Leff, 1999: 205–35).

Under Khrushchev and Brezhnev it appeared for a long time as if the decision to take local national elites into partnership in ruling their own areas (though they were given only a tiny share of power in central Soviet institutions) had succeeded in taking the sting out of the national problem. The only serious challenges to the constitutional structure came from national groups which felt that their interests had been recognized insufficiently under this cosy arrangement, in particular the Armenians of Nagornyi Karabagh, and the Abkhazians in Georgia.

Nagornyi Karabagh (Mountain, or Upper, Karabagh), a largely Armenian enclave surrounded by Azerbaijani territory, was incorporated into Soviet Azerbaijan in 1921. Abkhazia (or 'Abkhazeti' in Georgian) was an area adjoining the west of Georgia, claimed by the Georgians as part of their country (a claim now disputed by most Abkhazians) and incorporated into Soviet Georgia in 1931 (after ten years of uncertainty about the precise relationship between the two areas). In view of the relevance of these two cases to later ethnic conflicts, we shall examine them in some detail here, dealing first with Nagornyi Karabagh, and then with Abkhazia.

The documents on the process by which Karabagh (including Nagornyi Karabagh, which was its southern, largely Armenian, part) became incorporated into Soviet Azerbaijan in the early 1920s demonstrate a considerable degree of incoherence in early Soviet nationality policy. On 30 November 1920, the following solemn declaration was made by Nariman Narimanov, the head of the Communist Party of Azerbaijan, and M. D. Guseinov, Azerbaijan's Commissar for Foreign Affairs: 'With effect from today, the former boundaries between Armenia and Azerbaijan are proclaimed annulled. Nagornyi Karabagh, Zangezur and Nakhichevan are recognized as a constituent part of the Armenian Socialist Republic' (Galoian and Khudaverdian, 1988: 28).

In the light of future decisions, this looks like a remarkable act of self-abnegation on Narimanov's part: in the interests of national reconciliation he simply handed these long disputed territories to Armenia. This, indeed, is the way Stalin presented it in *Pravda* a few days later: 'On December 1st, Soviet Azerbaijan voluntarily renounced its claim to the disputed provinces and proclaimed the handing over of Zangezur, Nakhichevan and Nagornyi Karabagh to Soviet Armenia' (Stalin, 1947: 414). The decision was confirmed on 12 June 1921 in relation to Nagornyi Karabagh by a vote of the Caucasian Bureau of the Russian Communist Party, and reconfirmed on 4 July 1921.

By now, however, Narimanov had changed his mind. The vote of 4 July 1921 was very close – four in favour, including Stalin's right-hand man in the Caucasus, Sergo Ordzhonikidze, and three against, including the representatives of both Azerbaijan and Georgia. On 5 July, the original decision was overturned, because Ordzhonikidze changed sides, and now Nagornyi Karabagh was included in Azerbaijan, though with the proviso that it would receive a degree of regional autonomy (Chorbajian *et al.*, 1994: 178–9).

It is generally assumed that Stalin was behind this change of heart, and that he had decided it was more important to placate the Azerbaijanis and the Turks, for foreign policy reasons, rather than the Armenians. According to the Armenian Communist leader, Alexander

Miasnikian, 'Azerbaijan said, if Armenia gets Karabagh, we shan't let it have any oil' (Galoian and Khudaverdian, 1988: 33). Geographical and economic arguments were also advanced, and, indeed, even a quick glance at the map of the region would show how 'natural' it looked to include in Azerbaijan what would otherwise be an entirely isolated enclave of Armenian territory (though the same argument applies in reverse to Nakhichevan, which was made part of Azerbaijan although it did not touch that republic at any point).

The future stability of the new arrangement would depend inevitably on how the Azerbaijanis treated this compactly Armenian area in the middle of their republic. As the sequel showed, Nagornyi Karabagh fell victim to one of the normal rules of Soviet nationality policy: where a union republic was set up, the titular nation tended to treat the whole of its national territory as a mini-empire. Moreover, Nagornyi Karabagh was not even an Autonomous Republic (ASSR): it was established in 1923 as an Autonomous District (AO), lower down the scale of Soviet autonomies, with fewer prerogatives. Its borders were drawn deliberately to make sure that it was separated from the territory of the Armenian SSR by an Azerbaijani corridor. For all these reasons, the next sixty years saw a continuous deterioration in the position of Armenian culture and the Armenian language. The Baku authorities' investment decisions bypassed the area,[13] and the local Armenian population began to emigrate in search of better economic opportunities. As a result, the proportion of Armenians in the population of Nagornyi Karabagh fell considerably, from 89.1 per cent in 1926 to 75.9 per cent in 1979 (Galoian and Khudaverdian, 1988: 47).

We now turn to developments in Abkhazia during the same period. Although the region had long been connected intimately with Georgia it was not a foregone conclusion when the Soviet Union was set up that it would be incorporated into that republic. On 31 March 1921 an independent Abkhazian SSR was proclaimed; this status lasted until December 1921, when Abkhazia entered the Georgian SSR, but through a treaty between equals, not as a subordinate territory. In fact, the first constitution of what was still described as the Abkhazian SSR, adopted in 1925, guaranteed the country independence and, just like any other SSR at the time, the right of free exit from both the TSFSR and the Soviet Union. The relevant paragraph was altered under Georgian pressure in 1927 to read: 'power is exercised subject to treaty relations with the Georgian SSR' (Beradze and Apakidze, 1991: 94).

A few years later (1931) Abkhazia was incorporated into Georgia as an ASSR. Resistance to this initially was muted. The Abkhazians hoped that their semi-independent status would be preserved. It was not. The big change in policy came in the late 1930s, the turning point being the liquidation in December 1936 of Nestor Lakoba, chair of the Abkhazian Central Executive Committee (Chervonnaya, 1994: 29). After that, the majority of the Abkhazian intelligentsia were eliminated in a series of purges, and the Abkhazian language was phased out of secondary schools; people were still allowed to write in it, but after 1938 they had to use Georgian characters rather than the Latin ones introduced in the 1920s (Comrie, 1981: 33). From 1936 onwards all leading party posts in the area were held by Georgians. The twin processes of Georgian immigration and assimilation of local people into the Georgian nation ('kartvelianization') reduced the ethnically Abkhazian proportion of the population of the Abkhaz ASSR drastically (between 1926 and 1959 this fell from 27.8 per cent to 15.1 per cent) (Hewitt, 1999: 466).

But, as elsewhere, policy changes after the death of Stalin allowed some degree of recovery. The Abkhaz proportion of the population rose from 15.1 per cent in 1959 to 17.7 per cent in 1989 (it is now estimated at 20 per cent); the separateness of the Abkhaz language was recognized in 1954, when the Georgian alphabet was replaced by the Cyrillic one; and, in general, the atmosphere became freer. This had an unexpected result: it allowed Abkhazian resentment to come to the surface. This was an indication that a serious problem existed. In response to repeated petitions from Abkhazian intellectuals and party officials (in 1956, 1967 and 1978), Nikita Khrushchev and his successors pursued a rather conciliatory line. The Abkhazians were the only ethnic group able to enforce a compromise on the central power by their protests. The reason was simple: they had a direct line to Moscow, through the fact that the Black Sea coast, where Abkhazia was located, was a favourite holiday destination for Kremlin policy-makers.

The more extreme Abkhazian demands (such as the call for secession from Georgia and the abolition of the Georgian language's official status) were rejected in 1978. But a party commission, headed by I. V. Kapitonov, was sent from Moscow to defuse the situation. The Kapitonov Commission advised a range of conciliatory measures in the areas of education and investment allocations. These were imposed on the Georgian party leadership, thereby 'defusing a potentially explosive situation' (Slider, 1985: 65).

The Abkhazians now began to enjoy the fruits of positive discrimination. More and more books were published in Abkhazian. As a result, the Abkhaz language ranked first in the whole of the Soviet Union in terms of book titles per person (the 1988 figures were 4.3 book titles for every 10 000 Abkhazians). An Abkhaz State University was established, TV broadcasts in the language began, and the level of investment in the area was raised. By 1989, Abkhazians held 40 per cent of the seats on local elected bodies and 50 per cent of local executive posts, although they constituted only 17.7 per cent of the population (Chervonnaya, 1994: 34). Abkhazians were appointed as first and second secretaries of the local Communist party, and they were also well represented in other party posts. As the Abkhazian writer, Konstantin Ozgan, concedes, there was 'over-representation of Abkhazian nationals in some ... posts in the autonomous republic' (he adds, however, that these posts were 'sinecures') (Ozgan, 1998: 187).

Nations and nationalism in Communist East Central Europe: the Polish example

In some ways, the events of the Second World War and its aftermath, horrifying though they were, reduced the possibility of ethnic conflict in the future by simply removing one or more of the contending parties. Most of the Jewish minorities of the region disappeared in the Holocaust, and after 1945 11 730 000 Germans fled or were expelled (6.9 million from future Polish territory). A further 2.1 million lost their lives in the process.[14] That is not to say that conflict was thereby ruled out; but there is a clear distinction between countries where this kind of 'solution' came about and those where it did not. Thus Poland, which was the scene of numerous ethnic conflicts of various kinds in the 1920s and 1930s, did not see a recrudescence of them in the 1990s.

With few exceptions, Polish politics after 1989 has been about issues of economic and political reform, social justice and the role of religion. Attempts to introduce anti-Semitism on to the agenda have largely been unsuccessful, given the lack of a substantial Jewish minority. Similarly, the Ukrainian question has not been raised, except in a very minor way. Divisive historical issues do exist: the UPA (Ukrainian Insurgent Army) carried out massacres of roughly 60 000 Poles in 1943–4 with German help, while the Polish army replied with the 'Vistula Operation' of 1947, which involved the uprooting of approximately 140 000 Ukrainians and Lemkos[15] from south-eastern Poland. They were resettled in the newly recovered northern and western territories, but dispersed among hundreds of villages to reduce their resistance to Polonization (Mucha, 1998: 174). 'In this manner,' writes

Orest Subtelny (1994: 490), 'the Poles finally rid themselves of the Ukrainian problem' (although it should be added that the Ukrainians and Lemkos did not entirely disappear through assimilation; many retained their identity).

After that, the policy pursued towards the remnants of minority groups that remained on Polish territory varied with the general political situation. Until 1952 the policy was assimilatory; between 1952 and 1966 there was a gradual improvement, culminating in the granting of permission to minorities to form their own cultural organizations. The main minorities in 1962 were 180 000 Ukrainians, 165 000 Belarusans, and 31 000 Jews. After 1966 the situation worsened again (particularly for Jews, with the anti-Zionist campaign of 1968, which resulted in the emigration of most of them, leaving 5000 still in Poland). The end of Communism brought an improvement: the Solidarity movement put forward Belarusan and Ukrainian candidates for election in 1989, and Solidarity's Prime Minister Tadeusz Mazowiecki proclaimed that 'Poland is the motherland for its minorities as well' (Gantskaia, 2000: 88–99). Since 1991 the Polish and Ukrainian governments have been determined to stay on good terms, and the Polish Constitution of 1997 provides stronger rights for minorities.[16] The contrast with Yugoslavia is clear: there the images and memories of atrocities committed between 1941 and 1945 were used to provide justification for the atrocities of the 1990s (Hayden, 1995: 213).

Communism and nationalism in South East Europe

One post-1945 'solution' to the problem of ethnic minorities within states which defined themselves ethnically, that is, as states belonging to a particular nation, was to encourage these groups to emigrate. Sometimes this formed part of an ethnic exchange with neighbouring territories (Slovaks moved from Hungary to Czechoslovakia, while Hungarians moved in the reverse direction). Usually, there was simply an outflow of people without any counter-current. In Bulgaria, the surviving Jewish minority and some of the Turkish-speaking inhabitants were persuaded to leave. Most of the 48 000 Jews went to Israel, with only 5000 staying in Bulgaria. In 1950–1, 150 000 Bulgarian Turks left, roughly a quarter of the total.

In the short term, this made things easier for those left behind: Turks were recruited into the Communist party and they were allowed Turkish-language education. Bulgarian policy changed after 1956, however. The April 1956 Plenum of the BCP resolved to merge Turkish and Bulgarian schools, to treat Muslims as an indissoluble part of the Bulgarian people, and to intensify atheist propaganda, which was directed mainly against Islam. Moreover, the Muslim women's veil (*feredzhe*), previously left untouched, was now subjected to attack. A deveiling campaign began in the late 1950s.

A little later (1962) came the first campaign to change the surnames used by the Pomaks (Stoianov, 1998: 64). These Bulgarian-speaking Muslims had already been forced to abandon their original homes during the Pomak Relocation Campaign of 1949–51, by which the authorities shifted them away from the borders of Bulgaria because they were thought to be potentially disloyal. Although they were later allowed back, most remained in their new locations. They were extremely vulnerable to assimilation, because they lacked their own language. Even so, they maintained a 'clandestine ethnicity' throughout this period, based on a number of common distinguishing features: kinship structure, concentration in one area (Rhodope), largely rural residence patterns, and a tendency to find employment in the Construction Corps set up to carry out heavy jobs and staffed by ethnic minorities (Konstantinou, 1997: 34).

Signs of economic and political decline in the 1980s strengthened the temptation to supplement Communist with nationalist ideology. In 1984, the Bulgarian government launched the so-called 'process of rebirth', which was intended to 'strengthen national unity' by a forced assimilation of ethnic Turks. The Communist party's leader, Todor Zhivkov, proclaimed in 1985: 'There are no Turks in Bulgaria.' In line with this slogan, they were forced to change their names from Turkish to Slavonic. The veil, already barely tolerated, was now made illegal, as were Turkish-style trousers (*shalvari*). Islamic religious rites were prohibited (Neuburger, 1997a: 178).

Zhivkov's policy had the opposite effect from the one intended. As Eminov points out, 'it acted as a powerful force of ethnic consolidation', welding Bulgarian Turks together, reinforcing links between them and turning them inwards (Eminov, 1997: 137). This new-found sense of solidarity was to result first in a mass wave of emigration to Turkey during the summer of 1989, when 300 000 ethnic Turks left (in fact, 100 000 returned immediately to Bulgaria because Turkey's welcome was not as warm as it had been in 1950), and then, after November 1989, in a religious revival, accompanied by a heightened degree of political awareness. A political party was formed, the

Movement for Rights and Freedoms (DPS). The DPS drew support over-whelmingly from ethnic Turks, although it should be added that it pre-sented itself as a secularist party agitating for minority rights rather than a Muslim or Turkish pressure group.

A similar change, from an initial Communist policy of recognition of ethnic differences to a nationalist campaign to construct a single, unified nation, took place in Romania. There were two phases in post-war Romanian policy towards the largest minority, the Hungarians. The first phase, lasting from 1945 to 1956, was relatively mild. Hungarian schools, theatres, newspapers and political associations were allowed to exist, and in 1952 a Hungarian autonomous region was established in eastern Transylvania, the area of strongest minority concentration. Seventy per cent of local officials in the autonomous region were ethnic Hungarians. The year 1956 marked the beginning of a new phase. Hungarian-language education was progressively restricted, so that by the mid-1960s there were no more Hungarian schools, and only 30 per cent of the classes at Cluj University were taught in Hungarian. The boundaries of the Hungarian autonomous region were changed in 1960, reducing the concentration of Hungarians there from 77 per cent to 62 per cent. In 1965, Nicolae Ceauşescu took over as party leader, and in 1968 he abolished the Hungarian autonomous region, dividing it into three separate counties (King, 1973: 152–62).

After this, assimilation proceeded by leaps and bounds, thanks to the migration of ethnic Romanians into Transylvania, the outmigration of Hungarians and Germans, and the campaign promoting the Romanian language as essential even for the minorities. Later, in 1988, Ceauşescu introduced the policy of 'systematization', which, if fully imple-mented, would have involved the destruction of many of the country's villages and the relocation of the inhabitants to urban centres. Although not directed specifically against the Hungarian minority, it affected them, and it met with resistance in the ethnically mixed city of Timişoara which sparked off the revolution of 1989.

That was the negative aspect; the positive side of Ceauşescu's policies was his defiance of the Soviet Union and his identification of the Romanian Communist party with Romanian national interests. When Soviet forces invaded Czechoslovakia in 1968, Ceauşescu condemned the action, and countered by using the language of national identity: 'Be sure, comrades ... that we shall never betray our homeland, we shall never betray the interests of our people' (Verdery, 1991: 123).

From that time, national values were stressed in literature and the writing of history. In the 1970s, not content with asserting an unbroken continuity between ancient Romans and modern Romanians, Ceauşescu launched the theory of 'Protochronism': the historians were now forced to proclaim that the Dacian ancestors of the Romanians were on a higher cultural level than the Romans who conquered them in the first century (Gilberg, 1990: 176). For a long time, Ceauşescu's strategy appeared to work: David Kideckel has noted that the dictator's downfall was 'long postponed' by popular acceptance of his nationalist credentials (Kideckel, 1993: 175). This could not have been achieved if the ideology had remained a purely external imposition; Ceauşescu's 'national discourse' owed its power to the fact that it 'emanated from many quarters of Romanian society', and not just the Communist party (Verdery, 1991: 182).

In Albania, as we have already seen, the Communist regime was never plagued by the severe ethnic divisions that existed elsewhere in South East Europe. The two major sub-ethnic groupings, the Tosks and the Gegs, had no difficulty in communicating with each other. Religion was not a particularly divisive force, as most Albanians, both Tosks and Gegs, were Muslim, and the Roman Catholic and Greek Orthodox minorities never developed a separate ethnic identity. It is true that what is seen as the major Eastern European cultural fault-line, between the Roman Catholic and the Greek Orthodox/Ottoman Muslim traditions, ran through the country. Yet this was never a cause of conflict (except at a very local level, in the context of the blood feud, where reconciliation was almost impossible if rival families belonged to different religious communities).

The uneasy course of Yugoslav multiculturalism

The policy of the Communist party of Yugoslavia in its first fifteen years of power was a kind of compulsory multiculturalism (from which at first the Kosovo Albanians and the Bosnian Muslims were excluded). There is some dispute about how genuine the Belgrade authorities' commitment was to this line of approach. Non-Serbian authors tend to point to the continuing dominance of the Serbian variant of the language in the mass media, the administration and the army. Formally, at least, the linguistic position from 1954 onwards was laid down in the Novi Sad Resolutions, signed by twenty-five authors and linguists (two-thirds of them Serbs, admittedly), according to which there was a common literary language, Serbo-Croat (Croatoserbian) containing both Croatian and Serbian variants. This reflected the endeavour to retain Yugoslav unity. But the reforms of the 1960s led to a considerable degree of decentralization, which had an impact in turn on the cultural sphere; the loosening of censorship also played a part.

In the 1940s and 1950s, the Communist party's aim had been to get beyond ethnic differences and produce 'Yugoslavs'. But at some point in the early 1960s the party leader, Josip Broz Tito, gave up the idea of creating a single Yugoslav nation. In 1964, while continuing to denounce 'nationalism', he announced his opposition to 'the establishment of some kind of artificial, that is one single, Yugoslav nation' (Vuckovic, 1997: 117). This change of approach had considerable consequences in the cultural sphere; the cultural changes that ensued were decisive for the later fate of the country. The contest between the minority of intellectuals who still held on to the supra-national vision of Yugoslav culture and the particularist majority who wanted to develop the separate cultural traditions of each nation ended with the victory of the latter. As Andrew Wachtel comments, 'it was the victory of cultural particularism that laid the crucial groundwork for the ultimate political collapse of Yugoslavia' (Wachtel, 1998: 174).

In referring to a 'decline of multiculturalism' we have in mind a number of linked phenomena: the decline of the notion of 'Yugoslavism' among all the country's constituent nations except the Serbs;[17] the reassertion of ethnic identity among the Slovenes and Croats; the rise of new Bosnian Muslim and Kosovo Albanian ethnicities; and the reaction of the Serbs (and to some extent the Montenegrins) to these developments.

The reassertion of ethnic identity in Croatia was expressed most notably in a fierce agitation against the common 'Serbo-Croat' language. On 15 March 1967, eighteen leading Croatian cultural institutions issued a declaration protesting against 'domination by the Serbian literary language'. They called collectively for the establishment of a separate Croatian literary language, which would be used in all educational institutions and in the mass media (Cohen and Warwick, 1983: 144). Tito denounced this declaration, and a campaign was mounted against its initiators. Nevertheless, the agitation continued and in 1971 *Matica Hrvatska*, the main Croatian cultural association, declared that the Novi Sad agreement of 1954 was no longer valid. The Croatian movement then moved on from cultural demands to a broad spectrum of complaints about such things as the continuing hegemony of Belgrade, the fall in the birth rate among ethnic Croats, the excessive representation of Serbs in the ruling parties of Croatia and Bosnia-Hercegovina, the budgetary contributions the Croatian republic had to make to the Fund for Accelerated Development of the Less Developed Republics and Kosovo (FADURK), and the way hard currency earned by the tourist industry in Croatia tended to end up in the coffers of banks located in the Yugoslav capital.

This first wave of Croatian national resurgence was crushed by the Communist authorities, who ordered the seizure and destruction of a manual of Croatian orthography, of which 40 000 copies were printed in 1971 (Franolić 1983: 108). This was followed in 1972 by a severe purge of the local section of the League of Communists. Fifty thousand members were expelled, and between 2000 and 5000 imprisoned, including the later president of the country, Franjo Tudjman, who received three years in jail for 'spreading anti-Yugoslav propaganda'. Croatian nationalism was driven back underground. But all the issues remained there in the wings, ready to resurface in the late 1980s.

The rise of a Bosnian Muslim sense of identity was reflected in the decision in 1961 to introduce the category 'Muslim' into the Yugoslav census; and in the move away from Bosnian multiculturalism towards a narrower Muslim consciousness. This is clear in Meša Selimović's 1966 novel, *Death and the Dervish*, which 'implicitly repudiates' the vision of 'multicultural Yugoslavism' presented previously in the novels of the most renowned Bosnian writer, Ivo Andrić. For Selimović, to be Bosnian was to be Muslim (Wachtel, 1998: 183). In 1968, the Bosnian Muslims were recognized officially as a nation,[18] while the anti-Islamic measures in force in Bosnia up to that time were relaxed. The pilgrimage to Mecca was permitted, and students were allowed to study in Muslim countries. This relaxation lasted until 1979, when fear of an Islamic revolution similar to that in Iran led the Communist authorities to mount a show trial against Muslim leaders.

The chief person accused was Alija Izetbegović, a veteran Islamic activist whose 'Islamic Declaration', written in 1966, but not published at the time, was used as the basis for his trial and condemnation to fourteen years' imprisonment in 1983 (he remained in prison until 1988). The document is open to varying interpretations, and one passage in particular was picked out by his opponents: 'There can be no peace or coexistence between the Islamic faith and non-Islamic societies and political institutions ... the state should be an expression of religion and should support its moral concepts' (Izetbegović, 1990: 22). As Noel Malcolm has pointed out, this injunction only applies to countries where the majority of the population are practising Muslims, hence 'the entire discussion of the nature of an Islamic political system is inapplicable to Bosnia' (Malcolm, 1994: 220). Certainly, the assertion of a Bosnian Muslim sense of identity did not necessarily mean the end of inter-ethnic harmony, as Izetbegovic's opponents claimed. The practice of *komšiluk* (good-neighbourliness) between the three ethnic communities continued to prevail until the emergence of the three communally-based parties, the Muslim SDA (Party of Democratic Action), the Serb SDS (Serbian Democratic Party) and the Croat HDZ (Croatian Democratic Union), which were all founded in 1990 (Bougarel, 1996: 91).

Under Izetbegovic's leadership the SDA initially saw itself purely as a Muslim party, appealing to Muslims alone. A rival, secularist, party, the Bosnian Muslim Organization (MBO), which was led by Adil Zulfikarpašić, tried to bridge the sectional divide, but it did not do well in the December 1990 elections (it gained two seats as against the SDA's 86) and soon faded from view. The SDA, having won the elections, went on to try to create a coalition government with the two other communal parties, the Croat HDZ and the Serb SDS. There was a period of euphoria after the defeat of the Communists in December 1990, during which 'the three parties began to celebrate each other's holidays with brotherly enthusiasm' (Burg and Shoup, 1999: 61) but this did not last. We shall examine the descent into conflict in the next chapter.

Like the Bosnian Muslims, the Kosovo Albanians also benefited from the relatively liberal atmosphere in Tito's later years, and from the general post–1968 policy of solving national problems by making concessions to local interests. In 1968, the Albanians of Kosovo were put in charge of the province where they were in a numerical majority, and where until then they had been ruled by representatives of the much smaller Serbian minority. This began a process of cultural and demographic expansion which continued for the next twenty years. By the end of the 1970s, Albanians made up 72 per cent of the student population in Kosovo, two thirds of the members of the local League of Communists, the ruling party, and possibly three quarters of the police (Malcolm, 1998: 326). The Albanians seemed to understand 'what it takes to make numerical majorities' (Jackson, 1987: 100). The number of Albanians in Yugoslavia rose from 505 000 in 1931 to 1 309 000 in 1971 (2.4 per cent per annum) and to 1 731 000 in 1981 (2.8 per cent per annum). The number of Albanians in Kosovo alone rose even more dramatically, from 525 000 in 1953 (65 per cent) to 1 227 000 in 1981 (77 per cent) (Judah, 2000: 313).

In 1981, the Kosovan Albanians began to demonstrate for their province to be upgraded to the level of a republic within Yugoslavia;

the authorities replied with a policy of repression, as a result of which roughly a hundred Albanians were killed. But while intervening to stamp out what they saw as manifestations of nationalism the Serbian authorities did not venture to suppress the autonomy of the province. As a result, the process of Albanian self-assertion continued throughout the next decade. Serbs continued to leave the province; Albanians continued to have more children. Later we shall see the impact this had on opinion in Serbia, and the use made by unscrupulous politicians of allegations that Serbs were being driven out of Kosovo.

There were substantial Albanian minorities in Serbia proper, Montenegro and Macedonia. They were also highly visible, because they were concentrated in certain localities. For example, in 1981, Albanians made up 85.3 per cent of the commune of Preševo (southern Serbia), 55.4 per cent of Bujanovac (southern Serbia), 72.6 per cent of Ulcinj (Montenegro), 62.5 per cent of Gostivar (Macedonia), and 69.8 per cent of Tetovo (Macedonia). The Albanian share of the total population of Yugoslav Macedonia rose from 12.5 per cent in 1953 to 21.5 per cent in 1991, according to official census figures.

The reassertion of ethnic identities in Yugoslavia was helped by the relative infrequency of intermarriage between different ethnic groups. Yugoslavia was 'ethnically endogamous', argues Nikolai Botev (1994: 461–80). First, there was no clear upward trend in mixed marriages: in the period 1962–4 they represented 12.7 per cent of the total; and in 1987–9, 13.0 per cent. Intermarriage was always highest in Vojvodina (22.5 per cent in 1962–4; 28.4 per cent in 1987–9) and lowest in Kosovo (9.4 per cent in 1962–4; 4.7 per cent in 1987–9). Second, an analysis of the propensity to intermarry shows that even the Serbs (the most exogamous group) were between 2 and 8.5 times more likely to marry within their own ethnic group than random mating would imply. In Bosnia, where ethnic mixture was at its greatest, outside observers stressed the social distance between the different nations (*nacije*) in the mixed villages, despite traditions of good-neighbourliness (*komšiluk*). Contacts, though regular, were 'likely to be superficial' and 'in-group feeling and ethnocentrism' remained high (Lockwood, 1975: 220).

It is interesting to note that Yugoslavia in the 1980s presented most of the features identified by Robin M. Williams as making up 'the most lethal configuration for ethnic conflict', namely (i) a multi-ethnic population; (ii) a centralized state with redistributive powers, (iii) substantial military forces, (iv) a few large *ethnies* of nearly equal strength; (v) territorial concentration of ethnic groups as opposed to ethnic mixture; (vi) marked inequality between ethnic groups; and (vii) ethnic political struggles for collective goals (Williams, 1994: 72). Six of Williams' criteria fit the Yugoslav case well, though presumably this is not an accident, since they were developed with Yugoslavia in mind. Item (ii) is the only one that does not really apply, because by the 1970s Yugoslavia was no longer centralized, as we shall now explain.

The suppression of Croat nationalism at the beginning of the 1970s was, paradoxically, accompanied by constitutional changes which brought a tremendous accretion to the power of the constituent republics of the Yugoslav Federation. In 1969, the Ninth Congress of the LCY (League of Communists of Yugoslavia) set up a collective party leadership. From that point onwards there was no all-Yugoslav Communist organization. The task of each LCY Congress was henceforth to confirm (or compromise over) decisions already arrived at by the eight regional parties (the six original ones, plus the upgraded provincial parties of Vojvodina and Kosovo) (Vuckovic, 1997: 121). Moreover, the 1974 Constitution broadened the rights of the republics and reduced the federal authorities' jurisdiction, raised the status of Vojvodina and Kosovo so that they became in effect two extra republics, and established a 'decentralized federalism, with its sovereign basis in the nation, that is, in the republics as the nearest expression of that sovereignty' (Djordjevic, 1998: 192–3).[19]

A counter-attack on the view that multiculturalism was in decline in Yugoslavia has been mounted by a number of anthropologists, including Robert M. Hayden and Mary Gilliland. Hayden claims that there were many forces working to preserve the multicultural character of Yugoslavia, and he blames subsequent conflicts entirely on 'the political ideologies that won the elections of 1990' (Hayden, 1996: 783). He indicates five trends in the direction of multiculturalism. First there was the level of inter-republican migration: between 1953 and 1981 almost all the republics became more heterogeneous ethnically, exceptions being Vojvodina and Kosovo. Second there was the rising rate of intermarriage.[20] Third, the rising number of children of mixed marriages (15.9 per cent in Bosnia-Hercegovina, 7.4 per cent in Slovenia). Fourth, the rising proportion of people who declared themselves to be 'Yugoslavs' in the census (this rose from 1.3 per cent in 1971 to 5.4 per cent in 1981). Fifth, the generally low level of tension in mixed areas in the 1980s.

It is quite possible to quote examples of inter-ethnic co-operation to back up this more positive view of post-Tito Yugoslavia. In an opinion survey of a broad sample of Yugoslavs conducted in 1966, 60 per cent of the respondents said they were 'ready to accept members of other national groups in friendship or even marriage' (MacKenzie, 1977: 453). Here, among many similar comments, we can quote the words of a thirty-five-year-old Serbian woman in Bosnia: 'Before the war it was super. My neighbours were Muslims and Croats. We celebrated all the holidays together' (Laber, 1993: 3).

The forces indicated by Hayden were probably operating effectively at an earlier stage of Yugoslav Communist history, but the statistics he used did not cover the 1980s, and that was when everything went into reverse. Between 1981 and 1991, Croatia and Bosnia became ethnically less heterogeneous, rather than more. Between 1981 and 1991, the proportion of declared 'Yugoslavs' declined sharply, from 5.45 per cent to 3 per cent. In Croatia, it fell dramatically, from 8.2 per cent to 2.2 per cent (Petrović, 1992).

The same point can be made about Mary Gilliland's personal observation that there was a strong sense of Yugoslav identity in the Croatian town of Slavonski Brod, the location of her ethnographic field research in 1982–3. 'People rarely spoke of ethnonationality,' she reports. 'Many people appeared to have redefined themselves not as Croats, Serbs and so on but as Yugoslavs. In Brod, they seemed attached to the town and the region as much as to ethnic nationality. Croats and Serbs alike expressed this attachment in the sentimental way they talked about the region.' A friend, Nina, wrote to her in retrospect: 'We were Yugoslavs. My generation grew up believing that' (Gilliland, 1995: 199–201). As Gilliland herself stresses (1995: 202), there was 'a complete change of atmosphere' on her return in 1991. In general, the forces of multiculturalism proved incapable of restraining the shift of the 1980s towards ethnic intolerance.

It was the Serbian reaction of the 1980s to the partly-real, partly-imagined onslaught by the Albanians of Kosovo that really sounded the death-knell for Yugoslavia, a state that could continue to exist only while there was a readiness to compromise. Even before that there were straws in the wind indicating an upsurge of nationalism among the Serbs. The novelist, Dobrica Ćosić, threatened the autonomists of Kosovo and Vojvodina in 1968 that 'if particularist orientalisms endure and conquer in Yugoslavia' this would result in 'the unification of the Serbian people in a single state': thus the programme that Milošević and his supporters would later try to implement had already been in existence for twenty years.[21]

Three years later, the philosopher Mihailo Đurić said much the same thing as did Ćosić: 'with the rise of independent and even opposing national states' in Yugoslavia 'the existing borders are not adequate for any republic – except perhaps Slovenia – and least of all for Serbia' (Budding, 1997: 415–6). Serb historians were also thinking along the same lines. In 1979, Momčilo Zečević told a congress of historians in Belgrade that the Yugoslav historians of the previous thirty years were wrong on several counts: they had overstated the importance of trends towards Yugoslav unity, they had ignored Serb national interests, and they had failed to underline the role of the Vatican in stirring up religious divisions (Banac, 1992b: 1093).

However, the conflict over Kosovo in 1981 was the real turningpoint in this process; it was seen by many Serbian intellectuals as a fight against rising Muslim nationalism and Islamic fundamentalism (they were also influenced by the world context, in particular the war in Afghanistan, and in general the higher profile of Muslims in the 1980s). In 1982, Vuk Drašković brought out his novel *Noz* (The Knife), which painted Muslims in dark colours. The radical Serbian nationalist, Darko Tanasković, claimed that the Muslims were conducting 'an economic, diplomatic and demographic jihad' (Cigar, 1995: 22). The very popular novel by Danko Popović, *Knjiga o Milutinu*, about an aged peasant who fought for Yugoslavia in the Balkan and world conflicts of the early twentieth century, presents the underlying message that these sacrifices were completely pointless, and the hero should have been fighting for the narrower interests of Serbia (Pavković, 1994). At a more literary level, the world-famed novel by Milorad Pavić, *The Dictionary of the Khazars*, published in 1984, was read, by Serbs at least, as an attack on the Yugoslav idea and a warning of the dangers of full assimilation into Yugoslavia (Wachtel, 1998: 218).

The Serbian campaign took a further step with the drawing up in 1986 of a Memorandum by the Serbian Academy of Arts and Sciences (SANU), the most prestigious academic institution in the country, which portrayed the Serbs as the victim nation that had sacrificed its own interests for the good of Yugoslavia and received no thanks; now it was time for the Serbs to act in their own interests. Although the Memorandum was leaked rather than published officially, it still represented the state of mind of a good part of the Serbian intelligentsia. It has been described as 'a sketch of a new Serb national programme' (Grmek *et al.*, 1993: 235).

Ordinary people in Serbia still retained their faith in Yugoslavia in the mid-1980s, but their replies to Alvin Magid's in-depth investigation of Serb attitudes in Belgrade also showed the extent to which this was combined with a growing level of ethnic self-identification as 'proud

Serbs'. Here are some comments made by Magid's interlocutors: 'I am a proud Serb who is a loyal Yugoslav'; 'I want my family to be secure in the new Yugoslavia'; 'We are many different people – Serbs, Croats, Slovenes etc. – held together mostly by the social compact. God help us when it is damaged beyond repair!'; 'Many of my compatriots despair for the future of Yugoslavia. I do not.'; 'I will pray that Yugoslavia does not fall apart before an alternative way of governing it can be found'; 'I am a Serbian cultural nationalist but I am perfectly content to see Serbia survive and flourish in our multinational Yugoslav society'; 'First and foremost I am a patriotic Yugoslav who is a loyal Serb'; 'It probably seems to you that I am in deep despair about the future of Yugoslavia. Believe me, it is not so. I myself am a proud Serb, but I do not have the mad dream of a Great Serbia at the centre of Socialist Yugoslavia'; and 'I feel myself a citizen of Yugoslavia and of the world' (Magid, 1991).

We should note that the Kosovo question was well to the forefront of the minds of ordinary Serbs even before the 1986 SANU Memorandum was compiled. The only factory worker Magid interviewed had this to say: 'Tito's vice-president, Ranković, was sent to beat up the restless Albanians in Kosovo. Was this a practical solution, with long-term benefits? Look at what we have now – Albanians more rebellious and increasingly violent, taking out their wrath against the minority of Serbs and Montenegrins who live in the province' (Magid, 1991: 253). At the other end of the social scale, a lawyer said something very similar: 'Perhaps it was Tito who watered the seeds of Albanian nationalism in Kosovo by alternately beating those people over the head and then trying to buy them off with political appointments and money' (Magid, 1991: 474).

One of the interviewees ventured a remarkably accurate prophecy: 'I fear that some day there will emerge in Serbia a demagogic element that will want to whip up our ancient Serbian nationalism as a way of undermining the growing political power of the Albanians in Kosovo.' Two years later the prophecy was fulfilled: Slobodan Milošević rode to power on the back of one short phrase, pregnant with meaning, which he uttered in front of a large protest demonstration of Kosovo Serbs on 24 April 1987: 'Serbs! No one should be allowed to beat you'.

The decline of communism and the escalation of ethnic conflict

By the 1980s it was commonly agreed by students of nationalism all over the world that the phenomenon was on the upsurge. A. D. Smith, writing in 1981, pointed to the revival of ethnic sentiments among dominant nations, such as the French, the Romanians and the Poles, as well as to a surge of support for ethnic movements claiming autonomy from the states of which they were currently members. He gave as examples Scottish, Québécois, Croat and Slovak nationalism (Smith, 1981: 163). The anthropologist, E. E. Roosens, made a similar observation: 'Ethnic groups are affirming themselves more and more. They promote their own new, cultural identity, even as their old identity is eroded' (Roosens, 1989: 9). And he added that contact between cultures, far from eroding differences between them, as had previously been assumed, led rather to an increase in divergence.

Although Roosens' insights were derived from studies of movements located mainly outside Europe (one was European, the others were in Quebec, Morocco, Bolivia and Zaire), they were intended to apply generally, and indeed they could be applied by students of Soviet and Communist affairs to their own region too, though before the coming of *perestroika* and liberalization it was not easy to perceive this. The year Roosens was writing – 1988 – was the year when ethnicity and ethnic conflict first became burning questions in the Soviet Union, a development that was related directly to the freer atmosphere under Mikhail Gorbachev, who by his reforms made it permissible for the first time to raise questions of constitutional change in public. The process occurred somewhat later further west, in Eastern Europe proper, except in Yugoslavia, where the liberalization of the late 1960s had already produced the first signs of disintegration.

In every area where there was the potential for ethnic conflict, the decline and fall of Communist rule triggered this off. A full discussion of the general reasons for ethnic conflict will be reserved for Chapter 7. Here we shall simply examine the specific situation of the late 1980s to see how this led to disputes and, in many cases, to wars. From 1988 onwards national movements of various kinds began to come into conflict with each other and with the state authorities in the Soviet Union.[22] In the South Caucasian region (formerly Transcaucasia) the conflicts were particularly acute. All three South Caucasian republics were involved. Armenia and Azerbaijan were in conflict over the Nagorno-Karabagh autonomous region (also known as Nagornyi Karabagh, or, in its Armenian version, Artsakh); Georgia's drive to independence stimulated resistance from Abkhazia and South Ossetia. The growth of independence movements in the Baltic lands (Estonia, Latvia and Lithuania) met with resistance from local Russian minorities (in Lithuania there was also Polish resistance); moves towards independence in the Moldavian SSR (later Moldova) were resisted by Russian, Ukrainian and Gagauz minorities.

These developments gathered strength in the next few years (1989 to 1991) in a context of social and political collapse, hyperinflation and economic distress, and a loss of ideological landmarks resulting from the collapse (or sometimes the overthrow) of Communist rule. The process of emancipation from Communism seemed to spark off immediate ethnic conflict. Even the euphoria of the year 1989 did not prevent nationalists from misusing their new-found freedom to agitate against formerly deprived ethnic groups. This was clear particularly in Bulgaria (the Central Committee's resolution of 29 December 1989 guaranteeing the 'genuine exercise of rights' to all Bulgarian citizens irrespective of 'nationality, origin, creed, sex, race, education or social and material status' sparked off a wave of anti-Turkish protests from disappointed Bulgarian nationalists); in Romania (the post-1989 political mobilization of the Hungarian minority soon produced a reaction in the shape of the setting up in February 1990 of Romanian Cradle, and the March 1990 riots); and above all in Yugoslavia, where nationalism stepped into the shoes of Communism without any intervening honeymoon period at all. Similar events took place in the rest of the region. The next chapter will examine these developments in detail.

Economic difficulties were very visible in the dying days of Communism, and many writers have made a direct link between the arguments over how to solve these problems and the rise of ethnic conflict. This applies in particular to the Soviet Union and Yugoslavia (although one cannot exclude economic factors elsewhere). In Yugoslavia, the issue of economic reform led immediately on to the question of whether specific groups, or indeed specific regions, had to suffer sacrifices for the greater good.

Susan Woodward has examined this economic background in some detail. Her conclusion, that Yugoslavia's last chance of survival was the Marković government, which was pursuing a policy of reforming the economy without being tied to any particular regional grouping, is shared by several other commentators (though by no means all). Laszlo Sekelj, for instance, claims that 'the reform programme of the Marković government' was ruined by 'an aggressive and militant minority' (Sekelj, 1993: 277).

It would, however, be entirely mistaken to stress changes in the economic environment at the expense of cultural and intellectual factors. What was happening in the 1980s was an intensification of the gradual ideological decline that has been identifiable since the failure of Khrushchev's reform attempt in the Soviet Union (and the failure, but also the forcible suppression, of other more radical reform attempts in Eastern Europe). For the nations of the Soviet Union, this gave rise to a tendency on the part of local party leaders (who, as we saw earlier, were by this time usually members of the indigenous nation rather than Russians or other outsiders) to encourage the development of nationally-based histories and myths about history.

During the 1960s and 1970s, the local elites who now ran the union republics regarded the production of national histories as the most important task that academic historians could undertake. The first national history to reach completion was the Latvian one (1958). Over the next twenty years, every union republic produced a multi-volume history: some examples are Armenia in 1967–70, Georgia in 1970–6, and the Lithuania in 1957–75. They were all published first in the local language, and only later in Russian. National encyclope-dias, in the national language, were also published for the first time in this period. Here are some examples, with starting dates: Ukrainian, 1959; Lithuanian, 1966; Latvian, 1967; Estonian, 1968; Belarusan, 1969; Moldavian, 1970; Kazakh, 1972; Azerbaijani, 1976; and Kyrgyz, 1977.[23]

The later the date of publication, the less the work conformed to the pattern imposed centrally from Moscow. Versions of the past emerged which were tailor-made to the requirements of local ethnic elites. This process could be observed everywhere, but was naturally most marked where there were serious potential ethnic conflicts, where everyone wanted to get their claim in first. Whereas the central Soviet authorities endeavoured consistently to minimize points of national friction and to stress the 'eternal friendship' between the non-Russian nations, a different approach was taken on the Soviet Empire's periphery, as soon as local historians had the opportunity to publish more freely.[24]

In the Caucasus, the struggle of the historians over the past had already started in the 1960s, though it did not really take off until the 1980s. As Nora Dudwick has pointed out, historical arguments were in part a surrogate for discussions about the real subject under dispute: 'Conflicts were projected into the past' because 'interethnic tensions' were 'denied free political expression' (Dudwick, 1990: 377). The typical argument over priority of settlement on a given territory, which is so characteristic of rival nationalisms, took the form in Armenia and Azerbaijan of the discussion over the 'Caucasian Albanians'.

Azerbaijani scholars insisted that the Albanian civilization of the early centuries of the Christian era was not inferior to the contemporary Armenian or Georgian civilizations, that the Caucasian Albanians were the first to adopt Christianity and the first to produce a literature of their own – then the Armenians came and stole it by translating these works from Albanian to Armenian and destroying the originals. Armenian scholars replied that none of this was true; that 'Albania' was not an ethnic entity but an administrative region set up by the Persian Empire; and that the Azerbaijanis were not descendants of former Albanians but arose from a mixture of invading Turkic tribes and Islamicized Armenians and Georgians.[25]

The Caucasian Albanian issue was more important for the Azerbaijanis than for the Armenians. For the Armenians, the main issues were more recent in time. The three major historic themes that concerned them were the genocide of 1915, the loss of national territory in Anatolia, Karabagh and Nakhichevan, and the protection of Armenian identity against what was perceived as a threat of Russianization. Even diaspora Armenians living in Western countries were allowed to contribute to the new artistic and literary periodicals that sprang up in the 1980s. The history and culture of the lost homeland was investigated actively by Armenian scholars and promoted by Armenian artists. The agitation over Anatolia was tolerated by the Soviet authorities, reports Claire Mouradian, because 'it contributed to feeding the Armenians' visceral anti-Turkism without hindering the USSR's foreign policy or putting the regime itself into question' (Mouradian, 1984: 133).

In Georgia, similarly, the battle over the past began in the late Soviet era. At stake here were, respectively, the age-old unity of Georgia and the right of its component parts to separate. The Georgian line on South Ossetia was that the Ossetians were not 'truly indigenous': they came from outside, so while their presence could be tolerated, they could not be permitted to separate from Georgia, taking Georgian land with them. Moreover, they should not even have received the autonomy given to them by the Bolsheviks in 1922.

Here is a passionate disquisition on the subject by a leading Georgian historian:

> Why was the setting up of the autonomous region in 1922 in Samachablo, the so-called South Ossetia, unjustified? Because the Ossetians descend from the Alans, who had a state in the western part of the North Caucasus. Georgian sources localise the Alans

exclusively in the North Caucasus. Only after Tamerlane and later the Ottoman Turks had driven Georgians out of the mountains (between the fourteenth and sixteenth centuries) did the Ossetians have a chance to move in. There was no compact settlement of Ossetians south of the main Caucasian ridge until the seventeenth century. The Ossetians do have a right to live here. They have a right to cultural autonomy, and they have had that for a long time but they have no right to political independence, and no right to separate from Georgia and attach themselves to a separate political formation. Every nation has its historically formed territory and no one has the right to tear pieces away from it.[26]

The South Ossetians replied that, on the contrary, they were settled on the territory of Georgia as early as the fourth century CE.

In Central Asia, too, there were battles over the past, though they were waged less openly, since local ruling groups were not interested in promoting them; here, unlike in Armenia and Georgia, arguing over the past was a form of political dissent not tolerated by the authorities. Until 1990, nationalist arguments could only be presented in under-ground publications. In 1988, a well-known Tajik literary historian, Muhammadzhan Shukurov, launched an onslaught upon the official Uzbek view of Soviet history. He claimed that the Uzbeks had displayed consistent 'chauvinism' towards the Tajiks. They had 'denied the existence of the Tajik people, particularly in Bukhara and Samarqand' (Eisener, 1991: 13). Shukurov brought forward the usual arguments about ethnic population figures. In his view, there were far more Tajiks in what later became Uzbekistan than the Uzbeks claimed. Moreover, both the (Islamic reformist) *jadid* movement of the early twentieth century and the Bukhara Bolsheviks, despite the fact that they themselves were mainly ethnic Tajiks, had helped to obliterate the Tajik majority in the cities by launching the idea of a bilingual nation 'united by the cement of Turkism'.

Later, in the heyday of *glasnost'*, Shukurov was allowed to publish these views openly; but the battle over the past of Uzbekistan did not really get off the ground subsequently, because in both countries the political challenge from the semi-dissident, reform-orientated intellec-tuals was defeated quickly by the old guard, who have remained in power, and who have absolutely no interest in stirring up these murky ethnic waters.

5
The 1990s in Central and Eastern Europe

Yugoslavia: fertile ground for conflict theorists

Many attempts have been made to explain the conflicts that tore apart the former Yugoslavia in the 1990s. Serbia and the Serbs[1] have been the centre of attention here, given the role of Belgrade in sparking off four conflicts in succession – with Slovenia (1991), with Croatia (1991–5), with the Croats and Muslims of Bosnia-Hercegovina (1992–5), and with the Kosovo Albanians (1998–9).[2] No explanation necessarily covers all four situations, and later we shall be looking in detail at each conflict, but first we shall present a few general, overarching theories.

The predominant role of historical myth is one such theory. In this context, Branimir Anzulović has centred attention recently on the role of two men – Bishop Petar II Petrović Njegoš (1813–51), prince and Orthodox bishop of Montenegro, whose poem 'The Mountain Wreath' allegedly shows a 'hatred of Islam and a contempt for the West', and Dr Justin Popović, a contemporary figure, the leading Serbian Orthodox theologian, who has 'fulminated against Catholicism, Protestantism and humanism' in his works since the 1980s (Anzulovic, 1999: 345). This view of Popović is not new. It has already been advanced by Radmila Radić, who analyzed his work in the context of what she called the 'return of the Serbian Orthodox Church from the margin of society' to centre stage (Radić, 2000: 247). In the case of Njegoš, we saw in an earlier chapter that his work can be interpreted in many different ways. It is the use made of his poem rather than the poem itself which may have played a part in creating a paranoid Serb consciousness.

Much of the psychological background to the conflicts that tore Yugoslavia apart in the 1990s can be gleaned from the record made by

Brian Hall of conversations with Yugoslavs of all ethnic groups (except the Macedonians and certain minorities) during a trip he made in 1991 (Hall, 1994). His book is the closest anyone has yet come to repeating Rebecca West's achievement of the 1930s. He noted carefully the fears, prejudices, legends, and sometimes the insights, of people he met, in the context of the impending conflict.

Hall restricted himself to reporting what he heard and saw, but the cultural psychologist John Borneman took a different approach, using similar evidence to develop not one but two theories to explain the extreme brutality that often disfigured the conflicts in Yugoslavia. One of Borneman's theories is sexual in character; the other legal. The sexual theory is that 'the Mediterranean male dreads assuming a feminine posture'; he fears 'an awakened sexual desire to be penetrated by men'. He reacts to this fear by raping the opponent's womenfolk, because 'to rape the enemy's women is to attack their husbands and in fact to feminize them' (Borneman, 1998). The legal explanation runs as follows: 'retributive violence is an effect of the absence of retributive justice'. In a state where there is 'public enactment of retributive justice' this does not happen. Where this is absent, people have recourse to 'collective retributive violence' (Borneman, 1997: 155). Let us throw in for good measure the explanation in terms of historical culture favoured by Stjepan Meštrović: 'power-hungry, aggressive Dinaric tribesmen' practised 'brutality, hatred and excessive violence' over a thousand years ago, and their descendants are simply repeating this behaviour (Meštrović, 1993: 50, 51, 61, 65).

The above theories are applicable to the brutality with which the wars have been fought, but they do not tell us why the conflicts broke out in the first place. For this, there are two explanations specific to Yugoslavia. The first relates to the constitutional structure of the country. The establishment of a largely federal system of nationally-based republics 'reified nationality' and thus created automatically nationalist responses to crisis situations (Verdery, 1993b: 182). The new constitutions established after or during the disintegration of the country worked in the same direction, since they were based on the sovereignty of the majority ethnic group, and not the individual citizen. Citizens of minority ethnic groups tended to be excluded to various degrees, and this increased the likelihood of a nationalist response from them (Hayden, 1992: 657–8).

The second explanation is in terms of the personality and ambitions of one man: Slobodan Milošević. He had everything to gain politically from the conflicts between Serbia and its successive opponents. In the case of Kosovo, a former aide has assured us that Milošević was not interested in the province itself. It 'served as a kind of supply base for seats in the Serbian and Yugoslav parliaments. He preferred a chaotic situation that brought him fifty deputies' mandates to a solution of the problem that would have cost him his power' (Reuter, 1999: 643). But we can only decide the validity of these explanations and of the more general explanations to be presented in Chapter 7 by examining each of the conflicts in the former Yugoslavia in more detail. This is the task of the next section.

Slovenia: the one that got away

The first stage in the disintegration of Yugoslavia, the achievement of independence by Slovenia, did not result in, and was not accompanied by, ethnic conflict, although from the outset the ethnic issue was very much present as a factor in the drive for independence. The Slovene Communist leadership's decision in February 1989 to support the demands of the Kosovo Albanians for a restoration of their rights, which had been eroded by the Serbian government over the previous two years, has been described by Susan Woodward as a 'critical transition on the way to the dissolution of Yugoslavia' which made it impossible to settle the conflicts in the other republics by negotiation (Woodward, 1995: 98).

Slovenia, unlike all other Yugoslav republics, was ethnically almost homogeneous (non-Slovenes made up only 12 per cent of the population in 1991). There were few Serbs resident in the republic (2.4 per cent) and they were not concentrated in any particular area. Historically, Slovenia had never been an area of Serb settlement, which meant that no Serb national claims were at stake. President Milošević of Serbia had no interest in stirring up a prolonged struggle. There was a war, certainly, but it was waged between the Yugoslav army (JNA) and the Slovene militia, and it was very short (it began on 25 June 1991 when Slovenia declared independence, and ended on 3 July 1991 with a ceasefire, confirmed on 25 October by the withdrawal of the army from the newly independent republic).

This apparent defeat for the JNA was not so much a result of the clever tactics of the Slovene defence minister, Janez Janša, who had for some time been diverting Yugoslav army recruits to Slovene republican barracks, although that played a part, as it was of the divisions within the army itself, which was only half-heartedly in favour of the action. Three JNA soldiers were killed during the fighting, but 3200 surrendered (Cohen, 1995: 214). Things were very different further south, in

Croatia. Here the first round of war started in June 1991 and continued until January 1992 (there was to be a later round in 1995).

War for Croatia

Brian Hall reports an interesting conversation with a certain Nataša in, 1991: 'Serbs aren't normal,' she said, screwing her index finger into her temple, 'they were right to be angry, but not like this. You bump into a Serb and he pulls out a gun and shoots you' (Hall, 1994: 22). And it was true, the Croats did bump into the Serbs in the dying days of Yugoslavia. There were several ways in which the Serb minority within Croatia (12.1 per cent of the population) were provoked by the party that won the May 1990 elections, the Croatian Democratic Union (HDZ). One was the constitutional amendment that changed the Serbs' status from that of a 'titular nationality' within Croatia under the 1974 Constitution to that of a 'national minority' in a state where there was only one titular nation (Sekelj, 2000: 57). In the 1990 Constitution, Croatia was defined as 'the national state of the Croatian people' (Hayden, 1996: 785).

These constitutional provisions reflected a general atmosphere in Croatia in which national definition was required of everyone; whereas previously it had been possible to claim to be a Yugoslav or a human being, from 1990 onwards it was impossible to avoid being branded as either a Croat, and therefore a rightful member of the community, or an enemy. Dubravka Ugrešić, a victim of this branding process, described it in 1992 in this way:

> To start with there was mild, secret counting, then somewhat more obvious dividing, and then very clear branding. How else can one mark one's stock, distinguish one's own herd from someone else's? Branding was not a sweet which could be accepted or politely refused. If you can't yourself think who you are, I'll help you, grinned the people from the Great Manipulators' teams, holding glowing national branding irons in their hands. (Ugrešić, 1998: 40–1)

And, as she makes clear, an identical process took place among Serbs.

Did powerful forces in the Western world also help to promote the conflict in Croatia? This is the view advanced by several respected analysts, including Susan Woodward and Misha Glenny. They claim that the recognition of Croatian independence by the EC, under strong

German pressure, both prevented a peaceful settlement of the Serb–Croat conflict and sparked off the war in Bosnia-Hercegovina. The argument here is that whereas the Badinter Commission in its report of 15 January 1992 distinguished between Slovenia and Croatia, saying the former could be recognized immediately while Croatia could not, because 'it had not provided sufficient guarantees for the protection of minorities' (meaning above all the Serbs), the German government had already ignored this, recognizing both Slovenia and Croatia unilaterally on 23 December 1991, despite a warning from Lord Carrington on 2 December that 'premature recognition might well be the spark that sets Bosnia-Hercegovina alight' (Woodward, 1995: 184–90). The EC was forced to follow suit on 15 January 1992, ignoring the Badinter Commission's reservations. The war in Bosnia broke out soon afterwards.

However, strong arguments have been advanced against this interpretation. In the first place, fighting between Croatia and Serbia was not prolonged by the EC's intervention; a ceasefire between Croatia and Serbia was signed on 3 January 1992 – in other words, shortly after Croatia's independence had been recognized (Goldstein, 1999: 236). In the second place, as we shall see in the next section, the internal dynamism in the direction of war within Bosnia was far too strong to be affected by the recognition or non-recognition of a neighbouring state; and there was after all a gap of roughly four months between EC recognition of Croatia and the outbreak of war in its neighbour.

The January 1992 ceasefire which ended the military conflict between Croatia and Serbia was inherently unstable, since no one in Croatia (or indeed in the world at large, since UN Resolution 871 of 4 October 1993 reaffirmed Croatia's territorial integrity) accepted the Krajina Serbs' claim to independence, and also since the Krajina state (the Serbian Republic of Krajina, or RSK) could only exist with Belgrade's support. The truce was broken repeatedly. In June 1993, fighting began again, and continued until a further ceasefire agreement on 15 September 1993, which was policed by a United Nations force, UNPROFOR. The Krajina Serbs resisted signing the agreement until 30 March 1994. On 23 September 1994, the Croatian Chamber of Deputies called for the cancellation of UNPROFOR's mandate, and demanded 'the disarming of Serb rebels'. On 26 October a group of powers working under UN auspices proposed the 're-integration of the RSK into Croatia', a proposal which, naturally, was rejected by the RSK authorities.

On 25 January 1995, President Tudjman announced that Croatia would retake the RSK 'by force if necessary'. On 12 March 1995 the mandate of UNPROFOR was extended on Croatia's terms, with a proclaimed purpose of 'expediting the re-integration of Krajina into Croatia'. On 2 May 1995, Croatian forces fought their way into the formerly Serb Okučani-Pakrac enclave of West Slavonia. This was just the beginning. On 4 August, the Croatian reconquest of Krajina began: in 'Operation Storm', 200 000 Croatian soldiers were pitted against 40 000 Krajina Serbs. The campaign took just four days. The international situation was favourable, with diplomatic support coming from the USA and Germany. Hundreds of thousands of Serbs were driven across the border or fled voluntarily. Some stopped in Serb-held Bosnia; others went all the way to Serbia. Shortly afterwards, the Serb authorities in East Slavonia, seeing the writing on the wall, agreed to reintegrate their territory peacefully into Croatia. By the agreement of 12 November 1995, East Slavonia was to be returned to Croatia after two years, without any referendum. In the interim the area would be administered by a body set up by the United Nations, with the acronym UNTAES – the United Nations Transitional Administration of East Slavonia. On 15 January 1998, after the expiry of the UNTAES mandate, Croatia formally resumed control of the area. All the territories cut off in 1991 by the Serb onslaught had now been, or were about to be, returned. The country was at last in a position to begin its recovery from wartime devastation.

The Bosnian triangle[3]

Despite having won a relative majority in the November 1990 elections, with 37.8 per cent of the vote and 86 out of 240 seats in the Bosnian representative assemblies, the party of Bosnian Muslims, the SDA, was in no position to copy the provocative behaviour of the HDZ in neighbouring Croatia. The Bosnian Muslims were, of course, faced with a different situation. They could not claim to represent more than about two-fifths of the country, whereas the HDZ represented four-fifths of Croatians. They needed to conciliate the other two major politico-ethnic blocs, the Bosnian Croat HDZ and the Bosnian Serb SDS, which had similarly swept the board in their own communities.

As a result, and uniquely in former Yugoslavia, they avoided drawing up the constitution in such a way as to ensure the supremacy of their own ethnic group. They did not change Amendment 60 to the Constitution of Bosnia and Hercegovina, dated 31 July 1990, which states that 'the Socialist Republic of Bosnia-Hercegovina is a state of equal citizens, of the nations of Bosnia and Hercegovina–Muslims, Serbo-

Croats and the other nations and nationalities living within it' and they immediately formed a coalition government with the HDZ and the SDS (20 December 1990). Not until March 1994, when the Constitution of the Federation of Bosnia and Hercegovina was signed, did they exclude those Bosnian Serbs who found themselves within the borders of the Federation, referring instead to 'Bosniaks[4] and Croats' as the 'constituent peoples' of Bosnia and Hercegovina (Hayden, 1996: 792).

There was also little sign of the 'Islamic fundamentalism' repeatedly agitated as a scarecrow by their Catholic and Orthodox opponents. Alija Izetbegović, party leader of the SDA and, after December 1990, the president of the State Presidency of Bosnia-Hercegovina, had the reputation of being a militant pan-Islamist , but he presided over a government of a purely secular nature. This fact was obscured at the time by the expulsion from the SDA on 23 September 1990 of the secularist faction around Adil Zulfikarpašić (Bougarel, 1990: 548).

Once it became clear that the Slovenes and Croats were not prepared to stay within Yugoslavia, Izetbegović decided to take Bosnia-Hercegovina out of the federation, but only as a single unit. This unity could, however, only be achieved against the wishes of the other two nations. Despite his fundamentally secular and inclusive view of Bosnia, Izetbegović contributed to the fears of the Bosnian Croats and Serbs by his tendency to waver on the key issue of whether the future state was to belong to the Muslim nation, or to be a continuation of the multi-ethnic and multi-confessional entity of Communist times (Woodward, 1995: 301). The Bosnian Serbs, in the shape of their main political party, the SDS, walked out in protest against the Bosnian parliament's decision of 26 January 1992 to conduct a referendum on independence. They had already held their own private referendum (9–10 November 1991), which delivered an overwhelming vote in favour of staying in Yugoslavia. The Croats, for their part, disavowed the actions of their leader, Stjepan Kljujić, who had helped Izetbegović's SDA to carry the independence referendum through parliament. Kljujić was forced to resign as head of the HDZ in Bosnia-Hercegovina shortly afterwards, handing over the leadership to Mate Boban, a hard-line Hercegovinan Croat nationalist (February 1992).

The EC now tried to secure a compromise between the rival parties. This was the Lisbon Agreement, by which Bosnia-Hercegovina was to be partitioned into ethnic cantons. All three sides signed this agreement on 23 February, Karadzić of the SDS and the HDZ representative Miro Lasić willingly, Izetbegović unwillingly, because he thought he would never be able to achieve a better result. Back home, his actions were immediately disavowed by the majority of his SDA colleagues, and he had to withdraw his signature.[5] As he commented subsequently: 'We decided for independence. Of course, we could have chosen the other option.'[6] The Bosnian independence referendum followed shortly afterwards (29 February–1 March 1992). With a 99.7 per cent vote in favour (the turnout, however, was 64.4 per cent, which demonstrated the unanimity of the Serb boycott), the way was clear for a declaration of independence. The next day the barricades went up in Sarajevo, allegedly in reaction to the shooting by Muslim gunmen of some members of a Serbian wedding party who had been carrying Serbian flags in a Muslim-inhabited part of the town. On the political level, the Serbian reaction to Izetbegović's 3 March declaration of independence was to proclaim their own 'Serbian Republic of Bosnia-Hercegovina' (27 March).

Fighting broke out during the month, though oddly enough it was largely between Croats and Serbs, or Croats and the JNA (the Bosnian Croats had plans to set up their own state of 'Herceg-Bosna,' and at this stage their main opponents in this endeavour were the Serbs and the Yugoslav Army). It was accompanied by reciprocal ethnic cleansing (against Croats in Hercegovina and Serbs in Posavina). A further step towards full-blown conflict came on 1 April, when the Serbian paramilitary leader Željko Ražnjatović (known as Arkan) crossed into the north-eastern corner of Bosnia with his private militia, entered the town of Bijeljina, rounded up the leading local Muslims and executed some of them in front of the mosque. He then moved southwards and drove the Muslim inhabitants out of the town of Zvornik. By the time the EC recognized Bosnia as an independent state (6 April) it was too late to stop the fighting. The 'Serbian invasion of eastern Bosnia,' which some commentators regard as having been sparked off by EC recognition, was already well under way (Burg and Shoup, 1999: 117–20). In the course of the month the Muslims were driven out of two further towns, Višegrad and Foča, by Arkan's Tigers and other Serb paramilitary groups. Recognition did not cause the war, and withholding recognition would not have prevented the spread of war.

For the first year of war, the protagonists were the Bosnian Serbs on one side and the Muslims and Croats on the other; but tensions gradually developed between the Muslims and the Croats, so that eventually Bosnia was torn apart even more by a three-cornered conflict. In July 1992, Mate Boban, the head of the HDZ in Bosnia, declared a semi-autonomous state covering the Croat majority areas in the south, under the title 'Croatian Community of Herceg-Bosna'. In October

1992, Croatian paramilitary units acting under the orders of a Croatian Defence Council that had been set up by the HDZ seized the western part of the town of Mostar and made it the capital of Herceg-Bosna. Then in January 1993 Boban began to disarm Bosnian government police and soldiers in the area he claimed for his mini-state. Finally, open war broke out as a result of a massacre of Muslims carried out by the Croatian Defence League (HOS), the paramilitary wing of the extreme nationalist Party of Right (HSP–1861), in the village of Ahmići, near Vitez (April 1993).[7] This struggle was fierce and bloody, but fortunately brief. Its most dramatic episode was the deliberate destruction on 9 November 1993 of the bridge at Mostar by units of the Croatian Defence Council.

The war between Muslims and Croats ended on 23 February 1994 when a ceasefire was signed, followed by what President Tudjman described as the 'historic' agreement' of 18 March, which set up a 'Muslim–Croat Federation' within Bosnia-Hercegovina. Power in the Federation was to be shared between the two constituent ethnic groups, the Muslims and the Croats. This found expression in May 1994 in the election of a Muslim, Haris Silajdžić, as prime minister of the Federation, and a Croat, Kresimir Zubak, as president. Eleven of the cabinet ministers were Muslim, and six Croat. Four local government districts ('cantons') were recognized as Muslim, two as Croat, and two (Mostar and Travnik) were multi-ethnic. There were no further warlike confrontations between the Muslims and the Croats, but the Croat area of Bosnia ('Herceg-Bosna') retained its semi-independence.

The war with the Bosnian Serbs continued for two more years, despite successive ceasefires and peace plans. This war fell into a definite pattern, with Bosnian Serb forces replying to Bosnian Muslim (and sometimes also Bosnian Croat) offensives by shelling Sarajevo and any other Muslim-held towns (such as Tuzla) that were within the range of their heavy weapons. When the war eventually ended it was as a result of outside intervention, sparked off by three events: the conquest of two UN-designated 'safe areas' by Serb troops (Srebrenica fell on 11 July 1995, and Žepa on 28 July), and the killing of thirty-seven people in a Sarajevo market by shellfire from the Bosnian Serb positions around the city on 28 August. NATO, acting on behalf of the UN, responded with a series of air strikes during the months of August and September against the Bosnian Serb besiegers of the city. Strong international pressure was now put on President Slobodan Milošević of Serbia to abandon his Bosnian Serb allies; he did so. On 8 September 1995, an agreement was signed in Geneva establishing two 'entities' within Bosnia-Hercegovina: the Federation of Bosnia-Hercegovina, in other words the existing Muslim–Croat Federation, which was allotted 51 per cent of the territory, and the Serb Republic (Republika Srpska) which was to receive the remaining 49 per cent. This was not the situation on the ground (the Serbs were in occupation of 70 per cent), but three days later a joint Muslim–Croat offensive was launched to push the Serbs back to their allotted territory. The success of this offensive meant that when the ceasefire of 12 October was signed, the Federation had grown in size from 30 per cent to 52 per cent of the land, slightly more than it was due to receive.

After peace talks held at Dayton, Ohio during the month of November, an agreement was reached on this basis. The Bosnian Serbs kept Srebrenica and Žepa, the towns they had conquered in July, though they lost the part of Sarajevo they had previously controlled. An international Implementation Force, IFOR, was established to guard a four-kilometre boundary zone between the two 'entities'. The agreement was initialled at Dayton on 21 November, and finally signed in Paris on 14 December 1995.

The casualty figures for the four terrible years of the Bosnian war give a clear indication of the greater losses suffered by the Muslims: 141 000 Muslims were killed (51 per cent of the total); 97 000 Serbs (35 per cent); and 28 000 Croats (10 per cent). In terms of the proportion to each population, however, the figures are not so one-sided: 7.4 per cent of the Muslims were killed, 7.1 per cent of the Serbs, and 3.8 per cent of the Croats.

The world statesmen who constructed the Dayton Peace Accords intended them to be a rejection of ethnic cleansing and a framework for the restoration of the unity of Bosnia. A verdict delivered four years afterwards by one observer was that, on the contrary, all Dayton did was confirm the victory of the ethnic cleansers. Bosnia-Hercegovina, wrote J. M. B. Lyon, 'is ethnically divided, and without the scaffolding of international support it will collapse. It consists of three monoethnic entities' (Lyon, 2000: 110). The failure to reverse ethnic cleansing is sufficiently indicated by the fact that 1.2 million Bosnian refugees were still in search of permanent housing in August 1999. The officials charged with enforcing the Dayton Accords announced on 20 November 1999 that 'true peace remains a distant goal, and Bosnia has yet to become a united state which includes all ethnic groups'.

There were several obstacles to overcome before a genuine peace could be achieved in Bosnia-Hercegovina. One obstacle was the insistence of the Croats on maintaining their own mini-state of 'Herceg-

Bosna'; however, the change of government in Croatia as a result of the death of President Tudjman and the subsequent electoral defeat of the HDZ has resulted in some improvement in this area: on 24 March 2000 the new president of Croatia, Stipe Mešić, announced that Croatia would 'no longer provide funding for Herceg-Bosna'.

Another obstacle was the lack of any definitive territorial settlement. Certain parts of Bosnia were still disputed between rival claimants even after the Dayton Accords. For example, the fate of the Brčko corridor, connecting the two halves of Republika Srpska, remained uncertain, since the Muslims and Croats claimed the area on ethnic grounds, while the Serbs saw the town as being strategically vital. A decision was to have been reached by 15 February 1997, but there were repeated postponements. In the meantime, the area was governed by UN commissioners. Eventually, international arbitrators ruled that it be removed from Serb control and placed under 'a democratic alliance of Serbs, Muslims and Croats' (5 March 1999). On 19 August 1999, a 'final ruling' proclaimed that it would be 'permanently under the joint administration of Republika Srpska and the Federation of Bosnia and Hercegovina'.

The most fundamental obstacle of all to Bosnian unity was the overwhelming dominance of ethnically-based political parties in all three parts of the country. The elections of 11 November 2000 confirmed this situation as far as Republika Srpska was concerned, but in the Federation the results gave grounds for optimism. Here, a multi-ethnic party, the Social Democratic Party of Bosnia-Hercegovina (SDPBH), made considerable gains at the expense of both Muslim and Croat parties. The final results gave the SDPBH thirty-seven seats, the Muslim SDA thirty-eight and the Croat HDZ twenty-five. The remainder of the seats went to non-nationalist minority parties, and the SDPBH proclaimed that it would form a government coalition with these groups and not with either of the ethnically-based parties. This opened the way to the election of Božidar Matić, of the SDPBH, as chair of the Council of Ministers of Bosnia and Hercegovina, on 13 February 2001.

Serbs and Albanians in Kosovo

The reasons for the escalation of the Serbian–Albanian conflict after 1997 are to be sought very largely on the Albanian side; the repressive policy of the Serbian government under Slobodan Milošević had not varied for the previous ten years. Since the abolition of Kosovan autonomy in March 1989, accompanied as it was by severe conflict with the majority Albanian population, the Serbian security forces in the province had been, in practice, an army of occupation. The Albanian response to this was non-violent resistance. The Democratic League of Kosovo (LDK), the movement founded in December 1989 by Dr. Ibrahim Rugova, relied on peaceful, though necessarily unconstitutional methods. The LDK built up a 'phantom state behind the scenes', a 'simulated government structure' with an elected parliament and president, a parallel education system (made necessary because the official schools were by then purely Serbian in curriculum), and an alternative health service based on the 'Mother Teresa' clinics. At the same time, Rugova strove to achieve international legitimacy for the 'Kosovo republic', proclaimed in October 1991 by the underground parliament (Judah, 2000: 61–98).

The essential change of tactics by the Kosovo Albanians was the move from peaceful protest to armed guerrilla action, and this in turn provoked increasingly severe counter-action from the Serbian side. The requirements for a change in the method of resistance were twofold: first, the will to engage in armed struggle; and second, adequate supplies of weapons. The will to resist forcibly had been building up for a decade as a result of continuous humiliation at the hands of Serbia (or 'Yugoslavia') and the increasingly evident failure of the non-violence espoused by Ibrahim Rugova and the LDK. The last straw for many Kosovo Albanians was what they saw as the failure of the West to place Kosovo on the agenda of the Dayton Conference of 1995 (Judah, 2000: 124). The UÇK (Kosovo Liberation Army) was founded, it is claimed, as early as 1993, and had been making sporadic attacks on Serbian policemen and Albanian 'collaborators' since that time. But to make further progress it needed more plentiful supplies of arms (Judah, 2000: 129).

This problem was soon solved, and for a surprising reason: the temporary collapse of the neighbouring Albanian state which resulted from the pyramid finance scandal of 1997. In March of that year, the Albanian army 'dissolved, the police deserted their posts and the armouries were thrown open' (Judah, 1999: 13). Kalashnikov rifles were available for a few dollars each, and the UÇK could be armed. On 4 January 1998 it issued a proclamation that it would fight for the unification of Kosovo with Albania. A month later, it opened the guerrilla war by killing four Serbian policemen. The reply was drastic: twenty-four Albanians were killed by Serbian troops in an operation in the Drenica region of the province (28 February). A further eighty Albanians were killed on 5 March, including the alleged leader of the

UÇK, Adem Jashari, and the whole of his family. This outrage in turn led the very influential clan elders of Kosovo, who had held back until then, to decide that the time had come to fight the Serbs. Local militias started to form, in loose association with the UÇK. Meanwhile, Rugova's Democratic League continued the tactics of peaceful protest it had pursued for the previous eight years. On 13 March there was a mass demonstration in the Kosovan capital, Priština, which was not interfered with by the police, and on 22 March most Kosovo Albanians showed their continuing commitment to passive resistance by voting for Rugova's party at unofficial elections for a 'parliament of the republic of Kosovo'. The spring months of 1998 thus saw a combination of peaceful protest demonstrations in the towns (albeit under the radical slogan of independence) and violent guerrilla action in the countryside. This chaotic situation could not last; it reached its inevitable *dénouement* in July, when the Serbian government finally lost patience and a strong and successful offensive was mounted against the UÇK.

But this was not the end of the story. The international community began to get involved, drawn in by repeated evidence of brutality by the Serbian police and the Yugoslav army. On 12 October, David Holbrooke, a US special envoy, was able to secure an agreement with Milošević which provided for the stationing of unarmed OSCE observers. This did not, however, prevent the massacre of forty-five unarmed ethnic Albanians in January 1999, in the town of Racak. This was followed in March by the start of the NATO bombing campaign, which, though not particularly successful in strictly military terms (very few Yugoslav tanks were destroyed and most services continued to operate), did after seventy-eight days eventually lead Milošević to abandon the struggle and accept defeat. Approximately 850 000 Kosovo Albanians, who had been pushed out of their country by the fear of reprisals, or by direct government measures, were now given the opportunity to return to their homes. The vast majority did so.

The victory of NATO and the return of the Kosovan refugees to their homes did not mean a restoration of stable conditions, however. The material for ethnic conflict was still there, and indeed hatred was now stronger than at any previous time. The returning Kosovo Albanians did not believe in the possibility of peaceful coexistence with the remaining Serb population. According to a survey conducted in October 1999, 91 per cent of Kosovo Albanians did not think they would ever be able to live peacefully with the Serbs. An Albanian interviewed by David Rohde in 1999 expressed the general view: 'Local Serbs are worse than those from Serbia proper. Instead of protecting their Albanian neighbours, Kosovo Serbs facilitated their deaths' (Rohde, 2000: 68–9). Revenge attacks took place repeatedly; most of the remaining Serbs were driven out, as well as anyone who was felt to have been in league with them in previous years, a category which included Roma, Turks and Muslim Slavs.

By the autumn of 1999 a mere 100 000 Serbs were left in Kosovo, most of them in the north-west corner of the province, to the north of the town of Mitrovica. The UNMIK (United Nations Mission in Kosovo) hoped to establish a multi-ethnic Kosovo 'with substantial autonomy within the Federal Republic of Yugoslavia',[8] but this was doomed to failure. On the Serbian side, the reaction to defeat was to boycott any multi-ethnic institutions the UN set up; on the Albanian side, the unanimous objective was independence, and the complete ending of the Yugoslav connection. It was not surprising that Hashim Thaçi, the UÇK-affiliated prime minister of Kosovo, demanded independence for his region; but the events of the previous few years made it impossible even for a moderate like Ibrahim Rugova to stand out against this demand (Cohen, 2000: 122). The relative failure of the radical nationalists at the municipal elections of 28 October 2000 (the two radical parties together secured only 35 per cent of the vote, as against 58 per cent for Rugova's LDK) does not mean that the dream of independence has been abandoned by the Kosovo Albanians.

Transylvania: a conflict that stayed off the boil

The Transylvanian question could well have been a serious international issue in the 1990s, but as it has turned out, not only did the smouldering embers fail to ignite, but the smoke itself has begun to clear. Why was this?

The answer to the question lies on both sides of the Romanian–Hungarian border. In Hungary, the efforts of nationalist agitators to bring the fate of Hungarian minorities outside the country to the forefront of the political agenda have failed consistently. They hoped to gain the support of the MDF (Hungarian Democratic Forum), the party which came to power after winning the first post-Communist elections. But the MDF prime minister, József Antall, was far more interested in domestic issues. Even his statement of 23 May 1990 that he was 'spiritually the prime minister of all fifteen million Hungarians', which marks perhaps the highpoint of Hungarian official interest in the issue, and was interpreted by Romanians as an encouragement to irredentism, was meant as a general cultural commitment. It was not a call to tear up the Treaty of Trianon again. At the next elections the nationalist right failed miserably, and the conservative MDF was replaced in office by the Socialist Party under Gyula Horn. Horn's main foreign policy priority was to improve relations with Hungary's neighbours.

In Romania, in contrast, nationalist forces were a great deal stronger, but even so, in the long run, here too forces of conciliation and compromise prevailed. It did not always look as if this would happen. Very soon after the revolution of December 1989 (which looked at the time like a textbook example of inter-ethnic co-operation against national Communist oppression, with joint action by Magyars and Romanians in the town of Timişoara setting the tone of the struggle against Ceauşescu[9]) members of the Hungarian ethnic minority organized the Hungarian Democratic Union of Romania (UDMR) on a very moderate programme of educational and cultural demands. Certain Romanian journalists (the most prominent among them were Radu Ceontea, Gheorghe Funar and Corneliu Vadim Tudor) took this as a threat to Romanian identity, and proceeded to set up two extreme nationalist groupings, first, *Vatra Românească* (Romanian Cradle), which was initially a cultural organization, but later turned into a political party called the Party of Romanian National Unity, or PUNR, and second, *România Mare* (Greater Romania), a journal which gave birth in May 1991 to the Greater Romania Party (PRM). Members of the former group started to make physical attacks on ethnic Hungarians, which resulted in a series of inter-ethnic clashes in March 1990.

The new Romanian authorities, those recycled members of the old *nomenklatura* who called themselves the National Salvation Front (FSN), blamed the violence of March 1990 on Hungarian provocateurs from across the border. For the next few years the FSN was able to stay in power, partly with the help of the nationalists. Moreover, the FSN used xenophobic slogans to win both the May 1990 and September 1992 elections: 'the democratic parties have sold the country to foreigners' is one example (Durandin, 1994: 107). They therefore at first had no interest in taking the heat out of the national problem. They engaged in talks with the Hungarian community in Transylvania, admittedly, but simultaneously and contradictorily entered into an alliance with the forces of extreme Romanian nationalism. On 25 June 1993, a parliamentary alliance was formed between the government coalition of Nicolae Văcăroiu and both the PRM and PUNR. Văcăroiu moved still closer to the nationalist right by including a member of the

PUNR in the cabinet (6 March 1994). Two further PUNR ministers were appointed in August 1994.

The next two years saw a series of anti-Hungarian measures, culminating in the Education Law of 24 July 1995, which prescribed Romanian as the language of tuition in all universities and denied ethnic minorities the right to university education in their own language (except for courses in Fine Arts and Theatre Studies). But at this point there was a change of heart. In August, the Romanian prime minister told Max van der Stael, the OSCE high commissioner, that the situation of national minorities in Romania had improved substantially, and that the Education Law was not really directed against the Hungarians. President Iliescu added the weight of his authority by proposing a 'historic reconciliation' with them. On 2 September, the three PUNR ministers were dismissed from the cabinet. There followed serious negotiations with both the Hungarian minority community and the Hungarian government. The upshot of this was the Treaty of Understanding, Co-operation and Good Neighbourliness, signed by the prime ministers of Romania and Hungary on 16 September 1996. Hungary renounced any claim to Transylvania, and Romania agreed to guarantee the rights of ethnic Hungarians.

The chief opposition party in the country (the Party of Civic Alliance, subsequently transformed into the Democratic Convention of Romania) also changed its position towards Romanian nationalism at this time. After a short period during 1995 when, under its conservative leader Corneliu Coposu, it appeared to be drifting towards the nationalist right (the founder of Romanian Cradle was even allowed to take part in a Democratic Convention conference in September 1995), the party shifted back towards the political centre early in 1996, with the selection of Emil Constantinescu as its candidate for president.[10] This meant, in effect, that by mid-1996 there was a consensus between government and opposition in the area of ethnic minority policy. As a result, the election campaign of autumn 1996 was fought over economic rather than ethnic issues.

Having won the elections (November 1996) the Democratic Convention formed a government which included representatives of both the Hungarian and the Roma minorities (György Tokay and Vasile Burtea, respectively). Gradually, the main demands of the Hungarians were met: in May 1997 the law on local administration was changed to allow ethnic groups comprising more than 20 per cent of the population of a given area to use their own language for official written communications (Gabanyi, 1997: 350); and, after considerable hesitation, with pressures and counter-pressures coming from both sides, a compromise was reached over the issue of a Hungarian university: the UDMR agreed in October 1998 to the government's offer of a 'multicultural university' in which tuition would be given both in Hungarian and German (rather than just in Hungarian, as they had previously insisted).

Macedonia: the conflict with a delayed fuse

Macedonia is the other former Yugoslav republic with a potential for ethnic conflict. On 17 November 1991, the Macedonians adopted a Constitution defining citizenship in ethnic terms: 'Macedonia is established as a national state of the Macedonian people.' The claims of the national minorities were recognized grudgingly by a clause guaranteeing full equality as citizens and 'the permanent coexistence of the Macedonian nation' with them (Dimitrijević, 1993: 50).

The main form of ethnic conflict affecting the country was with the large Albanian minority. Relations with the other minorities in Macedonia have also been problematic, although their small numbers and dispersal throughout the country have meant that these issues are not of great significance. The Roma have had the least to complain of. They have been integrated successfully into Macedonia, and conflict is unlikely.[11] The Turks, Serbs and Vlachs all have their own political parties and have advanced national claims which the Macedonian government has not satisfied. The Greek issue, which had a high international profile in the early 1990s, is really a pseudo-conflict, since there are few Greeks on Macedonian territory (the Macedonians estimate 1 000), and Macedonia has denied repeatedly that it has any territorial claims on Greece. Conversely, there are no Greek claims on Macedonia. The quarrel with Greece was about symbols rather than hard facts on the ground. The Macedonians, who felt they needed a symbol of the past that would not be attached either to ethnicity or religion, and would therefore unite all Macedonians irrespective of origin, adopted the Star of Vergina as their emblem. However, the Greek reaction to this was very hostile, as the Greeks felt that the Star of Vergina belonged to their own history. To the astonishment of most of the outside world, the two nations were also in dispute about the name of the newly-independent state of Macedonia. The Greek government, backed unanimously by Greek public opinion, rejected Macedonia's right to describe itself as such; the word 'Macedonia' belonged to Greece by virtue of history and could not be appropriated by another nation.

Here is how Evangelos Kofos explained the Greek grievance in 1991: 'It is as if a robber came into my house and stole my most precious jewels – my history, my culture, my identity' (Danforth, 1993: 4). In accordance with this attitude, Greece prevented Macedonia from being recognized by the EU or admitted to the UN under its own name. A compromise solution, accepted by the United Nations on 7 April 1993, was to admit Macedonia under the name FYROM (the Former Yugoslav Republic of Macedonia). The name 'Macedonia' was still there, but safely wrapped in cotton wool.

Not safely enough for the Greeks, however. In Greece the preferred name for Macedonia was 'Skopje'. When the United States recognized Macedonia under the FYROM title (9 February 1994) the immediate Greek response was to impose a ban on trade with 'Skopje' (16 February). The conflict ran on until 13 September 1995, when, under a settlement brokered by the UN representative Cyrus Vance in New York, it was agreed that the Star of Vergina would be removed from the Macedonian flag and replaced by a sun symbol. In return, Greece lifted its trade embargo and its veto on Macedonian (that is, FYROM) membership of international organizations. These were substantial Greek concessions, which allowed the restoration of fairly normal relations between the two countries. But the republic of Macedonia was still unable to use its own preferred name, except internally.

The conflict with the Albanian minority in Macedonia is fraught with much greater dangers. Its large size (23 per cent of the Macedonian population according to the 1994 EU-funded census, which was, however, boycotted by many Albanians), its territorial compactness, and its proximity to the Kosovo flashpoint all strengthened the possibility of violent conflict with the Slav minority. In the Macedonian constitution, the Albanians were simply listed alongside the much smaller groups of Turks, Roma, Serbs, Vlachs and Greeks as a national minority. Their response was to complain that this gave them an inferior status, and to campaign for a change in the wording.

Social separation between ethnic groups, always a danger signal, was a feature of the Macedonian situation. The Albanians and the Macedonian Slavs were thoroughly self-segregated on ethnic lines within Macedonia throughout the 1990s. They constituted, in effect, 'two rival societies' (Willemsen and Troebst, 2001: 310). A survey made in 1993 showed that 75 per cent of Orthodox believers (overwhelmingly ethnic Macedonians) and 78 per cent of Muslims (overwhelmingly Albanians) would not marry across the religious divide; 75 per cent of Albanians wanted their identity cards to be issued in Albanian only; while 70 per cent of the Orthodox wanted them issued in Macedonian Cyrillic only. Ninety-one per cent of Muslims thought they didn't have enough rights, while 47 per cent of the Orthodox thought they already had too many (Najcevska *et al.* 1996: 81, 93). The first major source of conflict was education. The struggle for Albanian-language higher education has led to violent and forcibly-repressed demonstrations in the ethnically Albanian parts of the country.

Despite these danger signs, disagreements between the two groups were for a long time muted, largely because of the moderation and statesmanship displayed by the Albanian side. The main ethnic Albanian party (the PPD, or Party for Democratic Prosperity) did not call either for independence or attachment to Albania or Kosovo. There was some agitation in 1992 for the setting up of an autonomous province of 'Illyrida' in the north-west of the country, and an unofficial referendum was conducted on 11/12 January 1992 on the issue. There was a majority of 74 per cent in favour, and 93 per cent participation by the local population. But the PPD did not take this any further, preferring to place their faith in co-operation with the Macedonian majority in the hope of securing full equality by consent (Schmidt-Neke, 1999: 203). Thus the PPD entered Branko Crvenkovski's coalition cabinet in September 1992, and remained in successive Macedonian cabinets for the next six years, at the cost of a split in the party in 1994 and the formation of a more radical group, which eventually merged with a minor party in 1997 to become the PDSH (Albanian Democratic Party). The PPD's programme, issued in 1993, called for the conversion of the country into 'a federation on the Belgian model, formed from two constituent peoples' (Schmidt and Moore, 1995: 122) but it seemed to be prepared to wait for the Macedonians to decide on this in their own good time.

Albanian moderation did not meet with an adequate response from the Macedonian side. The former Communists, now Social Democrats (SDSM) who ruled either alone or in coalition from 1991 to 1998, were ready to include Albanians in the government (in the less important cabinet posts), but not prepared to make any other concessions. Willemsen and Troebst claim to have discerned a 'course correction' of Macedonian policy towards the Albanian question in 1992 (2001: 299), but there is little evidence of this. Ten ethnic Albanians were convicted in June 1994 for an alleged plot to set up an All-Albanian Army in Tetovo. Issues of language use and higher education continued to smoulder. Attempts to give the Albanian language a more official status were resisted by the Macedonian majority; a law prohibiting the use of Albanian on identity cards was passed by the Assembly on 9 February 1995, sparking off a boycott by all eighteen Albanian deputies. Attempts to set up an Albanian language university in Tetovo were suppressed forcibly (the Tetovo university building was demolished in December 1994, and ethnic Albanians demonstrating for the university were harshly dealt with in February 1995, with one death as a result). The display of the Albanian flag except on public holidays was outlawed (July 1997). The immediate result of this was the sentencing of the mayor of Gostivar, Rufi Osmani, to fourteen years in jail (commuted to seven years) for allowing the Albanian flag to fly over his offices. Most Albanian mayors (including the mayor of Tetovo) resigned their posts in protest.

Albanians feared that things would get even worse after the October–November 1998 election victory of the Macedonian nationalists (VMRO-DPMNE) over the socialists (SDSM). But the only change the nationalists made was to form a coalition with the other, more radical, Albanian party, the PDSH, led by Arben Xhaferi, an Albanian from Kosovo. The PPD, for its part, proclaimed that it was not prepared to join a Macedonian nationalist government under any circumstances. The PDSH were given five seats in Ljupčo Georgievski's coalition government formed on 30 November 1998. Georgievski's programme included offers of state funds for the Albanian university at Tetovo, more local government power in Albanian areas and the release of ethnic Albanian political prisoners. Not all of the promises were fulfilled, but 8000 prisoners were amnestied by the new, VMRO-dominated, parliament, including the two Albanian mayors who had been imprisoned by the previous government, despite opposition from both the socialists and President Gligorov (4 February 1999).

The VMRO candidate for president, Boris Trajkovski, reaped his reward later in the year in the elections of 14 November 1999 and 5 December 1999 which he won thanks to overwhelming Albanian support. Immediately afterwards a new cabinet was formed in which the PDSH kept its five ministerial portfolios (22 December 1999). It retained four members in the slimmed-down cabinet announced on 27 July 2000. The Albanian-language university at Tetovo was legalized on 26 July of that year, against the wishes of the Macedonian Academy of Sciences, which described it as 'one more step in the ethnic partition of Macedonia'. The PPD (now no longer a member of the government) was also dissatisfied, pointing out that the new university was a private, and not a state institution, although state funds had earlier been promised. In the reshuffled coalition announced by Georgievski on 30 November, Albanians obtained two key posts (Foreign Affairs and Economics) previously held by Macedonian politicians from the Democratic Alliance.

Perhaps these concessions might have been enough. But now a new factor entered the scene, largely as a result of the continuing instability in Kosovo. In 1997–8 a number of attacks had already been carried out on police stations by supporters of the Kosovo Liberation Army (UÇK). Then, in 2000, after the Kosovo victory and the official disbandment of the UÇK, veterans of that army crossed the border (without taking off their uniforms, on which UÇK insignia were clearly visible), and set up a National Liberation Army in Macedonia. In February 2001 they began to take over in ethnically Albanian areas of the country, including Tetovo, the second largest city. Fighting ensued, but by the time of writing it had proved very difficult for the Macedonian army to dislodge them.

Divisions have also appeared within the Macedonian government over the degree to which further concessions should be made to the Albanian minority. The foreign minister, Srgjan Karim, an ethnic Albanian who was a member of the PDSH, naturally supported a 'package of reforms' (19 March). President Trajkovski was also in favour of compromise. Hawks from the majority party, the Macedonian nationalist VMRO, led by Prime Minister Georgievski, have opposed this, although they have been forced into forming a Grand Coalition which includes both the PDSH and the PPD (13 May 2001). The issue is in the balance at the time of writing. A ceasefire was announced on 5 July, but it has not held. Fighting continues. Negotiations so far have taken place, not with the NLA fighters, but with the elected representatives of the Albanian minority. Their demands are moderate: the introduction of Albanian as second official language, more control over the local police, broader authority for local government bodies, an accurate ethnic census, and state-funded Albanian language higher education. A peace deal was made on this basis on 13 August 2001.[12]

Efforts to stabilize the situation will perhaps succeed. Provided that Macedonian authorities are prepared to proceed with a compromise, the rebels are prepared to hand over their arms, and the outside world continues to oppose the fragmentation of the country and to engage constructively in the situation. None of these points can be taken for granted, however. NATO is not prepared to send troops to police an agreement unless the Albanian rebels give up their weapons. The outbreak of more serious conflict is certainly possible, and it is impossible to predict the outcome of this fast-moving situation.

Bulgaria and its dissatisfied minorities

Ethnic conflict broke out in Bulgaria immediately after the end of the Communist monopoly of power in 1989. The nature of the initial spark is clear: the ethnic Turks had been repressed during the 1980s, and the new, somewhat more democratic regime of Petŭr Mladenov, which took power in November 1989, took a number of steps to remove the restrictions they had suffered. This was clearly a response to pressure from the Turks, who were soon to organize their own political party, the DPS (Movement for Rights and Freedoms) to press for further concessions. But there were immediate counter-demonstrations by hundreds of thousands of ethnic Bulgarians on 2 January 1990, followed by a warning strike on 5 January, under the slogan 'Bulgaria for the Bulgarians'. Yet subsequent years saw no repetition of this. It is tempting to agree with Vesselin Stoianov, who sees the hand of the local Communist *nomenklatura* behind the Bulgarian nationalist protests of 1990: 'there lay at the bottom of all this the associations of the local *nomenklatura*, who were seeking a nationalist way of avoiding the loss of power' (Stoianov, 1998: 222).

The next step taken by the ex-Communists to stir up ethnic conflict in Bulgaria was the attempt to ban the DPS, which they 'viewed as a Turkish party because of its Turkish constituency', although the DPS's programme was couched from the outset in non-ethnic terms. It called for 'respect for civil rights and the freedom of individuals and communities', and rejected explicitly 'any form of separatism, nationalism or fundamentalism' as well as 'any attempt to fuel ethnic hatred' (Neuburger 1997b: 9). Notwithstanding this, the Bulgarian Supreme Court in September 1991 rejected the DPS's effort to form a legal political party because 'ethnically based parties' were forbidden under the constitution (Bates, 1993: 193–4).

Yet in the longer term the attempt to promote a narrow Bulgarian nationalism was a failure. There were three reasons for this. The first was, simply, that Bulgarians in general were not susceptible to this sort of agitation. As Ivan Kraster commented in retrospect, with some exaggeration (in view of the record of the 1920s): 'Bulgaria was the only country where nationalism never became a dominant force' (Kraster,

1997: 12). The second reason was that there was a strong liberal faction within the BSP, the renamed Communist party, which opposed the nationalist tactic, and they were able to prevail on party members to abandon this line of approach. The third reason was that the BSP was not in power long enough to do much damage (they were removed from office in November 1990).

Their successor in office, the Union of Democratic Forces, or SDS, was reliant on the DPS for a parliamentary majority, and in fact it was the decision of the DPS leader, Ahmed Dogan, to abandon the SDS alliance (in October 1992) that opened the way to the return to power of the socialists. When the latter returned to power, under a new leader, Zhan Videnov, after an interval of non-party government, their political perspective had changed. It was not that the liberal faction in the BSP had come to the top. It was rather that Videnov felt he had more to gain by co-operation with the DPS (which still held the parliamentary balance of power) than by appealing to Bulgarian nationalist sentiment, especially as the explicitly nationalist parties had done very badly in the December 1994 Bulgarian elections (in contrast to their success in neighbouring Romania). Moreover, there was a very specific reason for a DPS–BSP alliance after 1992: the impact of property restitution on agriculture. The restitution process of 1991–2 had had a severe impact on the Turkish minority. The ethnic Turks had no inherited property in the land and this meant that, not having been dispossessed by the Communists after 1945, they did not benefit from the post-Communist restitution; in fact, in so far as they were agricultural workers they were likely to lose their jobs. This was also true of the Pomaks. The BSP offered the hope (not, in the event, justified) that this process could be, if not reversed, at least slowed down (Creed, 1995).

The alliance between the BSP and the DPS lasted until 1996, and it allowed the BSP to prolong its period of rule over Bulgaria beyond expectations. This did not, however, give rise to any apparent increase in ethnic tension; the SDS, now in opposition, continued to be committed to democracy and the preservation of the rights of ethnic minorities, so it was hardly in a position to make capital out of the DPS alliance with the socialists. In any case, the BSP did not give the Turkish minority much in return for their support; the last straw for the DPS was the annulment of its local election victory of October 1995 in Kŭrdzhali.

When the presidential elections took place, in November 1996, it was the condition of the economy that was the issue between the parties, and not the position of ethnic minorities. This statement also holds true for the subsequent general election (on 19 April 1997), as a result of which the Union for National Salvation (an electoral alliance comprising the DPS and a number of smaller groups) won nineteen seats. The Turkish minority therefore continued to be well represented in parliament and to play a balancing role there (it opposed the introduction of a Currency Board, for example). The Bulgarian nationalists, in contrast, failed even to pass the 4 per cent threshold and were unable to gain any parliamentary seats.

Slovaks and Hungarians in conflict

This conflict too was settled peacefully and by compromise. Its rather threatening aspect during the early 1990s was largely a result of the rise of national feeling among the Slovaks, which was connected inseparably with the process of building a new nation. The Slovaks' two main targets were the oppression they considered they had suffered at the hands of the Czechs during the period of Czechoslovakia's existence, and the claims advanced by the Hungarian minority for certain national rights. Former members of the Communist *nomenklatura* who had now found a political home in the party of the Democratic Left decided in March 1991 that it would be to their advantage to make an alliance with Slovak nationalism.

In addition, one man bears considerable responsibility for the ethnic tensions of the 1990s in Slovakia: Vladimír Mečiar, the leader of a faction within the VPN (Public against Violence), the Slovak half of the movement that took over Czechoslovakia after the fall of Communism. He left the VPN in March 1991, on the grounds that its current leader had 'failed to defend Slovak interests'. In June 1991 he set up his own party, the HZDS (Movement for a Democratic Slovakia), with a programme of Slovak sovereignty, amounting in effect to independence. When the first government of independent Slovakia was formed, in January 1993, it was naturally led by Mečiar, who had gained the reputation of being the 'strong man' of Slovak politics. He showed the future direction of his policy on the national issue by immediately including a member of the extreme nationalist Slovak National Party (SNS) in his cabinet.

There were a number of reasons for Slovak resentment against the Hungarian minority. First, there was the very fact of organizing politically on an ethnic basis (the largest of the ethnically Hungarian parties, Coexistence, founded in February 1990 by Miklós Duray, took up the cause of all ethnic minorities in Czechoslovakia, including Poles,

Germans, Ukrainians and Ruthenians[13], but it was single-mindedly concerned with the minority issue rather than broader questions of democratization). Second, there was the tendency to support the federal link with the Czech half of the country, out of fear that the Slovaks, left to themselves, would be less tolerant of ethnic differences than the Czechs had been. Third, there was the Hungarians' insistence that existing minority legislation was inadequate. They rejected the law of 25 October 1990 on the official language of Slovakia for several reasons: it required minorities to reach a level of 20 per cent of the population before they were permitted to use their mother tongue officially, and it did not provide for bilingual street and road signs in minority areas.

The first two years after independence were the most dangerous period for the minorities. The new Slovak constitution provided for the compulsory use of the Slovak language in state and local administration, and did not mention minority rights. In the course of 1993 the authorities changed district boundaries to ensure that there were no longer any administrative districts with Hungarian majorities. The government of neighbouring Hungary also became involved: in June 1993 it threatened to veto the admission of Slovakia to the Council of Europe over the minority issue, although it withdrew the threat once Slovakia promised to allow minorities to use place names in their own language.

The Slovak nationalists were in power for most of this period, in alliance with the Mečiar government. The short interval of the Moravčik government (March to November 1994), which relied on Hungarian minority support, resulted in the passage of two minority laws through parliament, but the trend towards compromise was quickly reversed by Mečiar when he returned to power in December 1994, having won the elections of 30 September/1 October. For the next four years he ruled Slovakia with the aid of what was known as the 'red-brown coalition', so called because it consisted of his own party, the HZDS, the SNS 'browns' (in other words, extreme nationalists) and the ZRS 'reds' (the extreme left Association of Workers of Slovakia).

The Mečiar government pursued a two-track policy on the ethnic minority question. On the one hand it negotiated with Hungary, in order to remove the international dimension from the problem. This was successful, partly because elections in that country had just removed the centre-right from power and brought in the Hungarian Socialist Party in coalition with the liberal Alliance of Free Democrats.

The new Hungarian prime minister, Gyula Horn, offered Slovakia what he called a 'historic reconciliation' (14 July 1994). The Slovak–Hungarian Friendship Treaty, signed on 19 March 1995, declared the borders of the two states to be 'inviolable' (which was intended to reassure the Slovaks that the Hungarians had abandoned irredentism once and for all), and guaranteed that existing international standards of minority rights would be maintained.

The force of this declaration was, on the other hand, somewhat reduced by Mečiar's behaviour within Slovakia. He continued to act as if the treaty had not been signed; he was, after all, in a coalition with the SNS and there was a nationally-inclined majority to be considered in the Slovak parliament. The leader of the SNS, Jan Slota, denounced the Slovak–Hungarian Treaty as 'unfortunate', and in May 1995 a group of Slovak football supporters threw some Hungarians out of a moving train (this was, admittedly, the only act of anti-Hungarian ethnic violence sufficiently important to be publicized during this time; the Roma suffered far more but they had no allies).

The next three years saw a series of anti-Hungarian measures by the Mečiar government. In June 1995, the Ministry of Education extended the range of Slovak language teaching in Hungarian schools, setting off months of Hungarian protests in southern Slovakia. In November, the Slovak parliament passed a law for the protection of the Slovak state language which did just that, but failed to protect the language rights of the minorities. On 22 March 1996, the country was divided into eight regions (*kraje*), only two of which possessed enough Hungarians to qualify for minority rights, despite the fact that according to the 1991 census there were 567 000 Hungarians in Slovakia (Bugajski, 1994: 322). In April 1997, the Slovak Ministry of Education decreed that in Hungarian schools history and geography must be taught by Slovaks in the Slovak language. In September 1997, Mečiar called for the voluntary repatriation of ethnic Hungarians from Slovakia, a proposal which the Hungarian prime minister refused to entertain. In April 1998, the HZDS proposed a new election law (approved on 20 May), by which each member of an electoral alliance (rather than the alliance as a whole) was obliged to pass the minimum threshold of 5 per cent to secure a seat in parliament. This compelled the Hungarian parties to merge if they wanted any parliamentary representation. They did so, and after the September 1998 elections the long night of HZDS rule was at an end. The HZDS secured a plurality of votes, but the opposition parties together held the majority.

A new government was formed on 30 October, and the Hungarian Coalition Party was given three cabinet posts in it. On 10 July 1999, a new minority language law was approved, essentially reaffirming the rule established in October 1990 that where the minority reached 20 per cent its language would be declared official. The ethnic Hungarians again complained that this was inadequate; nevertheless, it may be safely affirmed that the bitter confrontations of the early 1990s with the Hungarians have come to an end; the Roma now occupy the foreground as the main ethnic scapegoat in Slovakia.

Not every post-Communist country in Eastern Europe suffered from ethnic conflict. We shall now examine some cases where it was absent during the 1990s, either because the conditions for conflict were not present, or because its development was held back for certain specific reasons.

The Albanian case: a few minor problems

It might seem odd to include Albania as a country lacking in ethnic conflict. Yet it is a fact that over most of Albania (except the extreme south, where the presence of a Greek-speaking minority complicates matters) the very far-reaching differences between political factions and regions of the country have never taken on an ethnic colouring. Despite the polarization and personal enmity that divided Fatos Nano's PSSH (Socialist Party of Albania) from Sali Berisha's PDSH (Democratic Party of Albania) in the 1990s neither side was in a position to play the ethnic card. There were differences of view about Kosovo, with Nano making it clear that he did not want either a 'big Albania' or an 'independent Kosovo', and Berisha accusing him of betraying the nation by his moderate policies, but these were disputes over foreign policy and had no bearing on ethnic relations within the country.

Whether this lack of ethnic conflict is a sign of national maturity or its opposite is a moot point. We have seen that the Communist regime, despite its many faults, did at least succeed in welding the north and south together to form a single Albanian nation. But was this merely a temporary result of common oppression by a harsh dictatorship? Bruno Cabanes has recently noted that the predominant trait in the Albanian psyche is not a sense of national unity but its opposite: a 'wounded identity' and 'a loss of confidence in any kind of collective future at all' (Cabanes, 2000: 23).

The one major instance of ethnic conflict in Albania relates to the Greek minority in the south. This minority was small (59 000 people, or 1.9 per cent of the total population in 1989) but troublesome because there was a long-standing Greek nationalist claim on southern Albania. The Greeks preferred to describe the area as Northern Epirus, and claimed that there were 200 000 ethnic Greeks living there. After the fall of Communism, ethnic Greek activists were able to form their own organization, *Omonia* (Harmony) which stood successfully in the first multi-party elections, which took place in three stages, on 31 March, 7 April and 14 April 1991. They gained five seats. But they did not limit themselves to pressing for improvements in the Greek position within Albania; the chairman of *Omonia* in the town of Gjirokastër proclaimed in December 1991 that the organization would work for the unification of Greek minority zones in Albania with the Greek motherland. This naturally strengthened anti-Greek feeling in Albania, and, in February 1992, *Omonia* was excluded from future elections and in effect banned from political activities. It continued to work underground for a series of demands, including a referendum on a possible separation of the ethnically Greek region from Albania. Its public replacement, the Unity Party for Human Rights, entered the elections of March 1992 and gained two seats with 2.9 per cent of the vote. In local elections in July 1992 the party received 4.3 per cent (which would indicate that the Greek minority was much larger than Albanian figures suggested).

The Albanian–Greek issue continued to smoulder for the next three years, with claims from the Albanians that the Greeks were trying to 'Hellenize Southern Albania', and counter-claims from the Greeks that the Albanians were engaging in 'continuing persecution of the Greek minority' (foreign minister Kardos Papoulias, 20 April 1994) and 'terrorising the Greek minority into fleeing their homes' (also Papoulias, speaking on 26 May 1994). There was a brief flurry of excitement over the minority issue in September 1994, when five ethnic Greeks, members of *Omonia*, were imprisoned for terms of six to eight years for alleged 'treason' and 'conspiracy' against Albania. But, in December, President Berisha pardoned one prisoner and commuted the sentences of the rest, and on 9 February 1995 all the *Omonia* activists were freed.

On 26 February 1995, the OSCE's Human Rights Commission announced that there was 'no case to answer' in regard to alleged Albanian persecution of ethnic Greeks. Relations improved with Greece, and the Greek government played its part in this by arresting Greek nationalists, members of a so-called Northern Epirus Liberation Front, as they were preparing to attack Albanian border guards (20 March 1995). Two months later, the Albanian parliament approved an education law which included a guarantee of ethnic minority education in the relevant minority language (in this case, Greek). On 21 March 1996, an Albanian–Greek Friendship Treaty sealed the gradual improvement in relations between the two countries and this dispute can now be regarded as settled.

The Czech Republic and Czech-Slovak relations: the velvet divorce

Ethnic conflict has largely been absent from the Czech Republic, too. After all, the country is very homogeneous. If the 13.7 per cent who declared themselves Moravians or Silesians are added to the 81.3 per cent of Czechs, the total is 95 per cent. We shall deal later with the Moravian and Silesian cases. For the rest of the minorities, this is a question of past disputes which very few people have any desire to resuscitate. The hundred-year-old Sudeten question is the main issue. Yet this is largely a question of foreign policy now, and both partners, the Czech Republic and Germany, have adopted a moderate position, despite the attempts of extremists in both countries to stir up trouble.

Václav Havel has been notable for the strong line he has taken in favour of national reconciliation, both as president of Czechoslovakia (1989–92) and as president of the Czech Republic (from 1993 onwards). In 1990, he took what was at the time a very unpopular initiative when he apologized publicly for the 1945–6 expulsion of the Sudeten Germans from his country. Five years later, however, he adopted a somewhat different position. He gave a speech rejecting the idea of 'reawakening the past' which would 'bring to life all the demons that have laid dormant here', and announcing the passing of the 'time for apologies'. At the same time, he reaffirmed the need to 'replace confrontation with cooperation'.[14]

This proclamation that what had been done in 1945 could not be undone was welcomed by most people. Only the political extremes (the Communist party and the republicans in the Czech Republic, and the Sudeten German organizations in Germany) endeavoured to keep the conflict going. The head of the Sudeten organizations in Germany, Franz Neubauer, replied that the decisions of 1945 should be reversed, even in the 1990s; and if not, the Czechs ought not to be admitted to the EU. But Neubauer's views did not really represent German opinion or German policy. Similarly, the 100 Czech intellectuals who in 1995 called for direct negotiations between the Sudeten leaders and the

Czech government were also expressing a minority opinion (Bazin, 1997). Whatever the rights and wrongs of the question of the expulsion of the Germans, the issue is now dead.

The Moravian–Silesian movement (HSD-SMS), which emerged briefly in the early 1990s with a demand for autonomy for those two parts of the country was in fact a regionalist rather than an ethnic movement, even though its chief slogan 'We are not Czechs!' had ethnic overtones.[15] Its chairman, Jan Krycer, did not deny that Moravian and Silesia were integral parts of the Czech Republic, but he wanted to restore and extend the autonomy that had existed in the early twentieth century. For a short time it seemed that the movement was able to mobilize a substantial group of electors: in June 1990, the HSD-SMS gained 10 per cent of the vote in the Czech part of the republic, and in the 1991 census, 13.2 per cent of the population described themselves as 'Moravians' (though only 0.5 per cent called themselves 'Silesians'). In 1992, the Moravian autonomists took advantage of the dispute between Czechs and Slovaks by offering an alternative solution: the division of Czechoslovakia into three 'autonomous and equal entities' (Bugajski, 1994: 308). But they were unable to maintain their momentum: by 1996, the Moravian and Silesian regionalists had vanished from the parliamentary scene (Troebst, 1999: 598).

It is appropriate at this point to deal with the 'velvet divorce' between the Czechs and the Slovaks; in other words, the peaceful break-up of Czechoslovakia. Many Slovaks had long been resentful of what they viewed as Czech arrogance. The establishment of a federal Czechoslovakia in January 1969 did not genuinely mean that the Slovaks could now act autonomously, given the context of party dictatorship. As party leader Gustáv Husák (himself a Slovak) proclaimed in May 1969: 'The party is not federalized. On the contrary it is unified, and we are responsible for the work of Communists at all levels' (Leff, 1988: 246).

In a Communist-run state, the lack of any corresponding federalization of the Communist party inevitably meant a serious reduction in the area of autonomous decision-making. Hence the collapse of Communist rule in 1989 was seen by most Slovaks as an opportunity to achieve genuine federalization in a democratic context. Initially, this did not mean that they demanded the complete break-up of Czechoslovakia. But Slovak resentment continued to grow even after the measures of 1990, by which the country was renamed the 'Czech and Slovak Republic' and Slovakia received a very great degree of autonomy. A public opinion survey undertaken in March 1993 found that 62 per cent of a Slovak sample ascribed the division of Czechoslovakia to the unwillingness of Czechs to engage in an equal partnership with them (Bútoru and Bútorová, 1993: 127).

The Slovaks found this attitude even more galling, in that their image as a largely agricultural backwater was by now entirely inaccurate. The rapid economic development and urbanization of the Communist period in Slovakia had given rise to a situation in which social structure and employment patterns were pretty well identical in both parts of the country (Srubar, 1998: 56). But this was, in fact, one reason for the breakup of Czechoslovakia, because, while Czechs were in general prepared to support 'economic shock therapy', which would result in the devastation of large branches of Communist-era industries, Slovaks were more conservative; they thought, rightly, that Slovakia's industries would suffer severely from exposure to the competition of the world market and the imposition of stringent financial discipline. So while the Czechs just about favoured the introduction of a free market, on balance (52 per cent support during 1991), the Slovaks tended to oppose it (61 per cent were against this in January 1991, increasing to 67 per cent in November).

The change in the public mood among Slovaks was reflected in the split of 1991 in the VPN, which we mentioned earlier, and the setting up of the HZDS on a nationalist programme. Slovak Prime Minister Mečiar's nationalism was at first limited to economics: he was happy to retain a loose connection with the Czechs, but demanded absolute control of economic affairs. When his Czech counterpart, Václav Klaus, refused to concede this, the only alternative was complete independence. On 23 July 1992 agreement was reached between the two men on how the separation of the two halves of the former Czechoslovakia could be achieved. Somewhat paradoxically, public opinion in Slovakia, though strongly autonomist, was not generally in favour of complete independence. In June 1992, 30 per cent of Slovaks favoured this solution; even in September 1992 the figure had risen to only 41 per cent (Juchler, 1994: 342).

The potential ethnic conflict in Montenegro

It may seem strange to include Montenegrin–Serb relations in a discussion of potential ethnic conflict. The close religious and cultural affinity between Montenegrins and Serbs is well known. But there are also differences. Montenegro, under its prince-bishops, had a long, separate history. Whether this meant a separate Montenegrin identity was endlessly disputed. We reproduce here the judicious words of Ivo Banac: '[by the end of the nineteenth century] the Montenegrins had lost sight of their complex origins and thought of themselves as Serbs ... The contemporary claims over separate Montenegrin nationhood are on the whole a result of interwar Serbian misrule in Montenegro' (Banac, 1984: 45). This comment underlines both the lack of a separate Montenegrin national consciousness and the potentiality for its development.

Just as 'Serbian misrule' in the period between 1918 and 1941 stimulated the demand for an autonomous Montenegro within a federal Yugoslavia (a demand that the Communists adopted and put into effect formally after 1943 and in practice after 1971), so the 1990s were a period in which it became clear once again that Montenegro was not benefiting from its association with Serbia. The republic elected to stay in the Yugoslav Federation with Serbia in 1991, but there was already a strong current of opinion in favour of independence. This was, however, by no means unanimous; many Montenegrins continued to see themselves as Serbs. The ruling party split over the issue, and the faction that favoured gradually cutting links with Serbia, which was led by Milo Djukanović, came to the top first in the presidential elections of October 1997, and then in the legislative elections of May 1998.

Since June 1998, Montenegro has ceased to recognize federal authority, ostensibly because the appointment of the previous Montenegrin leader Momir Bulatović as president of Yugoslavia was unconstitutional. The real reason was this: Bulatović had already been removed from power in Montenegro because of his excessively pro-Serbian line, and the new appointment was an attempt by Bulatović's patron Milošević to restore his authority via the back door. President Djukanović of Montenegro has taken various measures to loosen the connection with Serbia, such as paying wages and pensions in German marks rather than Yugoslav dinars. The presence in the country of the Serb-dominated Yugoslav Army, and of a large faction of avowed supporters of the Yugoslav connection within the country, are deterrents to complete separation. What is clear is that the potential for conflict is there; and the change of government in Belgrade has not entirely removed this potential, since President Koštunica relies for his parliamentary majority on the Montenegrin supporters of Milošević. While another leading Serbian politician, Zoran Djindjić, supports Djukanović's efforts to separate Montenegro from Serbia, Koštunica has so far taken the middle position of calling for 'the two Montenegros' to enter a dialogue with each other. In Montenegro itself, the pro-Serbian and pro-independence factions are, at the time of writing, evenly balanced, with a slight tendency for the supporters of independence to predominate.

The Roma: an international ethnic minority

We shall conclude this section with some brief comments on the Roma. If this book were about ethnic minorities there would be much more to say, but in the context of ethnic conflict, the Roma are too scattered and powerless to be more than victims of ethnic intolerance. The Roma of Central and Eastern Europe had no particular ethnic claims to put forward, except to be allowed to continue living in their time-honoured manner. They suffered considerably from the problems associated with the process of transition after 1989. They were a very obvious target for resentment, because they could be used to symbolize the 'dislocating introduction of markets' into a formerly controlled economy, despite the fact that they themselves did not benefit from this (Verdery, 1993c: 42). They were by far the most disliked ethnic minority (78 per cent of respondents in a 1991 survey of opinion in Czechoslovakia, Hungary and Poland showed hostility) (Barany, 1994: 329).

Their fate varied, however, from country to country. The Macedonian Roma were perhaps best off. According to the 1981 census, there were 43 707 of them, although they had a tendency not to declare themselves as such on census forms.[16] In Macedonia, they functioned as 'an integral and accepted part of everyday life', receiving recognition in 1991 as a separate nationality (Friedman, 1999: 317). In Serbia, too, the 110 959 Roma (1981 census figures), many of whom lived in the province of Kosovo, were at first relatively fortunate. They were regarded by the Serbian government as useful allies against the claims of Albanians and other non-Serb groups; although they were also under pressure from Kosovo Albanians to declare themselves Albanian, for the same reason (Duijzings, 1997: 213). Their situation worsened considerably after Kosovo came under Albanian control again, as Albanians tend to regard Roma as complicit in the atrocities committed by Serb police and paramilitary units during the Kosovo conflict.

Elsewhere, the situation is bleak. In Romania, the large (11 per cent) Roma minority has had to face considerable hostility. In 1990–1 they were subjected to violent attacks in which the police did not intervene. They were generally presented as criminals in the mass media. Declining industries provided no opportunities for employment. The process of privatization in agriculture meant that they were thrown off the land (the majority received nothing in the redistribution). In 1993, four Roma were killed and 120 forced to flee from a Transylvanian village. Where possible, they have emigrated. In the Czech Republic, skinhead groups murdered twenty-six Roma between 1900 and 1993. Czech citizenship rules require at least two years of continuous residence and a clean police record for five years. The Czech government refuses to change this law, which in effect excludes Roma from citizenship (Barany, 1995). The situation in Slovakia is not much better. For the future, the hope must lie in two simultaneous processes: the integration of the Roma into society (through education and provision of employment) and a change in attitudes, allowing them to be embraced and welcomed into each society (Crowe, 1995: 238).

6
Ethnic Conflict and Compromise in the Former Soviet Union

Upon the breaking and shivering of a great state and empire, you may be sure to have wars. (Sir Francis Bacon)[1]

Without the Karabagh movement the flag of independence would not have been hoisted over the land of Armenia. (Balaian, 1995: 413)

We now move on to conflicts in the former Soviet Union. Pride of place must go as usual to the South Caucasus (Transcaucasia). We deal first with Armenian–Azerbaijani relations, then with Georgia's many problems.

There were three border issues at stake between Azerbaijan and Armenia: Zangezur (Armenian-inhabited territory within Armenia, claimed by Azerbaijan on historical grounds); Nakhichevan (Azerbaijani-inhabited territory with the status of an ASSR within Azerbaijan although geographically separated from it, as it lay on the border between Armenia and Turkey, and was claimed by Armenia on historical grounds); and Nagornyi Karabagh (the largely Armenian-inhabited enclave within Azerbaijan, which had the status of an Autonomous Region). Both sides were ready to compromise over Zangezur and Nakhichevan, despite a feeling of historic injustice, but Nagornyi Karabagh was another matter. This question remained as intractable in the 1990s as it had been in the 1920s.

The impact of the Karabagh issue

It is almost impossible to exaggerate the impact of the problem of Nagornyi Karabagh (NKAO)[2] on both Armenia and Azerbaijan in the late 1980s. The recent story starts in 1987 with the raising of the Armenian demand for a change in the status of NKAO. The demand itself was of long standing. What was new was the widespread feeling that, with the coming of *perestroika*, the Armenians had a much better chance of getting their way. Abel Aganbegyan, one of Gorbachev's main economic advisers, was an Armenian, and he associated himself publicly with the demand for the separation of NKAO from Azerbaijan when interviewed in November 1987. He was not disavowed; in fact, 'several prominent Soviet visitors to the US indicated that conditions were favourable for a solution of the Karabagh question' (Suny, 1993: 197).

The Armenian agitation fed on the hopes raised in this manner. The unanimous vote of the NKAO Supreme Soviet in favour of separation from Azerbaijan and inclusion in Armenia, in February 1988, alongside a series of tit-for-tat expulsions of Armenians and Azerbaijanis from each side's territory, in turn sparked off both violent pogroms against Armenians living in Azerbaijani territory and a mass political move-ment. In November 1988, public meetings on the subject in Baku were attended by nearly a million people. The local Communist party lead-ership was able to suppress the meetings after a few days, but this was the starting-point of a period of continuous political agitation among the Azerbaijanis. The situation was very tense in Armenia too, and an unofficial Karabakh Committee gained tremendous popular support. The party leadership was unable to control the situation, despite arrest-ing the committee's leaders.

In July 1989, an Azerbaijani Popular Front (APF) was formed in Baku. It had six demands, five of them unconnected with the Karabagh ques-tion, but the demand with the greatest emotional resonance was that for an end to direct (USSR government) rule over NKAO, imposed by Mikhail Gorbachev in despair in January 1989 because he was unable to find any solution to the problem that satisfied both parties. The objective of the Azerbaijanis was to keep things as they were, and to allow no changes in the constitutional framework set up by Stalin in 1921. One of the leaders of the APF, the lathe operator Neimat Panakhov, described the agitation over the NKAO as a 'cynical diver-sion which would melt away once republican self-rule was achieved and new relations between the republics established' (Dragadze, 1989: 2). This certainly did not mean that he envisaged giving the NKAO to Armenia once he came to power. Rather the reverse, in fact. The Popular Front countered Armenian complaints with its own call for the setting up of an autonomous *oblast'* in the Zangezur region of Armenia, as well as a cessation of Armenian nationalism and chauvinism, and an end to the destruction of Azerbaijani monuments in Armenia.[3]

Gorbachev claimed that the demonstrations in Baku were motivated purely by nationalism. It was certainly true that the ethnic issue was a vital part of the Popular Front's campaign. But the APF also wanted to create a non-Communist, democratic Azerbaijan. A year later they seemed close to achieving their goal. During the autumn of 1989, the party lost power progressively to the APF. The decision by the Moscow authorities in November 1989 to grant the main demand of the APF and return Karabagh to direct Azerbaijani control did not stop the agitation. Mass rallies in Baku in December 1989 called for secession of the republic from the Soviet Union; border posts between Azerbaijan and Iran were torn up; early in January, the Popular Front seized power at a local level in a number of outlying provinces; the situation looked to be dangerously out of control, with a renewed series of murderous attacks on Armenians in Baku and elsewhere (Swietochowski, 1993; Altstadt, 1994).

The Soviet leader decided to suppress the movement by force. On 19 January 1990, 17 000 Soviet troops, armed with tanks and automatic weapons, reconquered the capital of Azerbaijan for Communism, though after this 'tragedy of Black January' tens of thousands of Azerbaijani Communists burned their party cards (Zverev, 1996: 27). The official death toll was sixty-two, but the Popular Front claimed it was much higher. The Communist party was now back in the saddle, under a new leader, Ayaz Mutalibov, and he was able to stay in control for the next two years, until he was forced to resign by military defeat. The situation in NKAO remained deadlocked during this period, though the gradual decline of central Soviet institutions eventually left the two sides facing each other; the end of the Soviet Union was followed inevitably by the outbreak of war.

In the Armenian view, the war of 1992–94 in NKAO was fought between the Nagornyi Karabagh rebels and the army of Azerbaijan; but there was no secret about the close links between the Armenian patriots of Nagornyi Karabagh and other Armenians, and the Armenian army and state rapidly became involved as a third force. After all, the Armenian Minister of Defence at that time, Serzhik Sarkissian, was an MP in the Karabagh parliament. Azerbaijan did very badly in the war. The removal of Mutalibov in May 1992, and the electoral victory of the APF candidate Abulfaz Elchibey in June 1992, did not make any difference. By June 1993, when the town of Mardakert was surrendered, Azerbaijan had lost the whole of NKAO as well as the corridor that separated the district from Armenia, and an area stretching down to the border with Iran.

R. G. Suny claims that the reason for Azerbaijan's defeat and Armenia's victory in the war over Karabagh was that the Azerbaijanis lacked a strong sense of national identity (Suny, 1999–2000: 146). Robert D. Kaplan puts the same point even more strongly: 'The Turks of Azerbaijan had never become a nation, regardless of what the maps in the 1990s said' (Kaplan, 1996: 167). There are several problems with this argument. First, an Azerbaijani national identity *did* emerge before 1991, at least during the Soviet period and possibly earlier (Altstadt, 1992). Second, the overthrow of President Elchibey in June 1993 was caused by, not his attempt to project a Turkish identity, but by defeat at the hands of the Armenians. His successor, Geidar Aliev, hoped to gain more success by moving closer to Russia, but without abandoning the Turkish connection. He appealed to Turkey for military help, without success, and to Russia for mediation. Fighting gradually resumed in the autumn of 1993, with some slight gains for Azerbaijani forces. A ceasefire was agreed on 5 May 1994 (the Bishkek Protocol), but it did not entirely hold on the ground, and it has been impossible to arrive at a definitive peace settlement, despite round after round of wearisome negotiations.

These negotiations failed because, in an atmosphere of overheated nationalism, any attempt by political leaders on either side to settle things by compromise was a guarantee of their political, and sometimes also physical, demise. President Levon Ter Petrosian of Armenia seemed to be moving towards a compromise peace in the autumn of 1997. He rejected an independence demand by Arkadii Gukasian, president of Nagornyi Karabagh, as 'unrealistic' (26 September 1997). In November, he announced that Armenia just could not afford to support Nagornyi Karabagh any more: 'there is no other road for Armenia than a negotiated settlement with Azerbaijan' (Manutscharjan, 1998: 383).

The reaction of the authorities of the breakaway republic was to say that from now on Nagornyi Karabagh would deal directly with Baku over its problems; people in Armenia should keep quiet about the question. On 7 January 1998, the Armenian prime minister, Vazgen Sarkisian, demanded Ter Petrosian's resignation, on the absurd grounds that Petrosian's own party, the HHSh, was itself guilty of organizing terrorist attacks on Petrosian's colleagues so as to create an anti-Karabagh mood in Armenia. The pressure was increased by Armenia's association of war reservists, *Erkrapa*, who demanded the immediate unification of Nagornyi Karabagh with Armenia. The foreign minister, Aleksandr Argunian, who was associated closely with the peace negotiations, left the government on 2 February 1998. Ter Petrosian himself was forced to resign the next day. He declared in his resignation speech that 'the party of peace has suffered a bitter defeat'.

He was replaced by Robert Kocharian, known to be a hardliner on the Karabagh issue. Kocharian's position was confirmed a month later when he won the presidential elections. The extreme nationalist Dashnak party (the Armenian Revolutionary Federation, or ARF), banned in 1994 by Ter Petrosian, was relegalized, and given three seats in the cabinet (May 1998). Yet the peace negotiations continued, even under Kocharian. Having won the war, the Armenians needed to end it. This logic was inescapable, although the assassination of Vazgen Sarkisian in October 1999 by nationalist extremists indicated the personal cost involved in making concessions to the other side. Despite this warning, President Kocharian did not allow himself to be intimidated by the extremists. He supported the November 1998 plan of the Minsk Group of the OSCE for the setting up of a 'common state' of Azerbaijan and Karabagh, in which both parts would have equal rights. Under the Minsk Group's plan, Karabagh would have had 'de facto independent status, with its own constitution and armed forces' and would have been given 'the right to veto laws made by Azerbaijan'. In return, Armenia would have withdrawn its armed forces from Azerbaijani territory outside Karabagh.[4]

The Minsk plan was rejected by Baku on the grounds that it went too far towards the Armenian position. In fact, it requires both sides to make concessions. Yerevan has been able to bring Stepanakert into line on this; the same cannot be said of the authorities in Baku. Azerbaijan is prepared to grant 'the broadest autonomy' to Karabagh, but not 'independent status'. The appropriate analogy to apply, said President Aliev in March 2000, is with the status of Tatarstan within the Russian Federation (Meshcheriakov, 2000). For the Armenians, a subordinate status of this kind was completely inadequate. Deadlock continues; but at least fighting has been replaced by diplomacy.

Georgia: the triumph of ethnic separatism

The Soviet republic of Georgia was a 'little empire', as Andrei Sakharov pointed out in 1989 (Jones, 1997: 505). Hence, when the issue of Georgian independence was raised, the reaction of several of its component parts was to demand at least increased autonomy and in some cases full independence or separation. In Abkhazia and South Ossetia, the confrontation with Georgian nationalism was so fierce that it resulted in military conflict.

Abkhaz–Georgian conflict, as we saw earlier, was a constant theme during the Soviet period. Generally speaking, the centre tended to take the Georgian side, but the compromise settlement of the 1970s leaned somewhat more towards the Abkhazians, though certainly not granting any of their constitutional demands. The Soviet authorities hoped that concessions would make it possible for the Abkhaz to reconcile themselves with their position within the Georgian SSR. This did not happen. In fact, neither side was satisfied by the measures of the Brezhnev era. In 1980, a large number of prominent Georgians signed a letter to the 26th CPSU Congress complaining of discrimination against them locally, while the Abkhazians countered that they were now 'worse off than they had been under Beria' (the Georgian secret policeman who had run the area in the 1930s) (Lezhava, 1997: 224).[5] Thus a tense situation already existed when the coming of *perestroika* made it possible for both sides to voice their grievances publicly.

The Georgian nationalists stimulated Abkhazian resentment by calling for the immediate introduction of the Georgian language in every part of Georgia. The Abkhaz had until then shown a strong degree of resistance towards learning that language (only 2 per cent of them knew it in 1970); they preferred Russian (61 per cent spoke it as a second language).[6] Georgian nationalists also demanded the abolition of all autonomous districts (including Abkhazia), because of their alleged incompatibility with Georgian unity, and the recognition of Georgia's special character as a Christian state. One leading Georgian nationalist, Irakli Tsereteli, provocatively wiped out hundreds of years of Abkhazian history with this pronouncement: 'Those whom we call Abkhazians are not Abkhazians. The Abkhazians were a Georgian tribe. The present Abkhazians are the descendants of Kabardinians and Balkars who came to Georgia in the mid-nineteenth century.'[7]

One man, Vladimir Ardzinba, gained and retained the leading position in the Abkhazian movement. His evident Russian connections have given rise to the suspicion that the movement for Abkhazian independence from Georgia is really a Russian way of making sure that the pleasant seaside resorts by the Black Sea do not fall into Georgian hands. Ardzinba is, or was, a trained Moscow orientalist, specializing in the history of the Hittites. He worked at the Oriental Institute when Yevgenii Primakov (who later became Russian foreign minister) was its director. His eloquent speeches, in Russian rather than Abkhazian, in defence of the rights of small ethnic minorities, first brought him to the notice of the wider Russian public, and there is no doubt that there has been continuing unofficial support from Russia for his movement. Whether Georgian publicists, as well as the respected Russian specialist on ethnic questions, Svetlana Chervonnaya, are right in their claim that the whole Abkhazian movement was Russian-run and Russian-dominated is less certain (Chervonnaya, 1994: 58).

The movement for Georgian independence was intertwined fatefully with the Abkhazian question from the beginning. The Abkhazian People's Forum *Aidgylara* (Unity) was set up in the autumn of 1988 to press for the removal of Abkhazia from Georgian control and its direct subordination to Moscow. It held a rally in March 1989 at which calls were made for Abkhazia to be raised to the status of a union republic. Local Georgians in Gali (a town in the south of Abkhazia) protested immediately, and these anti-Abkhazian protests spread to the Georgian capital, Tbilisi. The protesters' demands escalated rapidly. They began to call for an independent Georgia. This was too much for the head of the Georgian Communist party, who arranged for Soviet troops to move in on 9 April 1989 and suppress the demonstrations by force. There were at least twenty deaths and hundreds of wounded. The well-nigh unanimous reaction of Georgians was to turn their backs on both the Communist party and the Soviet connection. The repercussions over the rest of the Soviet Union were also very serious: the nascent democratic movement recoiled in horror from the government's actions. It could well be said that the Tbilisi slaughter of 9 April 1989 was the first nail in the coffin of Soviet power.

In the course of the next two years, while the Georgians raced towards independence, the Abkhazians (encouraged by the Soviet authorities) cut their links progressively with Georgia. Abkhazia became independent of Georgia in practice during 1991, thanks to the presence of a strong contingent of Russian troops. (The actual declaration of Abkhazian independence took place on 23 July 1992.) While the Georgian Supreme Soviet was busily constructing a constitution that gave appointed prefects absolute powers over local representative bodies in the regions, thereby in practice abolishing local autonomy (Jones, 1993: 302),[8] the Abkhazians went on quietly consolidating their separate institutions, including a parliament in which they had majority representation. It was partly the Abkhazian issue (alongside other perhaps more vital questions) which led to the overthrow of President Zviad Gamsakhurdia, who was elected in May 1991 on a programme of extreme Georgian nationalism but was criticized for failing to do anything effective to counter Abkhazian separatism when in office. It is something of a paradox that Gamsakhurdia (having been overthrown by the Georgian National Guard on 6 January 1992) subsequently allied with Ardzinba in planning a joint campaign against the Military Council which had taken power in Tbilisi (Chervonnaya, 1994: 52). Shortly afterwards, a degree of political stability was restored to the country, with the return of Eduard Shevardnadze to power (March 1992).

Meanwhile, semi-independent Abkhazia became a safe haven for the Zviadists (the supporters of Zviad Gamsakhurdia), who seized prominent Georgians, including the vice-president, Alexander Karsadze, as hostages, and held them on Abkhazian territory.[9] Opinions in Moscow were divided over what line to take in this conflict, but on 14 August 1992 Russia finally gave Georgia the green light to invade Abkhazia, ostensibly to free the hostages. According to George Hewitt, Boris Yeltsin 'knew in advance of Shevardnadze's plan to invade Abkhazia and gave approval by silence afterwards' (Hewitt, 1999: 479).

Nevertheless, the general tendency of Russian policy was to maintain a balance between the two sides. They endeavoured repeatedly to arrange peace deals between Abkhazia and Georgia, and on 27 July 1993 Shevardnadze and Ardzinba signed a Russian-brokered peace agreement in Sochi by which the Russians would send peacekeeping troops while all Georgian forces would quit Abkhazia. With unofficial Russian support behind the scenes (denounced by the Georgian prime minister, Tengiz Segua, as 'Russia's undeclared war on Georgia'), the Abkhazian forces were able to resist Georgia very effectively. Whereas an Abkhaz assault on Sukhumi, the main town of the region, was defeated on 18 July 1993, before the agreement, by the Georgians, after the agreement the Georgians were defeated. On 27 September 1993, Sukhumi fell to Abkhazian forces, and by October 1993 Georgian troops had been driven out completely.

Shevardnadze blamed Russia for this debacle, accusing Yeltsin of betrayal. He said on 27 September that the plan to occupy Sukhumi 'was masterminded at Russian military headquarters'. His next move was to use diplomatic means to improve Georgia's position. He brought his country into the CIS and leased some bases to Russian troops (8–9 October 1993). The Russians responded by helping Georgian government forces to defeat the Zviadist rebels (November 1993) and they arranged a further round of peace talks, between 11 and 13 January 1994, which resulted in an agreement on the return of Georgian refugees and the deployment of Russian troops under the auspices of the United Nations to secure a buffer zone. But the agreement did not hold. The Abkhazians withdrew from renewed peace talks on 15 March in protest against Georgia's disbandment of their parliament.

Boris Yeltsin then stepped in and used his good offices to secure a peace agreement between the two sides – the Moscow Agreement of 4 April 1994 – which embodied a large number of Georgian concessions. The concessions were not a result of Russian pressure, however. They were a simple consequence of utter military defeat. The fact was that the Georgian army, which until 1994 was really no more than a collection of personal militias (Jones, 1997: 525), was no match for the combination of North Caucasian volunteers and sympathetic individuals from the Russian military who bore the brunt of the fighting on the other side.

Under the Moscow Agreement, Abkhazia received its own republic, constitution, flag, state emblem and national anthem, although it was not granted independent statehood. Russian troops were to be deployed as peacekeepers. The Abkhazians could vet applications for return from Georgian refugees,[10] on an individual basis, which did not satisfy the Georgians, who had wanted the 'instant mass return' of the exiles (Hewitt, 1999: 476). The Russians, for their part, were happy to allow all the Georgian exiles to return, and Shevardnadze and Viktor Chernomyrdin, the Russian prime minister, reached an agreement on 10 July 1995 on this subject; the Abkhazian leader, Vladimir Ardzinba, however, continued to oppose the idea. The Georgians offered autonomy to Abkhazia, but Abkhazia rejected the offer as insufficient; the Russians thereupon signed an agreement with Georgia that 'Georgia's territorial integrity should be restored', though not by military force (15 September 1995).

If military force was not to be used, the only other form of pressure the Russians could exert on Abkhazia was economic. When the 18th CIS summit met in Moscow on 19 January 1996 it decided to impose a complete blockade on Abkhazia until it agreed to reunite with Georgia. But economic pressure did not work either, perhaps because the blockade was ineffective. The Abkhazians remained stubbornly independent. In August 1997, Yeltsin announced further proposals for a settlement: Georgia's territorial integrity would be recognized, and Georgian refugees would be allowed to return, while Abkhazia would receive 'substantial autonomy'. Shevardnadze welcomed these proposals; but Ardzinba rejected them, adding on 14 August that Abkhazia 'would make no further concessions'.

In January 1998, Shevardnadze proposed a UN peacekeeping operation in Abkhazia similar to the one currently in force at the time of writing in Bosnia-Hercegovina; both Ardzinba and the Russians rejected this, on the grounds that 'only CIS troops would be acceptable' as peacekeeping forces. In May 1998, Abkhazia sent troops to drive the Georgians out of the southern town of Gali and the surrounding area; Georgian irregular forces fought back, but 35 000 Georgians were forced to flee. Yeltsin condemned Abkhazia for this invasion on 28 May, the UN joined in on 30 July (by UN Security Council Resolution No. 1187). This was further confirmed on 28 January 1999 by UN Security Council Resolution No. 1225, which expressed concern at the plight of Georgian refugees in the area. This forced the Abkhazians to make some concessions: Georgian refugees began to return to Gali on 1 March 1999. But on the main issue, which was independence, the Abkhazians were not to be moved. On 3 October 1999, a referendum was held in Abkhazia; 97 per cent of those who voted supported independence.

Eduard Shevardnadze, who remains, at the time of writing, the president of Georgia, would no doubt like to end the Abkhazian insurgency by compromise, since military victory seems impossible, but any concession on the vital issue of sovereignty would simply play into the hands of his turbulent opponents within the country. The situation could now be described as a stalemate, patrolled by UNOMIG (United Nations Observer Mission in Georgia), which has its mandate extended at regular, six-month intervals, and by Russian troops, who stand between the Abkhazian and Georgian forces.

Developments in South Ossetia followed a somewhat similar path to those in Abkhazia, and with similar results. The separate status of the South Ossetians was recognized in 1922 when they were granted an Autonomous District (AO) within Georgia – in other words, one rung below the Abkhazians. Georgian nationalists also tended to place them lower, claiming that they were recent immigrants with no right to the land. There was no such place as South Ossetia, said the Georgians: it was in fact 'Samochablo', a land named after Machabeli, a medieval Georgian prince. What was most immediately threatening to the South Ossetians, however, was the drive to make Georgian the sole official language: only 14 per cent of them knew Georgian (38 per cent knew Russian).

As in the case of Abkhazia, the rise of Georgian nationalism stimulated a corresponding Ossetian national movement, *Ademon Nykhas* (Popular Shrine), which gained control of the South Ossetian Supreme

Soviet in 1989 and forced through a resolution upgrading South Ossetia from an Autonomous District to an Autonomous Republic (10 November 1989). The Georgian reply was to annul the vote and send volunteers to the region to 'defend the Georgian population' (30 per cent of the total in South Ossetia in 1989). Fighting ensued. Negotiations with the Georgian leader, Zviad Gamsakhurdia, led nowhere, which is not surprising in view of his comment at the time: 'I shall bring an army of 300,000 here. Not a single Ossete shall remain in the land of Samachablo' (Zverev, 1996: 48). In August 1990, the Ossetian national movement was banned from taking part in elections; the South Ossetian Supreme Soviet replied by proclaiming a South Ossetian Soviet Democratic Republic (20 September 1990) which would be subordinate directly to Moscow rather than to Tbilisi; the Georgians responded, first by abolishing South Ossetian autonomy (11 December 1990) then by blockading and invading the territory (January 1991), although they did not succeed in conquering it.

Combat continued for the next two years, though at a low level, since the Georgians were prevented from devoting their full attention to South Ossetia by their many other problems, and the Russians tended to take the Ossetians under their wing. On 19 January 1992, 90 per cent of the South Ossetians voted to place their republic under Russia rather than Georgia; many of them wanted unification with North Ossetia. However, the widening of the conflict was prevented by the attitude of Akhsarbek Galazov, the North Ossetian leader, who refused to allow volunteers from the Confederation of Mountain Peoples of the Caucasus to pass through his territory to join in the fight against Georgia. The Russian nationalists and Communists pressed for more direct Russian involvement, but Yeltsin decided against this.

The alternative was mediation, and this resulted in the conclusion on 22 June 1992 of the Sochi Agreement, between the Georgian president, Eduard Shevardnadze, representatives of North and South Ossetia, and the Russians, for the stationing of joint Russian–Georgian peace-keeping forces in the disputed area. The South Ossetians have, however, retained their *de facto* independence since then. This is, of course, not recognized by Georgia (or by the international community).[11] The South Ossetian entity is something of a throwback to Soviet times: its passports are USSR passports on the 1974 model, its laws are Russian laws, its currency is the rouble, its largest political party (since the March 1994 elections) is the Communist party. The Georgian blockade has deprived it of electricity and gas; some inhabitants move north to North Ossetia in winter to avoid freezing. It can only survive with Russian support, and in fact its citizens would prefer to be citizens of the Russian Federation (Gusher, 2000: 6).

Finally, we need to examine a number of other regions of Georgia, where there were rather weaker grounds for separate status than in the cases of Abkhazia and South Ossetia, but where there were still significant differences between the 'Georgian nation' properly so-called and the predominant local ethnic group. The people of Ajaria, in the south-west of the country, spoke Georgian, but in the Guruli dialect. The important distinction, here, however, was in religion: the Ajarians were Muslims. This was considered to be enough, in Soviet times, to justify setting up an ASSR. After 1991, the Ajarian ASSR asserted and retained a semi-independent position, under its president, Aslan Abashidze. Abashidze's power rests not on mass support but on family and clan ties: he comes from a family which was already dominant in the region in the fifteenth century. The Bolshevik Revolution inevitably brought some changes, but even under Soviet rule Aslan's grandfather, Memed Abashidze, managed to retain a degree of control over the area, until he was shot by Beria in 1937. In November 1991, the Ajarians voted by an overwhelming majority (94 per cent) in favour of Abashidze's party, which entered the elections under the name 'The Union of Georgian Traditionalists'.

The Ajarians do not wish to secede from Georgia, but they are determined to preserve a high degree of autonomy. The Georgian attitude has evolved in the course of time from friendship to hostility. Whereas Gamsakhurdia himself had appointed Abashidze in 1991, by 1997 the Georgians were describing him as 'the head of a regionalist mafia'. Abashidze's alleged crimes included being secretly in league with the Russians, keeping Russian troops on the border with Turkey against Georgian wishes, and, perhaps worst of all, retaining two-thirds of the revenues from the lucrative customs dues levied on international trade passing to and from Turkey (Radvanyi and Berontchachvili, 1999: 231–2). Ever since 1997, the Georgians have made a determined attempt to throttle Ajaria economically. Abashidze's reply has been to try to create a confederation with the other troublesome southern province of Georgia, Dzhavakheti, and to enter Georgian politics directly, through his Batum Alliance, which did well enough in the 31 October 1999 Georgian elections to become the main opposition party.

Dzhavakheti, which is ethnically 90 per cent Armenian, supports a movement called Dzhavakhk that aims 'at least to obtain autonomy, if not to unite the region with Armenia' (Hewitt, 1999: 488). There is also continuing opposition to central rule in Mingrelia, which was previously a stronghold of support for Zviad Gamsakhurdia. These smaller movements suffer from the disadvantage of lacking the outside support enjoyed by the Abkhazian and South Ossetian nationalists, but given the weakness of the Georgian state at the time of writing, they may well succeed. If their demands were granted it would amount to the disintegration of historic Georgia into a congeries of small states, defined by George Hewitt, who advocates this solution, as Abkhazia, South Ossetia, Mingrelia, Svanetia, Ajaria, Dzhavakheti, Imereti, Kartli, K'akhetia, and 'the Azerbaijani area'[12] (which is located in the province of Kvemo Kartli, in the south-east of the country) (Hewitt, 1999: 490). In fact, there is already a distinct tendency for Georgia to fall apart into a number of independent states, based on regional elites. Of the ten regions enumerated by Hewitt, six were 'already autonomous in practice' by the year 2000 (Gusher, 2000: 8).

The Russian Federation and its problems

It will be convenient at this point to move to the other side of the Caucasian mountains, where there were also a number of violent conflicts in the 1990s, and where in one case, namely Chechnya, the issue was independence from Russia. In other instances, the Russians were not directly involved.

There were a number of unique features about the Chechen situation, and the Chechen–Russian relationship, which meant that Chechnya was the one part of the Russian Federation where an independence movement existed with mass backing and a chance of success. The Chechens were, first, almost the sole titular nationality which, in numerical terms, absolutely dominated their own autonomous republic in late Soviet times.[13] Second, the historical experience of the previous 200 years had both forged them into a nation with a very strong sense of solidarity and imbued most of them with a strong hatred of the Russian connection. Among these formative events were the long wars of conquest conducted by the Russian Empire in the early nineteenth century, the subsequent growth of Sufi brotherhoods, and the Russian reconquest, under Soviet auspices, in the 1920s. Finally, there was the mass deportation of 1944 and the long years in exile in Central Asia, an experience that not only underlined the alienation of the Chechens from Soviet society but also obliterated traditional tribal divisions and created a modern sense of nationality (Lieven, 1998: 338).

The two wars in Chechnya, terrible as they were for the local population, should not mislead us into an incorrect evaluation of the main-
springs of Russian policy. The ethnic policy of the Russian Federation
and of Russian governments has so far not been one of assimilation of
non-Russians into the Russian nationality. The Constitution of 1993
shows no signs of the identification of the state with the dominant
ethnic group, which is the rule in the constitutions of South East
Europe. The sovereign people in Russia are not the Russians (*russkie*)
but the 'Rossians' (*rossiiane*) (Geyer, 1998: 654).

Moreover, the years between 1994 and 1998 saw moves, not towards
increasing centralization but away from it, with the establishment of
asymmetrical arrangements between the entities that make up the
Russian Federation; in other words, the establishment of a hierarchy of
autonomies (such as existed also in the Soviet Union) with places like
Tatarstan at the top, enjoying very far-reaching autonomy, and with
the purely Russian provinces at the bottom. According to R. Sharlet, the
Constitutions of these new autonomous republics are 'infused with the
spirit of secessionism' (1993: 321), an alarmist view paralleled by the
opinion of the first deputy minister for Nationality Policy in the Russian
Federation, V. A. Pechenev, who complained in 1999 that 'in some areas
of the country the ethnic minorities enjoy greater rights than Russians',
and warned that any further evolution of the Federation in the direction
of a Confederation could lead to its disintegration.[14] The disintegration
of Russia is a possible scenario that cannot be excluded, but it would be
wrong to exaggerate the extent to which power has slipped away from
the centre. The recognition of the right of the major non-Russian ethnic
groups to autonomy strengthens the Federation by lessening centrifugal
tendencies, which are far more likely to gather strength in confrontation
with a more centralist state (Heinemann-Grüder, 1998: 688). In any case,
the last years of the 1990s saw a tendency for Russian power over the
regions to be reasserted, though at the time of writing this has not gone
so far as to cancel out the autonomy of the main non-Russian areas.

The case of Chechnya should be seen an exception, and not the har-
binger of a general collapse. This can be shown by an examination of
the situation in other parts of the North Caucasus. The Chechens were
unable to spread the fight against Russian hegemony either eastwards
or westwards. To the east of Chechnya lay Dagestan, an overwhelmingly Muslim, and overwhelmingly non-Russian, republic. Yet there
was little sign of any movement of resistance to the Russian connection in Dagestan in the 1990s, or any drive for independence on the
Chechen model.

One reason for this is clearly the lack of ethnic uniformity in Dagestan; the ethnic situation there is so complex that there was never any single titular nationality. The Avars come closest (with 27.5 per cent of the population), but they have always been held in check by the many other ethnic groups with equal claims. There is clearly the potential for ethnic conflict in Dagestan, but it is precisely the entrenched character of ethnicity that has prevented it: each ethnic group has its political representatives, under the system of 'ethnoparties' (Ware and Kisriev, 2000). The religious factions (among the Muslims, who form the overwhelming majority) tend to be tied to particular ethnic groups. Thus, in the early 1990s, separate Kumyk, Dargin, Lak and Lezgin Spiritual Directorates were formed to compete with the main Avar-run Spiritual Directorate of the Muslims of Dagestan (Bobrovnikov, 1996). This did not, however, result in conflict. Co-existence between ethnic groups is based partly on a common faith in Islam, and partly on the 'cooperative interaction between elites', under the 1994 Constitution, which provides in Article 88 that 'there cannot simultaneously be more than one representative of the fourteen major ethnic groups on the State Council'. Thus, if a Dargin replaces an Avar in a ministry, another Avar must receive a post in compensation, and so on down the line (Ware and Kisriev, 2001). This system has so far produced ethnic harmony, though the experience of analogous regimes in Lebanon and the former Yugoslavia is not a good omen for the future.

Appeals by the Chechens to the Dagestanis on the basis of Islamic or Caucasian solidarity in the 1990s generally fell on deaf ears. A Confederation of the Mountain Peoples of the Caucasus had indeed been set up in November 1991 in Abkhazia, with the declared aim of 'the collective defence of the Caucasus against Russian hegemony' (Bartak, 1993) but when, three years later, the time came to help Chechnya, minimal aid was given, partly because the Abkhazians could not afford to alienate the Russians, who were their allies against Georgia (Garb, 1998: 193).[15] There were no Dagestani uprisings in solidarity with the Chechen resistance in the first Chechen war; and Shamil Basayev's attempt to take over parts of Dagestan in August 1999, which was one of the reasons for the second Chechen war, was based on a similarly mistaken calculation that the common Islamic background of the North Caucasians would take precedence over the administrative divisions established by the Soviet leaders in the 1920s. Basayev assumed that the inhabitants of north Dagestan would join him in setting up an Islamic republic; he found to his surprise that popular resistance from the Dagestanis themselves (helped by the Russians) forced him to retreat back across the border (Longuet-Marx, 2000: 12). The Chechens were also unable to involve the nations living to the west of them. Even the Ingush, so close in language and culture, and with a common historical experience of deportation under Stalin, preferred to stay on good terms with Russia in the hope that the Russians would help them to recover at least part of their lost territory of Prigorodnyi. This land had been assigned to the North Ossetians in 1944 when the Ingush were deported; and on their return from deportation after 1956 they wanted it back. The two peoples had no other points of friction. The dispute over Prigorodnyi was created purely and simply by Soviet actions. But the Soviet authorities refused consistently to alter the borders Stalin had set in 1946, and that was also the attitude of the Russian Federation. After two years of conflict and the expulsion of 70 000 Ingush from North Ossetia, a four-day shooting war broke out at the end of October 1992 (Tscherwonnaja, 1995). The Russians moved troops in to keep the two sides apart, and eventually Yeltsin persuaded Ruslan Aushev and Akhsarbek Galazov, the respective leaders of Ingushetia and North Ossetia, to sign a statement whereby Ingushetia renounced its claims on the Prigorodnyi region and and North Ossetia promised to allow the Ingush refugees driven out in 1991 to return home (12 December 1993). The issue is by no means settled, in that the injustice done in 1944 has not been repaired, but it has not yet resurfaced.

There are two other North Caucasian issues which have the potential to develop into violent confrontations. They are both direct consequences of irrational Soviet decisions made in the 1920s. As we saw earlier, in two cases, completely unrelated nations were forced together into autonomies: the Karachai and the Cherkess in the Karachayevo–Cherkessian AO, and the Kabardinians and Balkars in the Kabardino–Balkarian ASSR. The differences between them were greatly heightened by unequal treatment in 1944: the Karachai and the Balkars were deported; the other two not. A movement grew up in 1991 among the Karachai for cutting the connection with the Cherkess and restoring the Karachai Republic. This failed, and instead the Karachai candidate General Vladimir Semionov entered and won an election contest (16 May 1999). The Cherkess, for their part, refused to accept this Karachai victory and demanded the right to secede. They were strong enough in the capital city to prevent Semionov from entering it. A similar conflict exists between the Kabardinians and the

Balkars, with the Balkars attempting to secede. They proclaimed the Balkar Republic on 17 November 1996 but were crushed by the Kabard president, V. M. Kokov. These conflicts have, however, not reached the level of civil war, and they are unlikely to do so (Tscherwonnaja, 2000). The Russians are not direct participants, but the March 2001 decision of President Putin to appoint Kokov to the post of one of a seven-member Presidium of the State Council which represents Russia's eighty-nine regions shows which side he favours.

The relative stability of the North Caucasus in the 1990s (except, of course, in the case of Chechnya) is shown by the absence of any population movement out of the area. In fact, rather the reverse. There was a population increase of 6.1 per cent there between 1989 and 1996, made up of 1.1 per cent natural increase, and 5 per cent immigration. The Russian population, which has been flowing away from freezing Siberia and unwelcoming Central Asia to the western regions, has tended to stay in, and indeed even to migrate into, the North Caucasus, during the 1990s (Heleniak, 1997b: 87).

Moldova and the former Soviet west

The western part of the former Soviet Union, too, was not without its ethnic conflicts in the 1990s. We look first at Moldova, where there were two areas of potential ethnic conflict: with the Gagauz minority in the south, and the Russians and Ukrainians who inhabited the more industrialized east of the country. Only in the latter case was the conflict violent enough to produce civil war. There is less to say about the former, for here a peaceful compromise was possible. The Gagauz were in language Turkic but in religion Orthodox Christian; they were a small group (153 000 in 1989) and they made up only 3.5 per cent of the population, though they were concentrated in a few particular districts. Their main grievance was the Moldovan language law of 31 August 1989, which made Moldovan the official language of the Moldovan republic (only 4.4 per cent of the Gagauz could speak Moldovan, as against 65 per cent who could speak Russian). They also feared that the objective of Moldovan nationalists was to unite the country with neighbouring Romania and carry out a policy of Romanianization. Hence a Gagauz National Movement (*Gagauz Khalki*) emerged during the next year. On 19 August 1990 it declared a Gagauz republic, to consist of the five allegedly Gagauz districts of Moldova. In fact, only two of them had Gagauz majorities.[16] The new republic would, the Gagauz nationalists said, remain part of the Soviet Union but not be part of Moldova.

The Moldovan response was to declare the movement illegal, but the movement of Moldovan nationalists into the area was blocked by the presence of Soviet troops. A tense stand-off followed, which did not, however, degenerate into violence. After the failure of the August 1991 coup (which many Gagauz had supported) a national Gagauz congress held in Komrat, the chief town of the area, declared an independent state.[17] Eventually, by Article 111 of the Constitution of 27 July 1994, the Gagauz people were guaranteed the autonomous republic for which they had been pressing; the promise was implemented by the law of 15 January 1995, providing 'administrative autonomy' for Gagauzia, an entity officially described as *Gagauz Yeri*. There are three recognized official languages: Gagauz, Moldovan and Russian. This solution seems unlikely to unravel as Gagauzia now generally regards autonomy within Moldova as sufficient, with the significant reservation that it will secede if Moldova unites with Romania.[18] There was thus a very clear link between the settlement of the Gagauz conflict and the decision of Moldova not to seek union with Romania (the referendum of 6 March 1994 delivered a 95.4 per cent vote in favour of Moldovan independence) (Gangloff, 1997).

The Russians and Ukrainians of the lands beyond the river Dniestr had more far-reaching objectives than the Gagauz: they did not want to be part of Moldova at all. Surprisingly, some of the local Moldovans took the same line. The reaction of these three groups of 'Transdniestrians' to Moldovan moves towards independence in the Gorbachev era was first to insist that they would stay in the Soviet Union (this was the meaning of the unilateral proclamation of a Dniestr Moldovan SSR on 2 September 1990) then, when that option was no longer available (with the failure of the coup of August 1991 and the subsequent collapse of the Soviet state) to set up a Transdniestr republic. A referendum held in December 1991 produced a 97.7 per cent vote in favour of independence, on a 78 per cent turnout. Given that 39.9 per cent of the population of the area was ethnically Moldovan, and assuming a fair count, the implication of these figures is that a large proportion of Moldovans (70 per cent has been claimed) supported the Transdniestr option (Kolstø *et al.*, 1993: 986).

After this, relations with Moldova worsened steadily, and a civil war broke out in March 1992. This lasted until July 1992, and resulted in a victory for Transdniestr, thanks to the involvement of the Russian 14th Army which was stationed there, as well as Cossack volunteers from other parts of Russia. By the agreement of 21 July, Moldova con-ceded the establishment of a security zone dividing Transdniestr from the rest of the country, to be policed by the Russian 14th. Army. The resulting entity, called the Transdniestr Moldovan Republic (PMR), has been described as 'a cross between a last relic of the Soviet Union and a giant smugglers' camp' (Lieven, 1998: 248). The reason for its survival throughout the 1990s was 'massive terror against opponents of separa-tion' combined with 'a population exchange governed by ideological criteria'. As a result, surviving opponents have simply left the area (Büscher, 1996: 863).

Some observers have taken a much more favourable view of the PMR. John O'Loughlin asserts that the new republic is a 'multi-cultural world' in which 'the majority of the political leaders and the personnel of the armed forces' are Moldovan (the ethnic Russian president, Ivan Smirnov and the ethnic Russian minister for State Security, Vadim Shevtsov, are the exceptions, he says), and in which all three languages have equal rights, where there is no ethnic strife, tremendous popular support for the republic, and a high degree of intermarriage between the three major national groups of Russians, Ukrainians and Moldovans (O'Loughlin *et al.*, 1998). Paul Kolstø, in similar vein, notes that members of all three groups fought on the Transdniestr side in the war, so that it would be 'an oversimplification to reduce the PMR–Moldova conflict to ethnic tensions' (Kolstø *et al.*, 1993: 974).[19] Instead of ethnicity, 'which is not the main driving force', the root of the conflict lies in a 'regionalism' which 'cuts across ethnic divisions' (Kolstø and Malgin, 1998: 103).

The trouble with this interpretation is that its exponents have not presented any strong evidence of ethnic Moldovan participation in the PMR, and they ignore evidence of ethnic Moldovan resistance (such as the schoolteachers' strike of September 1992 against the reintroduction of the Russian alphabet; the October 1993 protest in Bendery against the ban on the Latin script; and the growth of the pro-Moldovan 'Integrity' movement in the region). Apart from the chair of the Supreme Soviet, Grigorii Marakuţa, and the defence minister, Stefan Kitsak, all other prominent figures in the PMR are Slavs. One thing is clear: the part played by Soviet nostalgia in the situation. A 1998 survey revealed that 84 per cent of Russians, 82 per cent of Ukrainians and 70 per cent of Moldovans in the PMR considered themselves 'citi-zens of the former Soviet Union' (O'Loughlin *et al.*, 1998: 351). It should also be noted that the territory of the PMR is located in the same area as the old Moldavian ASSR, which existed within the Soviet

Union as an autonomous unit between 1924 and 1940. The territory of the pre-1940 Moldavian ASSR does not coincide exactly with that of the present Transdniestr republic, but the PMR leaders see themselves as the heirs of this earlier political formation.

The Russian 14th Army remained stationed in Transdniestr throughout the 1990s, which meant that Moldova had no chance of recovering the area by military force. The Moldovans conceded autonomy to the region, though they were not prepared to allow independence. For many years, this was the main stumbling block to agreement. Thus, talks between President Snegur of Moldova and Ivan Smirnov, the president of the Transdniestr republic, collapsed in September 1995 because Smirnov insisted on 'the recognition of the independent statehood of Dniestr', while Snegur would only offer 'autonomous republic status'.

Yet after a few years it turned out that an agreement could be made. There were two reasons for this. The first was a number of changes in the internal political scene in Moldova. By 1994, the Moldovans had abandoned their initial intention of joining the country to Romania, which the supporters of Transdniestr had found tremendously threatening. In 1990 and 1991 the Moldovan Popular Front pressed for reunification with Romania, arguing that the Moldovan state was a purely artificial Soviet creation, and that they were in fact Romanians.

After the fall of the Soviet Union, the pendulum began immediately to swing the other way. The Popular Front's enthusiasm for unification ceased to benefit it at the polls (Socor, 1992). The pro-Romanian parties lost the elections of 27 February 1994 (the Christian Democratic Popular Front received 8 per cent of the votes, and the Bloc of Peasants and Intellectuals 9 per cent). The winners were the Agrarian Democrats (43 per cent) and the Socialists (22 per cent). President Mircea Snegur proclaimed in a keynote speech of 5 February 1994 that 'Moldovans and Romanians are two different nations, and Moldova is entitled to be an independent state'. The referendum of 6 March, mentioned earlier, confirmed that almost all Moldovans now supported this position. The most contentious issue between Transdniestr and Moldova had thus been cleared away. But a settlement was now delayed by the president himself, who remained a Moldovan nationalist, although he had broken with the Popular Front. He was not prepared to compromise with the Transdniestr Russians on the question of Moldovan unity. Hence his defeat in the elections of December 1996 reopened the way to negotiations. The next president, Petru Lucinschi, inaugurated in January 1997, immediately began the search for an agreement with Smirnov, who had just been reelected president of the PMR.

Negotiations now began in earnest. Both parties agreed to sidestep the constitutional issue of whether an autonomous Dniestr republic would remain part of Moldova (as Lucinschi insisted) or be recognized as a state equal to Moldova but in partnership with it (which was Smirnov's formulation). The Memorandum of May 1997 on 'normalizing relations between Moldova and Dniestr' envisaged that 'the two governments' would 'develop relations as part of a single state'. But nowhere did it specify the constitutional status of the Dniestr Republic. This allowed Lucinschi and Smirnov to interpret the Memorandum in different ways. Subsequently, at further talks in July 1999, both sides 'agreed on a single economic, judicial and social sphere within Moldova's existing borders'.

At the time of writing, the Transdniestr conflict looks close to a definitive settlement. The likelihood of this was increased by the elections of 23 February 2001, at which the Communist party of Moldova (PCM) won an absolute majority of votes and seats (70 seats out of 101) in the legislative assembly. The party leader, Vladimir Voronin, announced that he favoured joining the Russo-Belarusan Union and making Russian the second official language in Moldova. If this happens the main issues driving the original conflict with the PMR will have disappeared.

Elsewhere in the western part of the former Soviet Union, ethnic conflict was deep-rooted and pervasive, but not sufficiently violent to result in war. We shall look first at the three Baltic republics of Estonia, Latvia and Lithuania and then move on to Ukraine and Belarus.

Estonia in the 1990s was a society strongly polarized along ethnic lines. There was very little intermarriage between the Estonian majority and the 30.3 per cent Russian minority, and the political attitudes of the two communities tended to be different. Most Russians were favourable to the Soviet connection and opposed independence (though approximately a third of the minority population voted for independence in the referendum of 3 March 1991) (Raun, 1997: 415). Ethnic Estonians overwhelmingly opposed the Soviet connection and supported independence. Once this goal had been achieved, they adopted an ethnically exclusive approach in building the new state, while the predominant Russian reaction to this was not to strive for assimilation in the dominant group via language change but to demand increased minority rights.

The ethnic schism persisted throughout the period because no one on the Estonian side wanted to introduce any incentives to weaken ethnic divisions. Thus Russian speakers could not vote without passing stringent language tests of Estonian competence, and the electoral system did not provide for ethnic minority representation (Evans, 1998). Estonia's citizenship law of 19 January 1995 was the harshest in the whole of the region and it was condemned by the Russian foreign ministry for 'legitimising discrimination against Russian speakers'. The minimum residence period for naturalization was set at five years. Only 150 000 out of the 475 000 Russians managed to become citizens of Estonia in the first seven years of independence.

Despite these disadvantages, the attitudes of the local Russian population did not tend towards extremism or nostalgia for the Soviet past. Instead, they demonstrated a wish for compromise and an awareness that the Estonians were calling the shots, given the unwillingness of the Russian Federation's government to intervene. Russians in Estonia surveyed by Geoffrey Evans in 1995 were keen to have the Russian Federation government concern itself with their rights (by 66 per cent to 13 per cent), but they were generally opposed to expanding the borders of Russia to include the parts of Estonia inhabited by Russian speakers (54 per cent against, and 17 per cent in favour) and they were inclined to give their allegiance to Estonia rather than to Russia (48 per cent in favour, 16 per cent against) (Evans, 1998: 68). Most Russians were non-nationalistic (in 1993, 72 per cent scored 'very low' or 'rather low' on an index of nationalism, and 60 per cent of them had a 'positive view' of Estonian independence) (Kirch and Kirch, 1995: 47; Raun, 1997: 419).

Hence the more radical Russian nationalist parties were in a minority position within the Russian electorate of Estonia. The nationalists did not stand in the first two elections (September 1992 and March 1995). In the elections of 10 March 1999, the nationalist Russian Party received only 4.5 per cent of the vote and failed to get into parliament. 'Our Home is Estonia', on the other hand, a moderate party representing all the ethnic minorities (which meant in effect the Russians, who were 79 per cent of the minority population), received 5.9 per cent of the vote and six seats in 1995. It stood again in 1999 under the name Estonian United People's Party, and increased its vote to 6.1 per cent, retaining its six members of parliament.

The Russians made up a sizeable minority of the population in Latvia (34 per cent in 1989, falling to 32 per cent in 1999). Their social presence was even more striking than these figures suggest, as they were concentrated in the cities, some of which still had Russian-speaking majorities at the end of the twentieth century (Daugavpils was 59 per cent Russian, and Rezekne 54 per cent). There were plenty of reasons for conflict with the Latvian majority. The Russians were associated in Latvian minds with Soviet rule, with deliberate Russification, and with unrestricted immigration, which had turned Latvians into minorities within their own cities, and looked as if it might now endanger the Latvian majority over the whole country, given the very low Latvian birthrate.

Apart from the usual conflicts over education and language, Latvians and Russians also clashed over national monuments. In February 1993, the Latvian parliament voted to remove the remains of Red Army soldiers from the Latvian national military cemetery, on the ground that 'soldiers who served in the Red Army were deliberately buried there to defile the place'. The Russian view was that this was rank ingratitude: the Soviets had saved Latvia from Nazism. The Latvian view was that they had not wanted to be saved by the Soviets, so there was nothing to be grateful for. In this case the crisis was defused by a delegation from the USA, which persuaded the Latvians to adopt a moratorium on any unilateral changes to cemeteries or monuments (Volkan, 1997: 144).

Latvian hostility to Russians was not matched by Russian hostility to Latvians. A poll taken in 1993 showed that while 64 per cent of Russian speakers felt they had much in common with Latvians, 46 per cent of Latvians felt they had nothing in common with Russians. Even so, 62 per cent of Latvians felt relations with the Russians were good, while only 22 per cent thought they were bad (Dreifelds, 1996: 164–8). Although Latvia's regulations on citizenship were at first extremely stringent (only pre-1940 nationals and their descendants had an automatic right to citizenship, while the rest had to have resided for ten years and passed a test of competence in Latvian) many local Russians were descended from pre-1940 residents. Hence, by January 1994, 38 per cent of the Russian population had qualified as citizens (Muiznieks, 1997: 392). As a result, a sizeable proportion of the electorate (21 per cent) was ethnically non-Latvian.

This provided a strong basis for Russian parliamentary representation. In voting at elections, as well in answering pollsters' questions, the Russians in Latvia revealed very little support for extreme nationalism. The Russian parties entering the elections concentrated on issues of minority rights and economic progress. In the elections of June 1993, the Russian-based party Harmony for Latvia–Rebirth of the Economy gained 12.0 per cent of the vote and 13 seats; its rival for the Russian vote, the ex-Communist Equal Rights group, doing less well, with 5.8 per cent and 7 seats. A stringent Naturalization Law was passed on 22 July 1994. This was a disappointment for the Russians as it required five years' residence and demonstrable command of the Latvian language, and may be the reason for the decline in support for Harmony for Latvia in the October 1995 elections (down to 5.6 per cent and 6 seats). The other moderate Russian party, Equal Rights' successor, the Socialist Party, also received 5.6 per cent of the vote. But the continuing weakness of overt Russian nationalism was demonstrated by the failure of the Party of Russian Citizens to pass the parliamentary threshold (with 1.25 per cent of the vote) (Pettai and Kreuzer 1999: 155).

In the third Baltic state, Lithuania, there were two substantial minorities: Russians (9.4 per cent in 1989) and Poles (7.0 per cent). Despite the ease with which they could acquire Lithuanian citizenship (under the 'zero-option' citizenship law of November 1989 which made all current residents eligible), the 340 000 strong Russian minority did not throw up any political parties until 1996. When a Russian party did emerge it secured only 1.6 per cent of the vote and no seats (November 1996). Russians showed their identification with Lithuania by supporting the ex-Communist Lithuanian Democratic Labour Party, which had paid its dues to Lithuanian nationalism by giving full support to independence at the crucial time. The Poles, in contrast, started by supporting the anti independence faction of the Communist Party of Lithuania (the LCP-CPSU set up by Mykolas Burokevičius), then, when it turned out that Lithuania's independence was irreversible, formed their own ethnic party, the Union of Poles, to press for recognition of Polish minority rights. In November 1992 this received 2.0 per cent of the vote.

In January 1995, the *Seimas* (parliament) declared Lithuanian the 'official state language' of the country. Polish agitation against this was seconded by the Council of Europe, which in April 1995 accused Lithuania of 'violating the rights of national minorities'. This did not stop the *Seimas* from raising the parliamentary threshold from 2 per cent to 5 per cent in June 1996, and abolishing the exception made for national minority parties. Hence, in November 1996, Polish Electoral Action received 2.9 per cent of the vote but remained unrepresented. Polish–Lithuanian relations continue to be uneasy, but the determination of successive governments on both sides to stay on friendly terms, despite the minority issue, has meant that politics in Lithuania have since 1996 revolved around domestic and economic issues.

We now move southwards to look at Ukraine and Belarus, parts of the former Soviet Union where independence was not an issue, since it was achieved without difficulty in 1991, and where ethnic conflict, though always present in the background, did not develop to any great degree during the 1990s.

In Ukraine, despite the Crimean issue, the 1990s have seen a decline rather than an increase in ethnic tension, and an increasing readiness to reach agreement with the large Russian minority. The Russians, for their part, have been ready to respond to advances from the Ukrainian side. Russian readiness to accept the new state has its roots in the events of the late 1980s. The new nation-state of Ukraine was built originally on a 'historic compromise' between the three strongest political groups in the country: the liberal nationalists around Rukh, the coal miners' movement and the 'national Communists', former nomenklaturists who adopted the cause of Ukrainian independence (Wittkowsky, 1999: 150–1). The last two of these groups were largely Russophone, yet they co-operated readily with subsequent official moves to promote the Ukrainian language and culture. The regional elites of the east of the country accepted the independence of Ukraine, and even in the case of Crimea, the only place where a movement in defence of Russian national interests had any success, the local leaders issued a communiqué on 3 June 1994 agreeing to maintain the 'territorial integrity of Ukraine', a position they did not later abandon, despite continuing argument over the precise nature of the future relationship between Crimea and Ukraine.

On the Ukrainian side, the chief reason for the decline in ethnic tension has been a shift in interest from nation-building to material and economic preoccupations. Thus whereas the Constitution of 1992 laid upon the Ukrainian state a duty to 'secure the national-cultural, spiritual and linguistic needs' of Ukrainians, the 1996 Constitution omits this provision (Wilson, 1997: 180).

The decline in the political influence of the western part of the country, formerly Galicia, a traditional stronghold of Ukrainian culture and nationalism, is another factor. Leonid Kuchma, who became prime minister in September 1992, and went on to replace Leonid Kravchuk as president in July 1994, played an important role in this process by conducting a rather clever balancing act. While refusing to take the nationalists into partnership, he continued to stress Ukraine's continuing independence of Russia, and to defend Ukrainian interests. Lev Chornovil, his nationalist opponent, claimed on 17 April 1994 that Kuchma was 'the most dangerous enemy of Ukraine', but this looked increasingly like a wild exaggeration. Despite coming to power with Communist support on a programme of closer links with Russia and the CIS, and the re-establishment of Russian as official language of the country, President Kuchma proceeded to water down these commitments as soon as he took office. He rejected any idea of political re-union with Russia (14 July 1994) and did nothing to implement his pledge to upgrade the role of the Russian language. Moreover, he learned Ukrainian, and started to speak it in public even though his mother tongue was Russian (Duncan, 1996: 207).

As a result, support for him increased, even in the heartland of Ukrainian nationalism, Galicia, where it went from 10 per cent in 1994 to 66 per cent in 1995 (Kubicek, 1999: 44, n.30). Moreover, surveys carried out in 1994 and 1995 showed that the majority of Ukrainians did not take an exclusivist attitude towards citizenship. This makes it possible for more recent immigrants, and in particular Russians, to feel that Ukraine is their state as well. In the south and east of the country, a mere 4 per cent of respondents thought the requirements for Ukrainian citizenship should be made more stringent; and even in the more nationalist west no more than 44 per cent took this view (Zimmerman, 1998).

Belarus can be dealt with very briefly. This republic gained independence in the backwash of the failure of the coup of August 1991 against Gorbachev. The conservative faction in the local Communist party was temporarily discredited, and this increased the influence of the democratic opposition, the Belarusan Popular Front. The chair of the Belarusan Supreme Soviet, N. I. Dzemantsei, was forced to resign, and replaced by the Popular Front leader, Stanislau Shushkevich. A series of measures transitional to independence were passed by the Supreme Soviet in September 1991, and the final step was taken at the meeting of 8 December 1991 between Boris Yeltsin, Kravchuk and Shushkevich, which declared the Soviet Union at an end and set up the Commonwealth of Independent States in its place.

The moderate Belarusan nationalist Shushkevich did not stay at the helm for very long. By 1993, he had lost the support of the Supreme Soviet, which was dominated by Russophil conservatives and he was ousted in January 1994. Presidential elections followed shortly afterwards (10 July 1994), won by Aleksandr Lukashenka on a programme of 'fighting corruption and crime and restoring ties with Soviet republics'. Lukashenka subsequently announced that 'Belarus should be more closely integrated politically with Russia than during the Soviet Union' (15 May 1995). The main issue was how far the victorious conservatives would be able to go in their nostalgic attempt to resurrect the Soviet Union by dismantling Belarusan independence and reintegrating the country with Russia.

They faced two obstacles: a weak one, the Belarusan Popular Front, which failed to secure a single seat at the elections of 14 and 28 May 1995, and a strong one, the unwillingness of President Yeltsin's more liberal advisers to go along with these plans. A formal Union Treaty, providing for a common foreign policy and military infrastructure, but not ending Belarusan independence, was signed on 2 April 1996 to come into force on 11 June 1997. Since then, successive protests by the Belarusan Popular Front have been suppressed violently; it would be fair to say that the issue here is democracy and civil rights in general, and not the rights of ethnic minorities. The Russian minority (13.2 per cent in 1989) feels perfectly content, at least from the ethnic aspect. Higher education is in Russian; more Russian than Belarusan is spoken in public; the president himself speaks Russian almost exclusively; many of the political parties are orientated towards Moscow; and the 83 per cent vote in the May 1995 referendum for the restoration of Russian as second official language showed that most Belarusans approved of this situation. Russian irredentism has no real reason for existence, given the continuing erosion of Belarusan ethnic identity, which independence has failed to halt.

Central Asia: the suppression of ethnic conflict

The other relatively conflict-free region of the former Soviet Union in the 1990s was Central Asia. The Central Asian republics gained independence in 1991 without really pressing for it. In this case, independence was really just a by-product of the decision made by Boris Yeltsin, in line with Russian opinion, to dissolve the Soviet Union (at the Minsk meeting of 8 December 1991, mentioned earlier). The point has been made by several analysts, each of them in a different way: for James Grant, the Central Asians underwent 'decolonization by default'; for Olga Bibikova, they 'drifted towards independence'; and for Martha Olcott, more dramatically, they were 'catapulted' in that direction. Finally, and still more dramatically, Svat Soucek has them being 'carried along by a torrent' created by 'the dam burst' of independence declarations (Grant, 1994; Bibikova, 1993; Olcott, 1992: 108; Soucek, 2000: 275).

As a result, the situation in Central Asia in 1992 was marked by a tremendous degree of continuity with the Soviet past. In view of this, it was only natural that the local Communist-era rulers should simply try to carry on as before (while making the necessary concessions to the market economy and introducing various formal aspects of democracy). Their opponents, the members of the existing dissident movements, were generally weak in numbers and influence, and in any case their objectives tended to be religious and democratic rather than, as elsewhere, nationalist. This did not preclude inter-ethnic disputes (which were at times very violent, especially while the Soviet Union still existed) but it did mean that there was little basis for either ethnic parties or national independence movements. There is a clear political contrast between Central Asia and the Caucasus, despite some similarities in culture and social structure. In South Caucasus there were, as we have seen, strong ethnically-based national independence movements, which either came to power (as in Armenia and Georgia) or (as in the case of Azerbaijan) forced existing rulers to conform to their objectives. North Caucasus occupied an intermediate position. There, numerous attempts were made to set up ethnically-based parties, but they generally failed. Only in Chechnya was success achieved, at least temporarily, with the establishment of *de facto* independence of Russia at the end of 1991.

In Central Asia, existing rulers have maintained complete control over their societies, defeating the two main threats to their power: the threat from religion, and the threat from nationalism. Let us look first at religion. Before 1991 there was a tendency in the West to exaggerate the role of Islamic fundamentalism in Central Asia and to claim that this was the major internal danger facing the Soviet Union. It was implied that the peoples of Central Asia had retained a strong attachment to their traditional faith, and that the ideology of Communism was only a superficial veneer.[20] Subsequent events during the 1990s have cast considerable doubt on this claim. Islamist movements have failed to make any headway in any part of Central Asia by political means.[21] Neither in Kazakhstan, nor Kyrgyzstan nor Turkmenistan, nor Uzbekistan, have political parties on an Islamist basis been able to survive. In Tajikistan, the Islamic Renaissance Party was a real force in the early 1990s, but its alliance with the democrats has compelled it to drop its Islamic objectives (Roy, 2000: 157).

One obvious reason for the failure of political Islam is the sheer strength of the forces of repression; the new regimes in most Central Asian states have, after all, retained many of the police state characteristics of old-style Communism. There are two other reasons. One is the fact that commitment to Islam, in the strict sense, was eroded successfully by the modernizing policies of Stalin and his successors; and the other is that the post-1991 regimes, essentially secular though they are, have generally practised a policy of religious co-optation rather than head-on confrontation. Thus President Karimov of Uzbekistan was prepared to make some concessions to Islamic opinion. He allowed religious education for the first time; and he took the leader of the Naqshbandi (Sufi) order with him on an official visit to Turkey; but the reality was that he retained the supreme power he inherited from Communist times and did not share a particle of it with local Islamists (Bibikova, 1993: 87). The other Central Asian states have made fewer concessions, so far without untoward consequences. But it is not just that the post-Communist regimes have defeated the Islamic challenge; they have also seen off nationalism, the other great threat to their authority.

The era of *perestroika* climaxed with a flurry of ethnic conflicts in Central Asia. In June 1989, Kazakhs fought Lezgins at Novy Uzen; Uzbeks fought Meskhetian Turks in the Ferghana valley; and Tajiks fought Kyrgyz on the borders of Tajikistan. Worse was to come in June 1990: 230 people were killed in fighting between Uzbeks and Kyrgyz at Osh in Kyrgyzstan (Huskey, 1997: 662). There was certainly enough explosive material there for aggressive nationalisms to triumph. None of the Central Asian states was ethnically homogeneous. All of them contained large European minorities as well as many members of other Central Asian ethnic groups. According to the 1989 census, there were: in Uzbekistan, substantial Russian (8.3 per cent), Tajik (4.7 per cent) and Kazakh (4.1 per cent) minorities; in Tajikistan, Russians (7.6 per cent) and Uzbeks (23.5 per cent); in Turkmenistan, Russians (9.5 per cent), Uzbeks (9.0 per cent) and Kazakhs (2.5 per cent); in Kyrgyzstan, Russians (21.5 per cent), Uzbeks (12.9 per cent) and Ukrainians (2.5 per cent); and, finally, in Kazakhstan, Russians (37.8 per cent), Germans (5.8 per cent) and Ukrainians (5.4 per cent).

In addition to ethnic divisions, there were also tribal and regional divisions in the states of Central Asia. The Turkmen continued to be divided among Teke, Yomud, Ersari, Salyr, Saryk and Chowder tribes; the Kyrgyz into Ong and Sol; Tajikistan was divided regionally between Kulyab, Hissar, Khujand and Gorno-Badakhshan (inhabited by seven groups of Pamiris). The Kazakhs, for their part, may have preserved their historic division into Great, Middle and Small Zhuz; on this point observers differ, with the claim that 'the Great Zhuz is still in power in Kazakhstan under Nazarbaev' (Edmunds, 1998: 465) being countered by an anthropologist's report that there is 'no evidence of clan structure in central Kazakhstan' (Esenova, 1998: 452). It is not disputed, however, that there is a division in Kazakhstan between town and country. Forty per cent of Kazakhstan's urban intellectuals have become linguistically Russianized; they may understand Kazakh but they do not speak it (Prazauskas, 1998: 67, n.6).

It is also possible to list further potential sources of conflict in Central Asia. There is land shortage, especially in the densely populated Ferghana Valley; there is the complexity of the ethno-territorial map, a result of waves of conquest and settlement over the centuries, but compounded by the artificiality of the Soviet-era territorial reorganizations of 1924 and 1936, which placed three Uzbek enclaves and two Tajik enclaves within Kyrgyzstan. There is the presence everywhere of ethnic Russians who identify with mother Russia rather than with their new homeland; and, finally, there is, as ever, the quarrel over who owns the past: each Central Asian state interprets the area's history differently.

But the 1990s were remarkably peaceful in Central Asia, apart from in Tajikistan, but even there it has been argued convincingly that religious and political rather than ethnic issues are involved (Kaiser, 1994: 256). The continuing civil war there admittedly has some ethnic elements: the Uzbeks of Leninobod province in the north are pitted against the mainly Tajik south, and the Pamir peoples of Gorno-Badakhshan, Iranian like the Tajiks but distinct from them, reject assimilation to the Tajik majority and want independence for their mountainous province. These sources of conflict are, however, far outweighed by the politico-religious struggle. The Tajik Communist elites, like their counterparts in Uzbekistan and Kazakhstan, have made little political use of the weapon of nationalism, which would have been a dangerous game to play, because their power centre was the city of Khujand, in Leninobod province, the Uzbek area of the country. The former party boss, Rahmon Nabiyev, who was dismissed by Gorbachev in 1985, managed to get back into power in September 1991. He was forced in May 1992 to share power with the opposition, and had to resign from the presidency in September 1992.

Now a civil war began in earnest, with the Pamiri party *La'li Bakakhshon*, the Party of Islamic Rebirth (*Rastokhez*) and the Democratic Party of Tajikistan on one side, and the Khujand-based Communists, the Uzbeks and some Russians on the other, welded together by a fear of 'Islamic fundamentalism' (Eisener, 1994: 777). The former Communists managed to regain control of the capital in November, but only with the help of the Kuljabis from the south of the country (Starchenkov and Makhkamov, 1993). This assistance was recognized by the appointment as president of Emomali Rakhmonov, who was chairman of the Kuljab Executive Committee (Geiss, 1995: 170; Payne, 1996: 382). One might say that the power in Tajikistan was now held by an ethnic alliance of Uzbeks from Khujand, and Kuljabis from the south. But it would be very superficial to see the civil war as a fight betweeen Uzbeks and Tajiks. The real conflict here is between the democratic and Islamic opposition, in uneasy alliance, and the Communist conservatives of the north, who are propped up by the presence of Russian and Uzbek troops under the auspices of the CIS. Even the apparently ethnic elements in this situation can be explained by continuing regionalism.

Elsewhere in Central Asia, there has been a remarkable absence of ethnic conflict, despite the gloomy prognoses uttered before 1991 by many observers. We can identify four reasons for this fortunate turn of events. First, the behaviour of the ethnic Russians of the area. They have reacted to independence and the downgrading of their importance not by fighting back but by leaving in fairly large numbers.[22] A Russian returnee interviewed by David Laitin gave this reason: 'It is better to leave now rather than face the inevitable crisis later ... They don't want us here' (Laitin, 1998: 175–6). The situation in Kazakhstan has been described as 'potentially explosive' (Prazauskas, 1998: 62), and ethnic Russian organizations have been banned. In November 1992, the Kazakh Supreme Soviet refused to register *Yedinstvo* thus effectively making it illegal; in November 1994 Cossack leaders were arrested for demanding that Kazakhstan rejoin Russia; and in November 1999 a number of Russians were sentenced to between four and eighteen years in prison on a charge of planning to overthrow Kazakh authority in the north and to set up a 'Russian Altai Republic' (Fuller, 2000). Despite all these signs of tension, there have been no reports of ethnic clashes between Russians and Kazakhs.

Second, the attitude of the Russian Federation itself. Boris Yeltsin, president of Russia for most of the 1990s, was always careful not to identify himself with the demands of Russian nationalists. Under the Yeltsin–Nazarbaev agreement of March 1994 for voluntary exchange of populations, any Russian was permitted to leave for Russia, and any Kazakh in Russia to move to Kazakhstan (Liu, 1998: 85). The immediate result was a flood of Russian emigrants, which President Nazarbaev does not in fact welcome, as Russians still provide much of the skilled labour.

Third, the insistence of the new rulers of Central Asia that all existing borders were sacrosanct, and their general refusal to follow the path demanded by the more extreme ethnic nationalists. If we take first Islam Karimov, head of the largest and most ethnically mixed state of Central Asia, Uzbekistan, we find that he approaches nationalism in the same way as he approaches Islam: he promotes Uzbek national culture but rejects exclusivist Uzbek nationalism, partly because he wants to keep skilled Russians and other foreigners in his republic, and partly because he rightly fears that the force of nationalism might sweep him away if it is unleashed. Like other post-Soviet rulers, he proclaimed the language of the relevant Soviet-era titular nationality – Uzbek – to be the official language of the state. Algimantas Prazauskas has claimed that this was an option for an 'ethnic model of nation building' which was likely to lead to an 'outburst of ethnic conflicts' (1998: 53). It was, in fact, a way of avoiding conflict. The nationalist agitation of both the majority Uzbeks and of the minority Tajiks has foundered on a combination of repression and mass indifference (Schoeberlein-Engel, 1996: 19).

Tajiks interviewed in 1997 in Uzbekistan referred to themselves alternately as Uzbeks or Tajiks without seeing any contradiction. Karimov's territorial concept of nationhood – that anyone who lives in Uzbekistan is an Uzbek – is 'acceptable both to the Uzbek state-forming nation and the ethnic minorities, which have been invited to share in it' (Koroteyeva and Makarova, 1998: 143). In line with this policy, Karimov also firmly opposed any suggestion that existing boundaries should be changed. This meant that the large Uzbek minority in Tajikistan were told to behave as Tajik citizens first and Uzbeks second. It also meant that the Uzbek president was able to defuse the situation which threatened to blow up over the deaths of many ethnic Uzbeks at the hands of the Kyrgyz police during the Osh riots of June 1990. Members of the democratic and nationalist Uzbek opposition immediately raised the demand for the transfer of the Osh region from Kyrgyzstan to Uzbekistan. Karimov, however, took the line that what happened in Osh was an internal matter for Kyrgyzstan. He was later praised for his statesmanship in this respect by his Kyrgyz opposite number, Askar Akaev.[23]

The story is similar in Kazakhstan. President Nazarbaev ruled throughout the 1990s in a rather authoritarian fashion, as befitted a member of the old Soviet-trained elite. He trod a cautious path between the extremes of, on the one hand, offending the Russians by too much Kazakh nation-building, and on the other hand destroying his local credit by giving way to Russian demands. As elsewhere, the basic guideline for constitutional policy is the maintenance of the integrity of the territories inherited from Soviet times. Thus the Kazakh response to calls from Russians (including no less a personage that Aleksandr Solzhenitsyn) for the separation of Northern Kazakhstan on ethnic grounds was a firm negative, accompanied by the deliberate decision to construct a new state capital at Akmola, close to the disputed area. 'Kazakhization' has been pushed forward, with the result that, by 1997, only 23 per cent of cabinet ministers and 6 per cent of presidential officials were ethnic non-Kazakhs (mainly Russians), although 49 per cent of the population were non-Kazakhs (Gumppenberg, 1999: 267).[24] But the paragraph of the 1993 constitution which defined Kazakhstan as the 'national homeland of the ethnic Kazakhs' was dropped in the constitution of 1995 in favour of a more inclusive formulation (Kolstø, 1998).

The fourth reason for the lack of ethnic conflict in Central Asia is rather a paradox: it is the absence of genuine democracy there. Central Asian rulers are able to act against irredentist groups without worrying about complaints from the neighbours, as they in their turn behave in exactly the same way. They also act against nationalist agitation by their own co-nationals. This is the authoritarian way to secure ethnic peace. One hopes it is not the only way. In Kazakhstan, President Nazarbaev dissolved parliament in March 1995, changed the constitution, and held new elections in December 1995. These produced a docile representative body without nationalist deputies. He even-handedly banned the democratic Alash Party, the Kazakh nationalist Zheltoqsan movement and Russian Cossack groups. The result has been that in opinion surveys both Kazakhs (83 per cent) and Russians (60 per cent) express their confidence in a continuation of ethnic stability (Kubicek, 1998: 35).

In Uzbekistan, President Karimov has forced opposition groups into exile and imprisoned the leader of the Tajik nationalist organization in Samarkand. In Kyrgyzstan, President Akaev dissolved his parliament in September 1994 to put a stop to the agitation of nationalists, who had been opposing his efforts to conciliate the Russians (and stem the flow of Russian emigration, which is depriving Kyrgyzstan of much-needed expertise) by setting up a Slavic University at Bishkek, the capital, and giving Russian the status of an official language in all Russian minority areas and in key branches of the national economy. The parliament that emerged from the elections of February and March 1995 was not quite as docile as others in Central Asia, but Akaev was able to persuade it to give Russian and other minority languages special protection (by the law of 11 March 1996). Has ethnic conflict been prevented in Central Asia by these authoritarian methods, or simply postponed and possibly made worse?[25] Future events alone can decide this.

7
Reasons for Conflict and Prospects for the Future

The reasons for ethnic conflict are many and various. In the summary that follows, a broad, general division into five categories will be used, namely material, intellectual, political, cultural, and finally, psychological. We shall begin on solid ground with the material reasons.

'Our taxes paid for that!' Such was the reported comment of the war criminal and Bosnian Serb leader Radovan Karadžić as he looked down on the Bosnian Muslim city of Sarajevo from the surrounding Serb-held hills during the recent war. The phrase can serve as a pithy illustration of the role of material factors in ethnic conflict. It gives utterance to a very specific emotion: the hatred of the countryman for the city. Karadžić had his own personal reasons for this, as indicated in a line of the poem 'Vuksan', dedicated to his father: 'Take no pity let's go/Kill that scum down in the city'.[1] This attitude was not new in Bosnia. Already by the 1930s Rebecca West was describing the behaviour of farmers (described by her as 'Christians': probably, but not necessarily, Serbs) coming down from the hills to the market in Sarajevo: 'They seem to clang with belligerence, as if they wore armour. In every way, I hear, they are a formidable lot' (West, 1993: vol. 1, 327). But at the same time the Serbs of Bosnia are an example of a general type: the impoverished villager who wishes to redistribute land and resources in favour of his own ethnic group.

The concept of 'distributive nationalism' has been developed to give a generalized explanation for this phenomenon. The aim of 'distributive nationalism' is to advantage one ethnic group by expropriating others. The theory, and the rationality, of this approach was analyzed critically as early as 1964 by Albert Breton. He came to the following conclusion: 'Even though the activities of nationalists have the appearance of redistributing income from one national or ethnic group to

167

another they only succeed in redistributing it from one social group to another within their own national or ethnic group' (1964: 380). This point can be illustrated by looking at Yugoslavia. Here, the new nationalist government of Croatia, and the not-so-new national-Communist government of Serbia, redistributed wealth and income to their own advantage, first by reducing the role of employee buy-outs in the privatization process, and, second, by renationalizing firms that had previously been social property under the system of self-management. Thus in Croatia, 46 per cent of social enterprises had been turned into state-owned enterprises by 1996, and in Serbia 37 per cent had become state property by 1993. This property thus reverted to the hands of the former Communist *nomenklatura*. The end result, according to B. Dallago and M. Uvalić, was 'the enormous enrichment of a privileged minority, to the detriment of the larger part of the population' (1998: 80–4).

The theory that envy of the rich and the desire to redistribute resources away from them was the driving force is not confirmed by the character of the regions that were the prime movers in the fragmentation of the countries of Eastern Europe. What kinds of region in Eastern Europe wanted to separate? Not the poor so much as the rich. Ten out of twelve seekers of independence in the 1990s were in economically more advanced regions. The exceptions were Slovakia and Kosovo, and even in the Slovak case it could well be argued that the motive for seeking independence was to retain the favourable economic position enjoyed by Slovak industry under the Communist regime, and to protect that industry's position against the harsh free-market policies emanating from Prague. We come finally to Kosovo. The temptation to redistribute economic resources was certainly present there. Material inequalities between the regions of Yugoslavia built up steadily in the 1970s and 1980s. The gap between Slovenia and Kosovo was large to start with, and it continued to widen (Uvalić, 1993). The countervailing effect of FADURK was infinitesimal. Kosovans could well feel that they gained nothing from the Yugoslav connection.

Another material factor in the growth of ethnic conflict is what Ashutosh Varshney has called 'economic separateness'. The arguments developed in his interesting study of intercommunal riots in different parts of India can also be applied to Yugoslavia. Varshney showed that the absence of intercommunal riots in Hyderabad was because of the 'constant interlocking of Muslims and Hindus in daily economic relationships'. Where economic separateness was the rule (as in Lucknow) there were frequent riots (Varshney, 1997: 15). Similarly, in Yugoslavia, different parts of the market became separated increasingly during the 1980s. Thus, between 1983 and 1987, the share of Serbian production that went to Serbia as its final destination rose from 52.1 per cent to 62 per cent. The comparable figures for Croatia were 59.7 per cent and 67 per cent. Growing economic separateness provided a clear inducement to political separatism.[2] The argument can also go some way to explaining why the contending nations were unable to settle their disagreements peacefully. We can see this very clearly in the case of Kosovo. One of the danger signs of the impending violent conflict there was the complete social and economic separation of the two ethnic groups. In the sphere of the economy, 'the Albanians controlled the private sector, the Serbs the public sector'. Socially, too, there was separation. Tim Judah reports an observation made by a local Serbian professor. In the town of Priština, where all the inhabitants take the customary evening stroll, the *corso*, 'they (the Albanians) have one side of the main street and we have the other' (2000: 81).

Are ethnic conflicts caused by 'sustained population growth and natural resource depletion' (Kaplan, 1996: 117)? One can certainly think of instances where unfavourable demographic and environmental situations form the background to severe ethnic conflicts. The outbursts of violence against Armenians in Sumgait in February 1988 and in Baku in January 1990 fall into this category to some extent: both a highly polluted environment and severe overcrowding sharpened the tensions. Such factors also played a part in stimulating ethnic conflict in Central Asia (in so far as there was ethnic conflict): in Tajikistan a combination of demographic and climatic factors led to conflicts between Tajiks and Kyrgyz, Tajiks and Uzbeks, and Tajiks and the mountain peoples of the Pamir region. What lay behind all these quarrels, according to the Russian analysts V. I. Bushkov and D. V. Mikul'skii, was 'uncontrolled demographic growth', resulting in a 'breakdown in ecological equilibrium'. The struggle for the control of resources, they say, led to the expulsion from the national territory of the surplus population, and in some degree its 'liquidation' (1997: 158).

But one must beware of laying too great a stress on material factors, considered in isolation. Bushkov and Mikul'skii, who generally favour this approach, are compelled to contradict their own thesis when they examine the origins of tension between Tajiks and Russians: they ascribe it to the 'growth of a myth about Russian exploitation of the Tajiks'. In other words, they supplement their economic analysis with a cultural and psychological explanation (1997: 153). Clearly, there have been many cases where ethnic conflict is exacerbated by a struggle between the haves and the have-nots; to put it another way, there have been occasions when class antagonisms have reinforced ethnic disagreements. But it would be a serious mistake to reduce all ethnic conflicts to this common denominator. Most of the recent ethnic conflicts have taken place between groups that are approximately equal in their command of resources or social position. In Yugoslavia, this was almost always the case: the Kosovo conflict is a possible exception, for, as we observed above, the hostility that was brewing in the 1980s was connected to the relative poverty of the area. The relative poverty argument is not entirely convincing, however. If the inhabitants of Kosovo could look enviously at more prosperous Yugoslavs further north and west of them they could also compare their situation with neighbouring Albania, where people were generally worse off.

In fact, one could make a case that material factors are irrelevant to national conflict. Steps may be taken by nationalists on grounds that are irrational economically but make perfectly good psychological sense. The gain that is made is not material but 'psychic' (Karcz, 1971: 233–4). Slobodan Milošević showed throughout the 1990s how successful this approach could be. The reflex of defiance against the outside (or at least the Western) world was exploited by him to destroy any opposition within the country, despite the continuing material hardships suffered by ordinary Serbs as a direct result of his wars. Opponents were simply portrayed as traitors. He continued to use the same technique with success until the year 2000. When in January 2000 his opponents issued a poster in which the images of Milošević and his wife were crossed out, with the accompanying legend 'The Nation Will Decide', he replied with a poster of Madeleine Albright together with the leaders of the Serbian opposition, with the legend 'Madeleine Will Decide' (Samary, 2000: 8). It was a good piece of propaganda, though for once it did not succeed in winning the election.

If we turn now to factors operating in the intellectual, or ideological, atmosphere, there are plenty of candidate theories to be considered. One superficial explanation often put forward is in terms of the re-emergence of atavistic hatreds, either reaching back to earlier parts of the twentieth century or to more remote epochs. The American journalist, Robert Kaplan, is a particularly eloquent exponent of this point of view in relation to the Balkans: 'This was a time-capsule world: a dim stage upon which people raged, spilled blood, experienced visions and ecstasies ... Here men have been isolated by poverty and ethnic rivalry, dooming them to hate. Here politics has been reduced to a level of near anarchy' (Kaplan, 1993: xxi, xxiii).

However, most specialists in the field reject the idea of ancient, primordial hatreds (Ridgeway, 1997: ix). To claim that Balkan ethnic groups hate each other so intensely that only compulsion can force them to live together is to ignore 'long periods of history when ethnic groups have got along well *despite* preserving ethnic distinctions' (Kuran, 1998: 56). Paul Brass has put a similar point, in the Indian context: 'Cultural cleavages ... are far from immutable. On the contrary, group definitions and boundaries, their political mobilization, and the content of their demands have been influenced by state policies and processes of competition between political parties' (Brass, 1990: 240). So, while memories of past ethnically based atrocities are present in people's minds, they only take on the strength of political factors when states and political parties enter the scene and appropriate these memories as their own.

Another form of ideological explanation often favoured points to the presence of religious antagonisms. In Bosnia, the religious element was present in the conflicts between the three groups, Serb (Orthodox), Croat (Roman Catholic) and Bosniak (Muslim). Mart Bax has shown that the ethnic cleansing of the (Croat) Republic of Herceg-Bosna had a combination of clan-based and confession-based motives. He describes the two-stage process whereby the village of Lakšić was first 'cleansed' of its Serbs in 1992, then a year later of its Muslims. In his view, the 'militant nationalists of the Province of the Franciscan Order of Hercegovina' played a major part in this.[3] Similarly, in the village of Gradiška, one clan, the Defterovči, Muslim by religion, were slaughtered by another clan, the Catholic Pavloviči (Bax, 2000: 19).

Jack Goody has recently put forward the view that religion is absolutely central to ethnic conflict in Kosovo, in Bosnia and in Northern Ireland (Goody, 2001: 5–15). This seems to be an exaggerated estimate. If we look at the major ethnic conflicts in the post-Communist world, we find that religious differences played the most important part in three cases – Croatia, Bosnia and Chechnya. In almost all other conflicts – Romania, Slovakia, Macedonia, Kosovo, Abkhazia, Ossetia and Moldova – we find driving forces of a predominantly ethnic rather than religious character. The civil war in Tajikistan is neither ethnic nor religious but regional.

Religious differences are part of the background of most conflicts, admittedly. They gain significance indirectly, in the sense that religious

associations have tended to create separate communities, which continue to exist even when the religious basis is largely a thing of the
past, or, as has so often occurred recently, it is artificially resuscitated
precisely as a side-effect of an ethnic conflict that already exists. Serb
paramilitaries in Bosnia took to using quasi-religious symbolism such
as the three-fingered hand gesture representing the Holy Trinity (Sells,
1996: 13–15). Their Croat opponents replied by singing: 'We'll break
all your fingers and not only those three' (Pettan, 1998: 17).

If we turn now to the role of political agents in the rise of ethnic
conflict, we find four essential explanations; political manipulation by
forces within the country, the use and abuse of the power of the mass
media; the policies of particular political leaders; and the impact of
external political forces.

Political manipulation from within each country certainly did not
start in 1989, but the space within which it could take place was
greatly enlarged. The new liberal freedoms experienced by the people
of the former Soviet bloc after 1989 created many opportunities for
ethnic conflict to grow (which is not to say that it did not exist before).
The means of communication, previously entirely in state hands, were
now opened up, and messages of hatred as well as love could be flashed
across screens or sent over the airwaves. Similarly, the new democratic
systems provided an opening for unscrupulous racist demagogues.
Extreme nationalist organizations such as *Vatra Românească* in
Romania made full use of this.

It should be noted, too, that the former Communists, who had generally (though not always) suppressed xenophobic tendencies when in
power (because such things tended to run out of control), now sometimes seized the opportunity to gain cheap popularity in explicit or
implicit alliance with nationalist extremists. The basis of this alliance
could even be the dream of returning to former certainties. Thus, in
Romania, *Vatra* not only agitated against Hungarians; it also called for
a reversal of the post-1989 changes. It wanted industry to be renation-
alized and the expropriated funds of the Romanian Communist party
given back (Verdery, 1993b: 188).

The National Salvation Front, made up for the most part of former
Communists, was not above using the violent events sparked off by
Vatra in March 1990 to its own advantage: instead of denouncing the
violence of the Romanian nationalists, its first response was to blame
the clashes on Hungarian agitators from across the border who had
'displayed anti-Romanian slogans' (FSN statement, 21 March)
(Gallagher, 1995: 88–9).[4] One of the FSN's election slogans in 1990 and

1992 was 'the democratic parties will sell the country to foreigners' (Durandin, 1994: 107). In Bulgaria too, the former Communists, who retained power until 1991 under the name 'Bulgarian Socialist Party', attempted to play the nationalist card by trying to prevent the party of the Turkish minority from registering for elections (they gave up when their electoral defeat of October 1991 demonstrated that this particular approach was ineffective).

If we turn now to the role of the media we find that media manipulation has played a decisive part in sparking off and prolonging successive Yugoslav conflicts. What we have said about the use of newly available means of communication by racist demagogues in Romania applies equally here. And in the Yugoslav case, thanks to republican decentralization followed by independence, the demagogues rapidly gained control of the state itself, so they were able to influence the media very strongly.

Mark Thompson has analyzed the role of the media in Yugoslavia carefully , showing, first, how President Milošević used his control of (RTS) Serbian Radio-Television in 1991 to convince Serbs in Croatia that they were in danger of suffering 'genocide', then in 1992 to convince Serbs in Serbia that the Bosnian Serbs were fighting a defensive war, protecting their native soil from Muslims, who were 'mujahedin' and 'jihad warriors' waging a religious war, and Croats, who wanted to unite with Croatia and renew the atrocities they committed in the Second World War (Thompson, 1994: 102). It should be added that by then the Serbian media campaign against the Kosovo Albanians had already been in progress for four years.[5] It would be unjustifiably one-sided, however, to concentrate one's fire exclusively on the Serbia of Slobodan Milošević. There are similar things to be said about President Tudjman's Croatia, where, in particular, the need to justify the attempt to seize territory in central Bosnia and set up a separate state of Herceg-Bosna 'triggered a most repressive and manipulative treatment of the media' (Thompson, 1994: 199).

Political leaders, new and old, often either stirred up or, more rarely, damped down, ethnic conflict. One notes the clear contrast between Milošević (and, to a lesser degree, Tudjman) in the former Yugoslavia and Boris Yeltsin in Russia. Milošević, for reasons of political ambition, took the lead in pushing Serbian policy towards a confrontation with the Albanians of Kosovo, and later with the Croats and the Bosnian Muslims. Yeltsin, perhaps for the same reasons, encouraged the Russians to support the endeavours of the non-Russian nations to secure political independence. In 1990 he called on the (Soviet) government to make 'fundamental changes in its relations with the republics to avoid a revolution' and told the autonomous republics to 'grab as much independence as you can' (Dunlop, 1993: 62). His actions matched his words. It is to Boris Yeltsin's lasting credit that he almost always[6] rejected the calls of both Russian nationalists and old-style Soviet loyalists for intervention in the non-Russian republics to uphold the interests of local Russian minorities.

In this case, then, the decisions of individual politicians played an important part in the course of events. Their room for manoeuvre was, however, predetermined by the historical background. In Russia, the failure of the Soviet Union to engage in decentralizing liberal reform over the previous twenty five years meant that the central Soviet apparatus was the chief point of attack for both non-Russian nationalists and Russian liberals, and in the last resort also for Russian nationalists. In Yugoslavia, in contrast, the thoroughgoing character of Titoist and post-Tito decentralization meant that the centre was already hollowed out: the confrontation when it came was, first and foremost, between the republics themselves. There was certainly conflict between the republics and the centre too, but this immediately took on an ethnic colouration, since the Serbs were perceived as its main upholders. Hence, if a Titoist solution to the Soviet Union's problems had been arrived at in the 1960s, its dissolution process might well have been much bloodier.

The development of ethnic conflicts within the region has also been influenced by external political forces, particularly where states contain ethnic minorities which are majorities in other states, giving rise to irredentism, but we must beware of exaggeration here. Recently, Rogers Brubaker has coined the expression 'the triadic nexus' to encompass the influence exerted on ethnic relations by the existence of external national homelands. He gives the example of Albania for the Kosovo Albanians, and of Hungary for the Hungarians of Slovakia, Yugoslavia and Romania. He refers to the 'multiplication and intensification' of ties between the Hungarians and their homeland, and the 'renewal and strengthening' of Kosovar ties with Albania. According to Brubaker, this 'potentially explosive dynamic interplay' is the central problem in ethnic relations (Brubaker, 1996: 56–7).

This claim is quite surprising, since it is hardly borne out by the recent historical record. For example, Hungarian policy towards Romania has played no part in exacerbating the ethnic conflict there; and the same is true of Albanian policy towards Serbia. Over the decade of the 1990s both Hungary and Albania have sought to avoid getting involved in the quarrels of their respective ethnic minorities in other countries – sympathy, certainly; intervention, never. This remained true even when right-wing governments more in tune with nationalist feeling came to power. Dr Sali Berisha's election victory in Albania in 1992 was regarded by the Kosovo Albanians as a golden opportunity, especially as Berisha came from the village of Tropoja in the north, which had close clan links with Kosovo, and had spent much of the previous two years denouncing the previous socialist (post-Communist) government for ignoring the Kosovo issue.

Disappointment soon set in, however. Berisha continued the foreign policy of his socialist predecessor, recommending to the Kosovo Albanians that they make a settlement with Belgrade and keeping his public interventions on the issue to a minimum. He earned high praise for this from the US envoy, who remarked on 1 February 1995 that Albania had 'taken a responsible attitude towards its neighbours'. 'Our priority,' Berisha explained, 'is the prevention of conflict' (Judah, 2000: 96). The same can be said of József Antall, prime minister of Hungary between 1990 and 1993, who made the absolute minimum of foreign policy concessions to nationalist elements in his party. In most cases we have examined, ethnic conflicts arose from domestic sources. There are only two cases that fit the Brubaker thesis: the war in Croatia and the triangular struggle in Bosnia. Neither in Slovenia, nor in Macedonia, nor in Kosovo was there any observable tendency towards 'triadic interplay' with co-ethnics across the border.

Brubaker's model is intended to apply to the former Soviet Union as well. 'These triadic relations,' he says, 'are replicated ... throughout the whole of post-Soviet Eurasia' (Brubaker, 1996: 44). Here too, we find on examination that the triadic model is derived from a tiny minority of cases (the most obvious one is the Armenian–Azerbaijani conflict over Nagornyi Karabagh) and does not help in analyzing the others. Although successive leaders of the Russian Federation have occasionally made threatening noises about the situation of ethnic Russians in the successor states, they have largely abstained from intervening in any decisive way (apart from the initial attempt, which did not last long, to make withdrawal of Russian troops conditional on improvements in ethnic relations in the Baltic). They are the 'abandoned brethren', to use A. J. Motyl's felicitous phrase (1998: 14). In the case of Lithuania, for instance, sarcastic comparisons have been drawn between the Polish ambassador's 'forceful action on behalf of his compatriots' and the inaction of the Russian ambassador (Senn, 1997: 363). No doubt one could put this down to a temporary sense of diplomatic weakness; but the replacement of Yeltsin by Vladimir Putin has by the time of writing made no difference.[7] We should also note that local Russian minorities have not tended to look to the mother country for diplomatic protection. They have relied instead on making complaints to the international community and calling for international standards of minority protection to be applied. The overall conclusion has to be that Brubaker is wrong: in the majority of cases examined, external influences have played little part in worsening existing conflicts.

Another political explanation offered for the growth of ethnic conflict in the 1990s is in terms of 'nation-building'. The new, or at least newly independent, states of the former Communist sphere have, it is claimed, been engaged in a process of nation-building on an ethnic basis. This view has also been expressed persuasively by Brubaker (1996).[8] He describes the new states of the formerly Communist part of the world as 'nationalising states', and claims that they have adopted an 'ethnocultural' rather than a 'civic' notion of citizenship. There is much to be said for this explanation, although its author is too hasty in generalizing certain features of specific situations to the whole region. As we have seen, the 'ethnocultural' definition was not applied in the Czech Republic, Poland, Hungary, Slovenia, Ukraine, Lithuania or any of the states of Central Asia.[9] Yet, in a way, these exceptions in fact strengthen Brubaker's case: none of them are characterized by severe ethnic conflict; this occurs where nation-building has been undertaken on a narrowly ethnic basis.

'Ethnocultural' nation-building of the kind just mentioned involves not just the reframing of laws on citizenship but the rewriting of history. This latter process did not begin in 1989, although it underwent a considerable acceleration after the fall of Communism. As we have seen, the period of Communist decline was marked by a rise of nationalism in the cultural and educational spheres. After 1989, all the newly independent nation-states set to work to produce both original works of historical research and educational textbooks with the common aim of restoring the 'lost past' of the nation: this often meant that neighbouring peoples promoted enthusiastically diametrically opposed versions of their, and their neighbours', past.

One example among many: the continuous existence of Slovakia from medieval times was an accepted fact among Slovaks; Hungarians, however, were taught that such a concept did not exist until the twentieth century. Slovak historiography turned Máté Csák, a Hungarian prince who ruled part of the area of present-day Slovakia in the fourteenth century, into a Slovak. Hungarian historiography viewed him simply as another Hungarian feudal baron. An analysis made in 1997 of the history textbooks in use in the schools of East Central Europe revealed that 'the schoolchildren of Hungary and neighbouring states' were now presented with 'a completely divergent picture of the past for every epoch' (Szarka, 1997: 525).

While admitting that the actions of modern politicians and political movements can increase the likelihood of ethnic conflict (and even, in rare cases, reduce it) it would be wrong to overestimate this factor. The merest glance at the history of some of the most serious ethnic conflicts would show that they all have a background, and do not strike from an unclouded sky. A comparison of, say, the Armenian–Azerbaijani conflict of the 1990s with similar conflicts in the early 1920s or in 1905, or of Serbian–Kosovan relations in the 1990s with Serbian–Kosovan relations in 1945 or 1912, would in each case clearly indicate that political manipulation or the agitation of extremist demagogues did not change the situation in any decisive way.

The cultural determinants of ethnic conflict

Next, a look at cultural factors. We can look at culture in both a broader and a narrower sense. Taking first the broad sense – in other words, what might be described as the whole complex of modes of behaviour and interpersonal interactions – it is clear that there are considerable cultural differences between the peoples of the former Communist sphere. One needs only to think of the distinctions between basic gestures. A line cuts across the Balkans dividing those (more northerly) people who say 'yes' by nodding the head and 'no' by shaking the head from those (more southerly) who do the opposite (Gavazzi, 1956: 12). Whether these symbolic cultural differences have a broader significance is a matter of dispute. According to the eminent Balkan philologist, Alois Schmaus, they do not; in his view, the floods and counterfloods of refugees and immigrants throughout Balkan history 'created an ethnic mixture and a new form of symbiosis, adaptation and cultural contact' between different groups. Hence 'the boundaries of cultural zones' did not coincide with 'confessional, linguistic or ethnic boundaries' (Schmaus, 1973: 294).

From the point of view of the analyst of culture, cultural differences of the behavioural type do not create unbridgeable gaps between communities. But the perception, the sense of separateness, is more important here than how outside observers see the matter: two different communities may feel so separate that nothing can bring them together. One obvious sign of this separation is endogamy; in other words, the tendency to marry within the group. This is 'an almost certain sign of hostility and conflict between groups', because it inhibits informal interaction between them (Wagley and Harris 1964: 260). This general sociological observation has been confirmed repeatedly in the cases we have examined in the former Yugoslavia, and in various parts of the former Soviet Union.

However, the converse does not necessarily hold. In other words, a readiness to marry and have children outside the group does not ultimately inhibit blood-letting between different communities. Laszlo Sekelj has pointed out that fierce inter-ethnic slaughter took place in areas of Yugoslavia where over 25 per cent of births were to mixed marriages. 'Relatives were killing each other', he says, 'while serving in different paramilitary formations' (Sekelj, 1993: 279). This observation loses some of its force, however, when one reflects that mixed areas tended to be fought over more often than ethnically homogeneous areas, so greater slaughter would be expected to take place there (and the participants may well have come from outside the region; the activities of non-local Serb paramilitary groups such as Vojislav Šešelj and his Chetniks, or Arkan and his Tigers in Croatia, Bosnia and Kosovo should not be forgotten). One may conclude that intermarriage does not solve the problems, but endogamy certainly makes them worse.

But what of culture in the narrower sense? In examining this issue we shall look first, and hardest, at music, not because it is necessarily more important than the other arts, but because, first, music, especially in the form of song, 'can be considered as a weapon' (Pettan, 1998: 10), and, second, in the later twentieth century the means of mass communication have given music a universal presence it did not possess before.

It seems that differences in mass musical culture provide pointers to deeper differences. Certain kinds of music have stimulated ethnic conflict in Yugoslavia (though less so elsewhere). Naturally, the impact of this, as of any other kind of culture, is dependent on how much coverage it receives in the mass media. Three kinds of music received saturation coverage in the Serbian and Yugoslav mass media, and all of them contributed to deepening Serb nationalism. First there was the 'newly composed folk music' (*Novokomponovana narodna muzika*) popular in the 1980s, which was later to develop into the 1990s phenomenon known as 'Turbo-folk'.[10] This genre covers traditional folk songs sung with modern instrumentation and influences from Western pop. One of the main performers at least (Ceca Ražnjatović, whose marriage to Arkan was a big media event in 1995) has associations with extreme Serbian nationalism. Janine Udovička and Sabrina Ramet both specifically target 'Turbo-folk' as being responsible for the brutality of ethnic conflict in Yugoslavia. Ramet comments that, in Serbia, 'folk music is more popular than rock music'. (It should be added that, in Serbia, rock music has been associated with opposition to the wars in Croatia and Bosnia, as, for example, in the case of the Belgrade Peace Concert of 22 April 1992.)

The rise of Slobodan Milošević to supreme power was accompanied by the emergence of folk groups issuing recordings of a nationalist character, often referring back to Chetnik exploits during the Second World War (Ramet, 1994: 105–6). These were freely available from street sellers in Belgrade, and were often bought by football supporters and sung provocatively in matches against teams from Croatia. Arkan, who began as the leader of a group of supporters of the Serbian team Red Star, was able to recruit many of them for his murderous enterprises when the war broke out (Čolovič 2000: 388).

The second musical engine of ethnic conflict is the traditional Serb song sung to *gusle* (one-stringed fiddle) accompaniment. This phenomenon has been studied in detail by the Croatian writer, Ivo Žanić (1998). The *gusle* is associated strongly with Serbian nationalism. The president of the Regional Committee of the SDS of Bosnia and Hercegovina, Božidar Vučurević, was a well known *guslar* (fiddler). Radovan Karadžić himself has been known to accompany recitations of his own poems on the instrument (Volkan, 1997: 71). The political character of *gusle* music is not just a recent development. As far back as 1918 the music of the *gusle* was being celebrated by Jovan Cvijić as demonstrating that 'Dinaric Serbs cannot be tamed by any earthly power. The *guslar* often flies into a rage when telling of the disasters his people have suffered, and it may happen that he throws his instrument to the ground and stamps on it to express his burning desire to bring injustice to an end. The listeners are moved to the depths of their soul, almost terrified' (Cvijić, 1918: 294).

As it was in 1918, so in the early 1990s: 'Photographs from the time of the Serbian aggression in Croatia and Bosnia-Hercegovina show how the *guslar* kept up or renewed the role of a military accompanist' (Žanić, 1998: 69). The impact of the *guslar's* songs has been described by Momo Kapor, a Serbian journalist originally from Sarajevo. Listening to a young Serb soldier in the Hercegovian town of Trebinje in 1992, Kapor became convinced, he says, of the 'worthlessness' of urban culture compared with this outpouring of the 'forgotten essence' of the nation: 'The sound of that young fighter's *gusle* travelled across the dark centuries uniting him with his ancestors who played on the same instruments' (Thomas, 1999: 172). Moreover, 'neither Bach nor Mozart can bring tears to my eyes or get under my skin the way this sound does, this sound which cries and rages, which threatens and sobs, which is capable of leading me wherever it wants. No one can resist the sound of the *gusle*, certainly not this boy in uniform, who grabs his automatic, raises it up and spills out bursts of fire into the sky' (Žanić, 1998: 71).

In the north-west of Yugoslavia, in contrast, the *gusle* was unknown. The folk instrument typical of the Croats is the *tambura* (a plucked string instrument similar to the mandolin), while the preferred instrument of the Bosnian Muslims, influenced as they are by the Ottoman cultural heritage, is the *saz* (the long-necked, seven-stringed lute). These cultural differences, on the face of it harmless, became fraught with danger in the 1980s: they were touchstones of ethnic identity.[11]

In fact, it is not quite as simple as this: the distribution of the different instruments and musical styles does not follow a strictly ethnic pattern. The *gusle*, and the folk epics it accompanies, are associated with the Balkan peninsula rather than the Serbs as such.[12] There are Croatian *guslars* too – for example, Željko Šimič – who celebrated the Bosnian Croat leader, Mate Boban, in his wartime songs. The instrument is also known in Albania and Bulgaria, where ethnic conflict has been muted (though not entirely absent) in modern times (Kremenchiev, 1956: 135). Curiously, the problem of the wide distribution of the *gusle*, which makes it impossible to regard it as a purely Serbian instrument, was already anticipated and brushed aside by the Serbian poet, Jovan Dučič in 1932. All *guslars*, asserted Dučič, were in fact Serbs by origin, even if they might have changed their religion (Wachtel, 1998: 113).

There is yet a third form of music that can be held responsible for the fierceness of the ethnic conflict in former Yugoslavia. This is the kind examined by the Dutch anthropologist, Mattijs van de Port. He returned from an eighteen-month field study in the Vojvodina town of Novi Sad with the insight that traditional explanations of the war in Bosnia failed to account for the sudden turn to brutality on the part of Serbs, who seemed until then to be tolerant and civilized. He decided that the main reason for this was the Serbian habit of listening to 'gypsy music'. The Serbs of Vojvodina, it seems, had a 'fascination with wild Gypsy bar life and music' (Port, 1998: 16).[13] There were no less than twenty of these bars *(kafane)* in Novi Sad, and while Serbs and

Roma did not usually come into contact socially, all restraints were abandoned in the frenetic atmosphere generated there. They would dance to songs such as the popular 1991 hit 'Dajte vina! Hoću lom!' (Give me wine! Let everything collapse!). 'The old songs of the Vojvodina were increasingly giving way to obscene bachelor songs, and others with rabidly nationalist lyrics, all to the frenetic accompaniment of the accordion. These Gypsies knew their audience' (Port, 1998: 3).

At this level, the explanation sounds extremely naïve; but van de Port has a more sophisticated thesis in mind. He considers that the Serbian habit (or, more precisely, middle-aged Serbian male habit) of letting their hair down in drunken orgies in bars where gypsy music is played is a sign of ambivalence or duality in the Serbian psyche.[14] What is expressed in this behaviour is the contradictory combination of the wish to be modern, European and cultured with the desire to be wild, oriental and brutal. Among the Serb warriors of the 1990s, the dream of transformation to modernity and Europeanness was countered and ultimately outweighed by the dream of 'a return to the Serbia of the epic poems when there was no electricity and no computers, when the Serbs were happy and had no cities, the breeding-ground of all evil' (Port, 1998: 17).

The authors we have quoted so far tend to lay the blame on music alone. Can this explanation possibly bear the weight that has been placed on it? Is music by itself really responsible for such catastrophic events? If we bear in mind the emotional resonance of the words that are sung and shouted in such a context, however, the cultural explanation begins to look more convincing. A leading characteristic of the songs sung to the accompaniment of the *gusle* is that they are renewed by each generation. But the model remains that of the bloodthirsty medieval epic. The hero of these epics is always the 'implacably vengeful solitary warrior' (Ling, 1997: 89). 'To kill a lot of Turks,' wrote Cvijić, 'is for the Dinaric peasant (he means the Serbian peasant) not only a means of avenging his ancestors but of softening the pain he shares with them. As the song says "Remember the Heroes of Old"' (Cvijić, 1918: 290).

The legend of Marko Kraljević is very characteristic: Prince Marko recognizes his father's sabre, and realizes that its possessor (a Turk) has killed his father to get it. So he draws it and cuts off the man's head. When the sultan hears of this he orders Marko's arrest. Marko's response is revealing: he goes to the sultan's tent and sits down on his prayer-mat wearing boots, knowing that this is a sacrilegious act to a Muslim (Wachtel, 1998: 7–8). But, as Svetozar Koljević has commented, 'while prepared to kill and maim in revenge or even out of spite', Marko is also 'ready to die for justice and honour' (Pennington and Levi, 1984: 30). The Bulgarian version of this legend is not very different from the Serbian one: the song of Krali Marko, popular in south-west Bulgaria, has him riding back to his village, which has been ravaged by a band of Turks, and beheading 'all three hundred of them' (Kremenchiev, 1956: 111).

The distinctive contribution made by the *guslars* of the 1990s to Serb nationalism was to give traditional songs new, patriotic and warlike texts. Many examples are quoted by both Ivo Žanić and Ivan Čolović.[15] The Serb fighters in Croatia and Bosnia were accompanied wherever they went either by the *guslar* in person (there is much photographic evidence of this in Žanić's book) or by tape-recordings of his songs. As we have seen, the Croatian counterpart of the *gusle* is the *tambura*,[16] and the short period of extreme national danger which started in 1991 saw the composition and wide distribution of many bloodthirsty songs by *tamburica* ensembles in Croatia. There were some differences from the Serbian situation, however: these songs were the products of a wartime defensive reflex, and after the war ended they sank without trace (Bonifačić, 1998: 131–49).[16]

It would be wrong to leave this subject without noting that music did not always divide people in the former Yugoslavia: the example of rock concerts for peace has already been quoted, and the traditional ring-dance or *kolo* is a supra-national phenomenon, though both Serbs and Croats have tended to claim it as their own. This is what Dubravka Ugrešić (herself a Croat) says: 'What it was that my countrymen were driving away with their stamping feet, I don't know ... It was an adrenalin *kolo*, a supernational *kolo*, it was a display of the brotherhood of strong rhythms. My countrymen used the rhythm to wipe away all meaning and all borders, including national ones' (Ugrešić, 1998: 146).

Alongside music, another cultural medium that has stimulated ethnic hatred has been the visual image. Television coverage of ethnic conflicts has been firmly under the control of the respective ethnic groups, in so far as they have achieved state status; so images of the other side's brutality are multiplied, while one's own side is presented as either the innocent victim or the brave resister. Cartoons are another favourite visual way of influencing popular perceptions. Ivo Banac has given several examples of the campaign waged in the Belgrade *Književne novine* (Literary Gazette) in 1989 and 1990 by the cartoonist Milenko Mihajlović to present Serbia's enemies (Albanians, Croats, Muslims and Roman Catholic bishops) as planning to repeat the atrocities they committed against Serbs during the Second World

War. Knife-wielding ustaše and Catholic prelates playing with gouged-out human eyes were a particularly striking feature of these cartoons (Banac, 1992a).

Propelled forward by the above-mentioned mechanisms and impulses, rival ethnic groups in the former Yugoslavia, in Moldova, in Armenia, in Azerbaijan and in Georgia entered into shooting wars with each other. Once that had happened, another factor came into play: the psychological impact of war. After the outbreak of an ethnic conflict, the pressure to take sides is very difficult to resist, while solidarity with co-ethnics is heightened. Slavenka Drakulić, another Croat writer, provides some eloquent comments on the psychological mechanism at work in the Yugoslav case: 'As it stands, noone in Croatia is permitted to feel non-Croat. And even if you did, it would still be morally wrong to tear this shirt [of Croat-ness] off the distressed state. It would not be right because of Vukovar ... and because of the shelling of Dubrovnik' (Drakulić, 1993: 101).

In Serbia too, practically no one was able to withstand the pressures towards ethnic solidarity. The parliamentary opposition in Belgrade certainly disliked Milošević, and blamed him for many of the misfortunes that befell the country; but not one of the parties represented in parliament put forward an alternative programme to Milošević's rallying cry: 'All Serbs in one state!'. Vuk Drašković's Serbian Renewal Movement, it has been said, 'did not have the strength to take the risk of national betrayal', hence it fell into 'a nationalistic political trap' set by Milošević (Stojanovic´, 2000: 466). The few individuals who dared to offer a different view were denounced as 'traitors to the nation' and 'NATO pacifists', and were marginalized politically (Šušak 2000: 488–9).

Similar factors operated in the course of the conflict that took place in Moldova. Stuart J. Kaufman has noted the 'mutual fears of extinction' felt by both Slavs and Moldovans engaged in the Transdniestr conflict (Kaufman, 1997: 170). This is a phenomenon generally observed in wartime situations. What appear to be (and may well in fact be) acts of aggression committed by the other side (once it has been defined as the other side) make it much easier for people to adopt a stance of national solidarity; the pressure to do so becomes irresistible.

National identity can thus actually be *imposed* by war; people respond to violence by feeling a stronger sense of belonging to their own region or their own nation. This has been demonstrated in the Croatian case by empirical ethnographical studies. There 'the strong sense of belonging to one's own region and nation ... is a "constructed essentialism" based on a cluster of responses to war violence' (Povrzanović, 2000: 154). This phenomenon can be observed in the case of Chechnya too. The war of 1994–95 between Chechnia and Russia 'made the decisive contribution to the homogenization of the Chechen people'; regional and clan divisions surfaced during the short period of *de facto* independence and uneasy peace, but once a life-and-death conflict was engaged the sense of common Chechen identity was much strengthened (Heinemann-Grüder, 1999: 173).

Prospects for the future

Here we shall attempt to draw a balance of ten years since 1990 and evaluate the reasons for ethnic discord and the prospects for a peaceful resolution of ethnic and national conflicts in the region. An analysis of this kind produces a rather remarkable result: the problem is going away. In a large number of cases existing conflicts reached a peaceful settlement during the 1990s. At first, the only example was the peaceful division of Czechoslovakia (1993), but during the late 1990s examples of settlement by compromise began to build up – Bulgaria, Romania, Slovakia and Moldova. It should be noted that the compromises were not all identical in their results. In Czechoslovakia (now the Czech Republic and Slovak Republic) and in Moldova there was territorial compromise; either the disputed territory was divided between the parties, or minority groups were allowed to exercise the autonomy they demanded. In the other cases, concessions were made to the national demands of minorities, certainly, but there was only a slight element of autonomy (at local government level). This seems to have been enough.

If we now proceed to enquire into the reasons for compromise, we find that there was usually a combination of external pressure from the UN, the OSCE and the EU, with a number of internal factors involving the decline of nationalist parties and a change of approach by post-Communist elites, often still in power.[17] There have been forcibly-imposed settlements in Bosnia-Hercegovina and Kosovo, and an agreed settlement in Macedonia. The longevity of these solutions is in some doubt, admittedly. In Macedonia, it is too early to tell. In Kosovo, ethnic conflict between Serbs and Albanians continues, despite the United Nations presence. In Bosnia, ethnically based parties are still the most significant elements of the political scene. The elections of November 2000 showed a welcome trend towards the fragmentation of two of the ethnic camps, though the Serb camp continues to be dominated by the SDS. The line dividing the two 'entities' into which Bosnia is divided is, in effect, a border between two separate states. The refusal of the Bosnian Serbs to 'certify in writing their support for multiethnicity' (a requirement not placed upon the Muslims and Croats of the other half of Bosnia) has meant that they have been deprived of international aid, 98 per cent of which goes to the Federation of Bosnia and Hercegovina. Ethnic cleansing has not been reversed. In fact there were 70 000 fewer people living in ethnically mixed areas in Bosnia after the Dayton Agreement than before. So there is still a long way to go (Boyd, 1998: 47). Nevertheless, the existence of the multi-ethnic Arizona Market on the road between Doboj and Tuzla is a hopeful sign; members of different ethnic groups can at least meet peacefully for commercial transactions (although this is to some extent a cover for drug-dealing and prostitution).

The prospect of entering the EU at some future date is a strong inducement towards negotiated compromise in Central and South East Europe, though this factor does not operate over most of the former Soviet Union. Even in the latter case, a peace of exhaustion seems to be emerging in the South Caucasus. By the end of the year 2000 there were no ongoing military conflicts in the region. Ceasefires reached in the mid-1990s have remained in operation in Nagornyi Karabagh, Abkhazia and South Ossetia. T. R. Gurr has recently examined the phenomenon on a world-wide scale. He has pointed out that out of a total of fifty-nine 'armed ethnic conflicts' during the early 1990s, twenty-three were 'de-escalating', twenty-nine were not getting any worse, and only seven were 'escalating' during 1999. Turning to 'separatist wars', a slightly narrower category, he noted that sixten had been settled by peace agreements, and ten by cease-fires, which left eighteen still proceeding (Gurr, 2000: 54).

This leads us on to the prognosis for ethnic conflict. Whether this is favourable or unfavourable varies according to the length of time selected for prediction. In the short term, it is favourable, as we have seen. But for the medium term the answer must be different. The ending of the majority of the ethnically-based conflicts of recent times should not mislead us. Peace has come about either through temporary exhaustion, through the exertion of strong pressure by outside forces, or through the victory of one side over the other. In all of these cases there is continuing resentment, and the wish to gain revenge merely lies dormant. We may expect a resurgence of most of the conflicts that appear to be settled, making necessary the further intervention of the international community. The underlying forces making for ethnic conflict, and above all the ethno-nationalist conception itself, continue to operate for the present. Everywhere in the post-Communist region people continue to identify more strongly with their own ethnic community than any other reference group. While this situation persists there will be renewed wars for the division and redivision of territory seen as ethnic property.

The long term prospects, however, are better than this. The present writer is inclined to adopt Walter L. Wallace's views on the future of ethnicity (Wallace, 1999). Just as ethnicity, and therefore ethnic conflict, grew up over time, so, in the course of time, they will decline. The task of the historian, who cannot after all remain neutral about the fate of humanity, is not to find reasons for ethnic division but rather reasons for unification and ethnic rapprochement. Taking this very long-term perspective, one can say that the long 'detour via ethnicity' which began in the nineteenth century is, for Europe at least, drawing to a close.

A process of what Wallace terms 'global species consolidation' is already under way, fuelled by the gradual 'equalization of the possession of the resources of human life', by the rise of international associations, by economic globalization, and by the global diffusion of scientific knowledge (Wallace, 1999: 5, 139–53). That is not to say that in the near future humanity will suddenly cease to be divided into ethnic groups,[18] but belonging to them will become less important. It has become sufficiently evident since the begining of the twentieth century that ethnic conflicts are the worst of all humanity's acts of self-destruction. They are the most ruthlessly conducted, and the most likely to result in dehumanization. In their absence, conflict between rival interest groups will still continue; but where the ethnic element does not enter the picture, such conflicts can be more easily settled by compromise rather than being pursued until one side or the other is exterminated.

Notes

1   Introduction

1   This view has been questioned. Fredrik Barth argued that 'the critical features of ethnic groups are first self-ascription and second ascription by others'. In other words, the possession of an inventory of cultural characteristics is not significant (Barth, 1969: 15). Katherine Verdery, writing almost thirty years later, also placed herself in this tradition: 'Ethnic identification is based on ascription, not on possessing a certain cultural inventory' (Verdery, 1996: 33).

2   The word 'Eurasia' is used here, not to signify agreement with the view recently advanced that this represents a geo-political entity, but as a convenient shorthand way of describing the part of the post-Communist landmass which is too far to the east to be covered by the term 'Eastern Europe'. A longer way of saying the same thing would be: 'the Former Soviet Union except the Baltic States, Belarus, Ukraine and Moldova'.

3   The distinction between 'nationhood' and 'nationalism' is not always made very clear in the literature of the subject. This is because either nationalism precedes nationhood, or, in the rare case where this course of events is reversed, nationhood develops quickly into nationalism.

4   T. H. Eriksen (1993: 116–8) has suggested that the island of Mauritius is one place where a 'non-ethnic nationalism' has developed, on the basis of both a multi-ethnic approach (in which the nation is seen as identical with the mosaic of cultures present on the island) and a supra-ethnic approach (in which the nation is seen as a community-transcending ethnicity).

5   See, in detail, Troebst (1999). For a different view, stressing the viability of a 'Ruthenian' nationality, see Magocsi (1997).

6   'The convergence of capitalism and print technology on the fatal diversity of human language created the possibility of a new form of imagined community, which in its basic morphology set the stage for the modern nation' (Anderson, 1991: 46).

7   One of these languages, Nostratic, is said to have extended over the whole of Europe and Asia, except China. It was a 'real language ... once spoken by real people' (Ramer *et al.*, 1993: 79).

8   There is, of course, much that is purely speculative about this delightful theory. The difficulties have recently been outlined by R. Wardhaugh (1993: 148–55).

9   This generalization is not intended to be a denial of the later medieval development of national languages, Slav and other, or of the introduction of Ottoman Turkish into South East Europe as a result of the Ottoman conquest of the fifteenth century.

10   It would take us too far afield to demonstrate in detail the problems the author creates for himself by assuming, instead of trying to investigate, the continued existence of 'Kosovo'. Here is one example: the local French

consul, Émile Wiet, reported that in 1843, 'Üsküb (Skopje) was made an independent pashalik and the eyalet of Prisrend was added to it' (Wiet, 1866: 283). N. Malcolm quotes this passage, and, in line with his general policy as enunciated earlier, quietly substitutes 'Kosovo' for 'Prisrend' (Malcolm, 1998: 186). It should be added that there is also no mention of Kosovo before 1843: Wiet notes that before that date the area was divided into six *pashaliks*: Djakova, Ipek, Pristina, Vrania, Tettova and Prisrend (Wiet, 1866: 284). Moreover, the Ottoman census of 1831 does not list Kosovo as an administrative subdivision on any level (see the complete list transcribed and published in 1951 – Akbal, 1951: 617–28).

11   Miranda Vickers takes exactly the same approach: 'For our purpose in this book the term Kosovo is used throughout' (Vickers, 1998: xv).

12   According to M. M. Atkepe (1986: 276), there was an Ottoman *sancak* of Kosovo during the sixteenth century. But the complete list of known *sancaks* in the *eyalet* of Rumeli given by Halil Inalcık (there were 17 in 1475, 33 in 1520, and 15 in 1644) does not include a Kosovo *sancak* (Inalcık, 1995: 610–11).

13   As G. Grimm notes: 'The Kosova region was not an administrative unit during the Turkish period until 1878. Before 1878 it was divided between the eyalets of Bosnia, Üsküb and Monastir. Afterwards a vilayet of Kosova was set up but it was much bigger than present-day Kosova' (Grimm, 1984: 41).

14   The Statutes of the League of Prizren, adopted on 18 June 1878, state this explicitly (Bartl, 1968: 120).

15   These strictures do not apply to Noel Malcolm's previous book, *Bosnia, A Short History* (1994). Unlike Kosovo, Bosnia has enjoyed a continuous existence as an administrative and territorial unit, starting in the year 1180. When the Ottoman Turks conquered it in the fifteenth century, they made it a major administrative division (*eyalet*), in line with their usual principle of maintaining pre-conquest boundaries.

16   The fight over the past now has its own historian: V. A. Shnirelman (1996).

17   The evidence in not very conclusive. Hrabak's comments relate above all to Montenegro in the sixteenth century, and to its relations with the Ottoman Turks. Bartl's article is a study of a single tribal association, the Mirdites of Northern Albania, who revolted in the nineteenth century, possibly with the aim of setting up a Roman Catholic principality in the area, but refraining from taking part in the early-twentieth-century struggle for Albanian independence. The distribution of clans (or 'tribes') in Montenegro and northern Albania is usefully shown in Map 3.3 of Banac, 1984: 273.

18   These initial comments are mainly for purposes of illustration. A more detailed treatment will be given in Chapter 2.

19   The term 'South Caucasia' is preferred here to Transcaucasia. Professor Cyril Toumanoff has pointed out (1963: 11–12) that 'Transcaucasia' implies a view from the north – in other words, a Russian perspective. Ciscaucasia would also be a possibility, but this would imply a view from the south.

20   'Central Asia' can be defined as the five former Soviet republics of Kazakhstan, Kyrgyzstan, Uzbekistan, Turkmenistan and Tajikistan. 'Inner Asia' is a larger unit taking in Mongolia and Sinkiang. There is a case for treating 'Inner Asia' as the appropriate unit before the twentieth century, though we shall look mainly at 'Central Asia'.

21 There can, of course, be different views about how many successive 'minor' changes add up to a 'major' change. The subsequent growth of towns and non-agricultural pursuits resulted in the gradual and progressive entry of German and Jewish settlers into East Central Europe, most of whom were then, respectively, expelled and exterminated in the mid-twentieth century.

22 In saying this, I am adopting the views of Halil Inalcık, who concluded that there was 'no large-scale colonisation at all in the Balkans by Anatolian Turks' (1951: 686). An estimate of 100 000 Turkish immigrant households was made by Speros Vryonis, Jr, on the basis of the 1520–30 census (Vryonis, 1972: 165–6). This is put into perspective by the estimated total population of the Ottoman Empire in Europe at the time: 8 000 000. See Chapter 2 for a more detailed discussion of this issue.

2   The Formation of Ethnic Groups

1 A useful guide to the main territorial changes in both East Central and South Eastern Europe is provided by both the maps and the accompanying text of Magocsi (1993).

2 The contrary position has been strongly put by some authors. One example is Larry Wolff: 'The attempt to distinguish cultural regions involves cultural construction and intellectual invention' (1994: 356). Another is P. M. Kitromilides: 'It is better to think of continuous and interpenetrating layers and fragments and mutual cultural osmosis across far from impenetrable cultural frontiers' (1994: xiii).

3 According to P. Gunst (1989: 53–91) there was already by 1400 a gap between the more advanced region of East Central Europe and a less advanced South East Europe. This gap widened in the next four centuries (Lampe, 1989: 184).

4 There is a considerable scholarly literature on the linguistic aspect of the question, beginning as far back as the early nineteenth century, when Bartholomy Kopitar compared the Albanian, Romanian ('Wallachian') and Bulgarian languages (1829). The notion of a specifically Balkan language cluster (*Sprachbund*) was put forward by N. N. Trubetskoi in 1928, and was generally accepted until recently, when Norbert Reiter subjected it to severe criticism. The most recent studies of linguistic borrowing between Balkan languages, with numerous examples, are Schaller (1996) and Hinrichs (1999: 429–760). Edgar Hösch has given a number of examples of cultural influence across Balkan borders, such as Byzantine elements in Dalmatian (Catholic) religious architecture, and the use in Bosnia, Serbia and Bulgaria of building styles characteristic of the Saxon miners of Transylvania (1998: 617).

5 There were, of course, exceptions. The rural population (the overwhelming majority) were already Bulgarian, Romanian, Serbian, Albanian, Greek and so on; what changed was the composition of the towns, which under Ottoman rule 'became the collecting points for a motley mixture of nationalities' thanks to the empire's readiness to accept recruits to its ruling class from anywhere, provided they converted to Islam. See E. Hösch (1972: 104–9). See also the evidence presented by P. F. Sugar (1977: 222–4), although his conclusion (that 'the demographic map of South-eastern Europe was completely changed' as a result of the migrations of the late

seventeenth century) cannot be accepted, since his evidence refers entirely to the growth of towns, with their mixed ethnic composition.

6 O. L. Barkan, as quoted by N. Todorov (1983: 47), tends to stress the role of immigration: 'there were major changes in the ethnic distribution of the population in ... the Balkans, as a result of the permanent colonisation of the land by newcomers.' However Todorov himself puts a different view, at least for Bosnia and Herzegovina. There, he says, 'Islamization took place without massive Turkish colonization' (1983: 51). As we saw earlier, Inalcık also rejects the theory of large-scale Turkish colonization. Vryonis, for his part, concludes his discussion by saying that 'the bulk of Turkish settlement took place in Asia Minor rather than in the Balkans' (1972: 171), although he also states, somewhat inconsistently, that '50 per cent of the Balkan Muslim population counted in 1520–30 came from outside the peninsula' (1972: 162). In any case, whether by conversion, immigration or a mixture of the two, an extra element was added to the ethnic mix: Slavs who were Muslim by religion. It was a slow process: in the mid-sixteenth century the proportion of Muslims in the Balkans was fairly small (18.8 per cent of the total, or 195 000 households).

7 For Albanian borrowings from Latin and Greek, and to a lesser degree the Slav languages, see H. W. Schaller (1999: 466).

8 The following authors excluded Romania from the Balkans: B. C. Wallis (in 1924), M. R. Shackleton (in 1954), E. W. Hoffman (in 1963), E. Hösch (in 1972) and A. Blanc (in 1977). See D. Hall and D. Danta (1996: 5).

9 The composition of this class changed somewhat as a result of Habsburg land grants. Haumant lists the names of Italians, Germans and Magyars who settled in Croatia and were ennobled in the sixteenth and seventeenth centuries (1930: 323). We may presume that gradually they took on a Croat identity.

10 The southern part of Bosnia held on to its independence until 1482, under its 'Herceg' Stephen Vukčić Kosača and his successors (hence 'Hercegovina').

11 In more detail: M. R. Hickok (1997).

12 As argued by N. Malcolm (1994: 73).

13 See the brief summary by A. Djilas (1991: 10–11).

14 The Livs, who gave their name to Livonia, may also have been absorbed by the Latvians despite their originally Finno-Ugritic character.

15 Most of this paragraph also applies to the conditions governing the growth of Latvian culture.

16 Ukrainian historians have tended to treat the Kievan state as part of Ukrainian history, and Russian historians look on it as part of Russian history. Thus N. V. Riasanovsky writes of the 'well-developed literary language of the Kievan Russians' and the 'rich legacy' that Kiev left to 'the Russians' (Riasanovsky, 2000: 59–60); O. Subtelny, in contrast, avoids any reference to Russians, although he does not endorse explicitly Mihailo Hrushevsky's claim that the Ukrainians rather than the Russians are the heirs of the Kievan state (Subtelny, 1994: 53).

17 Rather characteristically, the Russian historian, N. V. Riasanovsky, refers to this as the Lithuanian–Russian state, 'organized on the Russian pattern' with Russian as its 'official language' (2000: 134).

18 There is disagreement among scholars about the nature of this language. Some regard it as Old Russian, or West Russian. One can at least be certain that it was a type of East Slavic (Bojtár, 1997: 189, n.41).

19 The Albanian alphabet was rediscovered in 1937. It comprised 52 letters, some identical to Armenian and Greek letters, but most were different (Toumanoff, 1963: 106, n.160). Some fragmentary Albanian inscriptions have been found, but not deciphered.

20 An early example is Z. Buniiatov (1965). Azerbaijani views on the question of Caucasian Albania were controverted immediately by Armenian scholars, who asserted that, far from being the starting-point of Azerbaijani history, the Albanian kingdom was an Armenian state. The Armenian point of view has been presented in detail by H. S. Anassian (1969: 299–330).

21 The claim that Mashtots invented the Georgian alphabet has been disputed by Georgian historians (Suny, 1994: 23)

22 There is still a considerable Armenian minority in Dzavakheti.

23 We have attempted here to summarize a complex and highly controversial history in one paragraph. Most modern Western scholars regard Central Asian ethnicity as a Soviet invention. This is not the view currently taken by Central Asian writers.

24 This does not by any means exhaust the list of *ethnies* on the territory of the former Soviet Union. In all other cases, however, the overwhelming preponderance of the Russian element made the issue not one of ethnic conflict but of the degree to which the state was prepared to step in to prevent complete assimilation. The story is told in Forsyth (1992).

3 Ethnic Groups into Nations

1 These figures come from official Polish census returns. There is some doubt about their accuracy. The proportion of Poles should, if anything, be revised downwards, given that the proportion of Roman Catholics in the 1921 statistics was 63.8 per cent, and the overwhelming majority of Poles described themselves in this way (Rothschild, 1974: 36). This further strengthens the general point about ethnic diversity in inter-war Poland.

2 After 1989, Polish historians were free to examine this process in detail and in an unprejudiced way (the Communists were never interested in raking up these unsavoury details, even though they were not responsible for the policies of the 1920s and 1930s). See the brief English surveys by Brubaker (1996: ch. 4), and Hann (1996: 389–406).

3 One possible candidate for a medieval Slovak state is the principality ruled by Máté Csák in the early fourteenth century. He was a Slovak, not in any ethnic sense, but simply because his feudal realm covered much of what is now Slovakia. See J. M. Kirschbaum (1960: 68) for the claim, and C. A. Macartney (1962: 34) for a different view. Kirschbaum later modified his position, pointing out in 1995 that Csák was 'a non-Slovak', although 'given the nature of his rule ... his reign could not have been without some direct impact on the life of the Slovaks' (Kirschbaum, 1995: 46).

4 Out of a pre-war population of 3.2 million,165 000 remained behind.

5 Letter of 1929, printed by J. M. Kirschbaum (1960: 239).

6 *Financial Times*, 23 February 2000, p.15.

7 See the useful outline of the story by I. J. Lederer (1969: 427–8).

8 A separate sense of Montenegrin nationality seems not to have existed at this time: though politically independent, the Montenegrins were divided into

clans orientated either to their own district or to Serbia: 'Most Montenegrins did not consider themselves a separate nation from Serbs' (Djilas, 1991: 63).

9 In the original: *Dvije vjere mogu se složti ka u sakan što se čorbe slažu* (Njegoš, 1947: lines 1020–1).

10 The Yugoslav (Serbian) geographer, Jovan Cvijić, was well aware of this borderline case, waxing lyrical over the 'Catholics of Dalmatia, who were the healthiest elements of all, retaining their Dinaric way of life, including the custom of the *slava*' (Cvijić, 1918: 542).

11 Ivo Banac (1984: 291–306) provides a succinct treatment of the *kaćak* episode.

12 Edith Durham's expression (1905: ix).

13 The construction of a Greek identity in the nineteenth century (Herzfeld, 1982: 11–13) is one example.

14 Kállay's policy has been examined in detail by E.Redžić (1965: 367–79).

15 *Jugoslavenska Muslimanska Organizacija.*

16 Some historians regard this view as exaggerated. See my brief discussion (Fowkes, 1997: 12–13).

4 Ethnicity and Nationhood under Communism

1 For a more detailed account see, for example, Fowkes (1997: 35–61).

2 The Baltic nations were part of the Russian Empire and would no doubt have been incorporated in the Soviet Union in the early 1920s if things had gone according to plan. As noted in Chapter 3, they were included temporarily in June 1940, then more permanently after the end of German occupation, in 1944–5.

3 Jeremy Smith quotes from the archives a number of 1921 resolutions by congresses of local ethnic groups demanding separation from the GASSR (Smith, 1999: 53).

4 The relevant administrative units, with their dates, are: Dagestan ASSR, 1921; Karachay–Cherkess AO, 1922; Chechen AO, 1922; Adygey AO, 1922; North Ossetian AO, 1924; Ingush AO, 1924; Kabardino–Balkar ASSR, 1923. The Chechen and the Ingush autonomies were combined in 1936 and promoted one stage up the administrative hierarchy to form a 'Chechen–Ingush ASSR'.

5 This is the post-1936 form of words; before 1936, 'Socialist' came second, and 'Soviet' fourth, in the official title.

6 A representative sample of the critics would be: Alexandre Bennigsen (1971), Ronald Wixman (1980), Hélène Carrère d'Encausse (1992) and Boris Chichlo (1987). One recent exception is Jeremy Smith, who argues that the small nationalities of the North Caucasus were divided by a history of ethnic conflict, so that they needed separate territories to stop inter-ethnic violence. Moreover, autonomous territories were not set up lightly: there was 'extensive research and discussion of the status of the nationalities involved' (Smith, 1999: 53–5).

7 For example, A. G. Trofimova (1968: 311–12); and Iu. Poliakov, who said, in an interview printed in *Current Digest of the Soviet Press*, vol. XL, no.11, 13 April 1988: 'It soon became clear that uniting many nationalities in a single republic was not feasible. In place of one republic, several autonomous

republics emerged.' A similiar view has been taken recently by A. Kh. Daudov. In his view, the 'political purpose' of the Mountain Republic was 'extinguished' by the victory of Soviet power in Transcaucasia; in addition the 'economic interests' of various segments of the republic required separation (Daudov ,1997: 184-5).

8 It should be noted that Soucek rejects the widespread Western criticism that 'national delimitation' was an exercise in creating artificial borders. As he says: 'Perfectly monoethnic and monolingual populations ... are a rare occurrence ... and virtually every national state must devise a compromise on how to deal with one or more minorities' (Soucek, 2000: 225). This view is also taken by Jeremy Smith: 'While it was a somewhat artificial process to create national groups in Central Asia, the task was approached in a thoroughly scientific manner' (Smith, 1999: 84).

9 An exception was made for the Armenians and the Georgians, as well as for non-Georgians within Georgia, who all had to use the Georgian alphabet.

10 There was a trend towards an improvement of the situation of non-Russians in the ASSRs of the RSFSR, but it was far weaker. See Miller (1977: 3–36) and Simon (1991: 274).

11 This is Table 2.12 of Hodnett (1978). Hodnett's figures cover the period from 1955 to 1972.

12 This point has been well made by Rogers Brubaker (1996: 104).

13 An Armenian petition of 1963 claimed that 'in forty years not a single kilometre of road has been constructed to link the villages with the regional centre' (Mutafian, 1994: 145).

14 Varying figures are given in the sources. The statistics quoted here are taken from A.-M. de Zayas (1993: 152).

15 The Lemkos regard themselves as Ruthenian rather than Ukrainian, a view that is not accepted by most Ukrainians. A number of Lemko cultural associations have emerged in Poland since 1989.

16 The Polish government has nevertheless experienced some difficulty in preventing local Polish nationalists in Przemyśl from taking provocative anti-Ukrainian measures. Thus the attempt by Ukrainian Uniates to secure restitution of their church, handed to the Roman Catholics in 1946, was defeated by Polish pressure groups, and in 1996 the local authority demolished the dome of the church, because it was a 'symbol of Ukrainian culture' (Hann, 1998: 857).

17 Even in Serbia, however, there was a strong movement in the literature of the 1980s away from the idea of Yugoslavism, notably in the historical novels of Dobrica Ćosić and Danilo Popović. This trend of opinion considered that the Serbs had made a 'fatal error' in trying to liberate their brother Slavs during the two world wars (Melčić, 1999: 224).

18 J. D. Eller insists that there is 'no such ethnicity as Bosnian', and prefers instead to use the word 'Muslim' (Eller, 1999: 295). This term is equally problematic, because it is too broad. There are plenty of Muslim Slavs outside Bosnia (in the Sandžak, for example).

19 J. Djordjevic, 'The Creation of the 1974 Constitution of the SFRY', in R. A. Goldwin and A. Kaufman (eds), *Constitution Makers on Constitution Making*, (Washington, DC: American Enterprise Institute, 1988), pp. 192–3.

20 This involves rejecting Botev's views on the rate of intermarriage, on the grounds, first, that he ignores its 'great symbolic value', so that a merely sta-

tistical approach is inappropriate, and, second, that mixed marriages did, in fact, increase both 'in absolute numbers and as a percentage of all marriages' (Hayden, 1996: 797, n.6).

21   In a sense, it had existed since the time of Ilja Garašanin, but the traditional Greater Serbia programme differed from the new one in that it claimed to encompass the whole of Yugoslavia, not just the ethnically Serb areas.

22   A useful overview and statistical treatment is given by Beissinger (1998).

23   For a detailed study, see A.Martiny (1979).

24   A good picture, full of piquant details, of the historiography of the non-Russians prior to 1968 is given by Lowell Tillett (1969).

25   The views of the main protagonists in this dispute have been presented by Robert Hewsen (1982). He adopts an intermediate position, describing both sides as 'reckless with the sources and prone to overstatement'. The population of south-east Caucasia (that is, what is now Azerbaijan) was, he says, 'a heterogeneous mass' consisting of 'a great variety of people, e.g. Caucasian mountaineers, proto-Georgians, Iranians, Armenians, Arabs, and Turkic tribes' (Hewsen, 1982: 35).

26   From an article by Professor N. Lomouri in the Georgian newspaper *Zaria Vostoka*, 22 January 1991.

5   The 1990s in Central and Eastern Europe

1   I follow here the usual convention of describing the citizens of Serbia as Serbians, but ethnic Serbs, wherever they might be, as Serbs. The same distinction can be made between Croatians (citizens of Croatia) and ethnic Croats, Slovenians and Slovenes, and, perhaps, Bosnians and Bosniaks.

2   A fifth conflict, in Macedonia, not set off by Belgrade, will be examined later.

3   'Bosnia' is shorthand for 'Bosnia and Hercegovina'. It would be unnecessarily pedantic to add 'Hercegovina' every time Bosnia is mentioned. In some cases, however, it is necessary to use all three words.

4   The use of the word 'Bosniak' (*Bošnjak*) reflects the self-description now generally accepted by Bosnian Muslims. Previously, the word tended to be used (at least by the Muslims) to cover all inhabitants of Bosnia-Hercegovina; the change in meaning results from the abandonment of the view that a single Bosnian identity could exist (Bringa 1995: 35–6).

5   L. J. Cohen sees this as a partial justification for the attitude of the Bosnian Serbs: 'it is not surprising that in 1992 many Bosnian Serbs had serious reservations about their status in an Izetbegovic-led state, because of his rejection of the Lisbon Agreement under pressure from the Muslim side' (1995: 244).

6   *Summary of World Broadcasts, Eastern Europe*, 17 February 1993, 1615/C1.

7   Remarkably, in May 1993 the Zagreb weekly *Globus* published the UN Human Rights Commission report on this massacre (Thompson, 1994: 194).

8   This was the wording of UN Security Council Resolution 1244 of 10 June 1999.

9   See C. Durandin (1994: 105).

10   For the opposition's shift towards nationalism in 1995, see Tom Gallagher (1996). The article reflects the situation in 1995; by 1996, it was already out of date.

11 See below.

12 *Financial Times*, 14 August 2001, p. 5.

13 This inclusive approach was shown by the party's official name, which was 'Coexistence', written in four different languages (Együttéles, Spolužitie, Wspolnota and Soužití).

14 *Summary of World Broadcasts*, Part Two: Central Europe, the Balkans, Third Series, EE/2233, 21 February 1995, p. A/1, reporting Havel's speech of 17 February 1995.

15 Dušan Třeštík has described it as 'a particularly stupid case of nationalism *in statu nascendi*' (1995: 175).

16 The UN Human Rights Commission estimated that there were 750 000 Roma (gypsies) in Yugoslavia, whereas the 1981 census gave a total of 168 000 (Duijzings 1997: 196).

6 Ethnic Conflict and Compromise in the Former Soviet Union

1 F. Bacon, 'The Essayes or Counsels, Civill and Morall, 1625. LXIII: Of Vicissitude of Things', in S. Warhaft (ed.), *Francis Bacon: A Selection of His Works* (London: Macmillan, 1965), p. 193.

2 *Nagorno-Karabakhskaia Avtonomnaia Oblast'* (Nagornyi Karabagh Autonomous Region).

3 Appeal to Mikhail Gorbachev, published in *Central Asian Newsletter*, vol. 7, nos. 5–6, Dec. 1988–Jan. 1989, pp. 7–8.

4 The contents of the November 1998 plan were first made public by President Aliev on 21 February 2001, possibly to prepare Azerbaijani opinion for a peace agreement.

5 As usual, diametrically opposite positions can be found in the literature on this. As we saw earlier, Darrell Slider took an essentially favourable view of the Brezhnev measures (1985: 65). Svetlana Chervonnaya dismissed Abkhaz complaints as being without foundation (Chervonnaya, 1994: 34). But the English specialist on Abkhazia, George Hewitt, considers that the measures brought 'no long-lasting improvement' for the Abkhazians (Hewitt, 1999: 282).

6 Data from *Itogi Vsesoiuznoi Perepisi Naseleniia 1970 Goda*, vol. 4, table 16.

7 Interview in September 1989, quoted by Chervonnaya (1994: 197, n. 64).

8 See also the revised version of this article (Jones, 1997: 516).

9 Gamsakhurdia also received support from another minority group, the Mingrelians, although this did not prevent his later military defeat and death, which probably took place in December 1993.

10 These refugees, who were expelled from the country after the successful Abkhazian military offensive against Georgia, numbered some 160 000 (300 000 according to the Georgians).Their language (Mingrelian) was different from Georgian, although they did not claim to be a separate nation.

11 The course of events in South Ossetia between 1989 and 1992 has recently been summarized clearly by A. Zverev (1996: 48–54).

12 The Azerbaijanis made up 5.7 per cent of the population of Georgia in 1989. Despite being under some pressure to leave, they have tended to stay where they are. The main ethnically Azerbaijani districts are Marneuli (79 per cent), Bolnissi (60 per cent) and Dmanissi (64 per cent) (Serrano, 1999: 232).

13 Together with the closely related Ingush they made up 70.8 per cent of the population in 1989. The two other ASSRs with a dominant titular nationality were Chuvashia and Tuva (both over 60 per cent in 1989).

14 Speech of 28 April 1999, translated in *Current Digest of the Post-Soviet Press*, vol. 51, no. 18, 1999: 8.

15 Jane Ormrod refers to the sending of 'between 800 and 1,000 fighters to Chechnia' (Ormrod, 1997: 131).

16 It should be noted that the Gagauz movement did not stick to this demand, and the boundaries of the eventual autonomous Gagauzia were drawn so as to maximize the proportion of Gagauz citizens (it turned out to be 79 per cent).

17 For developments up to 1991, see Fane (1993: 142–5).

18 The right of secession in case of union with Romania is guaranteed to Gagauzia under the 1994 Moldovan Constitution (Crowther, 1997: 349).

19 It should be said that Kolstø and his co-authors do not take as extreme a position as O'Loughlin on this question. They write: 'the ethnic dimension cannot be denied altogether: Russians and Ukrainians are over-represented in the PMR leadership' and the 'language policy of the PMR tends to perpetuate Russian linguistic hegemony', while the Moldovan government, for its part, 'is almost entirely composed of ethnic Moldovans' (Kolstø *et al.*, 1993: 976, 983).

20 The late Alexandre Bennigsen, the doyen of modern Central Asian studies in the West, was the leading supporter of this view.

21 It still remains to be seen whether the victorious Taliban forces in Afghanistan will be able to export their revolution northwards by force.

22 Russian net migration from the republics of Central Asia has been calculated by Tim Heleniak for the years 1989 to 1996. A total of 1 325 000 Russians left over that period. Of these, 678 000 left Kazakhstan (reducing the Russian minority to 33.9 per cent), 363 000 left Uzbekistan (down to 5.6 per cent), 188 000 Tajikistan (down to 3.4 per cent), 55 000 Turkmenistan (down to 6.6 per cent), and 41 000 from Kyrgyzstan (down to 15.6 per cent) (Heleniak, 1997a).

23 *OE*, June 1993, p. A330.

24 Gumppenberg also notes that, by 1997, the ethnic Russian element in the population had fallen to 32.2 per cent, and the Kazakhs, with 50.6 per cent, had at last recovered the majority position they lost in the 1930s.

25 Optimistic views are given by P. Kubicek (1998), and A. Prazauskas, who claims that 'regimes of an authoritarian character remain the only effective instrument to prevent ethno-political polarisation and instability in the region' (1998: 66). For a pessimistic view, see I. Bremmer and C. Welt (1996: 197): 'What has been gained in the way of short-term stability looks to be squandered on the creation of a solid undemocratic foundation.'

7 Reasons for Conflict and Prospects for the Future

1 As quoted in Hukanović (1997: 56).

2 The relationship between demands for economic autarchy and a decline in trade interdependence has been analyzed by R. L. Rudolph (1994: 67-70).

3 The militant Croat nationalism of the Franciscans in Hercegovina is also stressed by Michael Sells (1996: 101–11).

4 Admittedly, President Iliescu took steps to defuse the situation shortly afterwards.

5 See R. Veljanovski's very detailed study (2000: 565–86).

6 The exception was Chechnya.

7 For a very different view, see T. Goltz (1993). Goltz claims that there is strong circumstantial evidence of Russian involvement in successive crises in Azerbaijan and Georgia. The Russians, he says, were responsible for a massacre of Azerbaijanis which took place in February 1992 in Khodjali (in Karabagh), after the town fell to Armenian forces (the Armenian side denies these rumours); and for the successful Armenian assault on the town of Kelbajar in April 1993. Russian aeroplanes bombed the Georgian occupiers of Sukhumi, in Abkhazia, in February and March 1992. He concedes, however, that 'finding a smoking gun is difficult' (Goltz, 1993: 98). While Russian units may well have been involved in these incidents, they have not yet been shown to have acted under the instructions of the Russian authorities themselves. Zverev (1996: 35) claims that the actions of alleged Russian units in Azerbaijan were in fact carried out by Armenian soldiers of the Russian army who had joined the Nagornyi Karabagh side out of ethnic solidarity. This remains an area where there are more rumours than hard facts.

8 It should be noted that this is a very general work, dealing with overarching hypotheses. The one case study included (pp. 64–103) deals with post-1918 Poland.

9 The states listed here share another common feature that is relevant in this context: the absence of troublesome ethnic minorities. They exist, but are either too small to be of concern (for example, Poles and Russians in Lithuania) or in too insecure a position to cause much trouble Russians in Central Asia, for example.

10 There is a brief English account of these styles, written by Kim Burton, stressing the musical rather than the political aspect, in Broughton *et al.* (1999: 273–6).

11 Ethnic differences in folk music in the former Yugoslavia have presented been succinctly presented by Kim Burton (1994).

12 Svanibor Pettan has commented that the *gusle* 'goes for a cross-ethnic tradition', although in the 1990s it was 'increasingly being experienced as the Serbian counterpart to the Croatian *tamburica*' (Pettan, 1998: 16).

13 Van de Port has been criticized by D. M. Crowe (in a review in *ERS*, vol. 23, no. 1, January 2000: 162) for allegedly stereotyping the Roma community.

14 The author compares his study of Serb behaviour in the *kafana* with Clifford Geertz's path-breaking 1966 study of the Balinese cockfight, and with Joseba Zulaika's 1988 study of Basque cultural activities, which was similarly aimed at explaining terrorism (Port, 1998: 216).

15 See Čolović (1994: 87–110) and Žanić (1998, *passim*). The latter gives fewer specific examples, but includes a wide-ranging general treatment of the whole subject of the historical role of South Slav epics.

16 The *tambura* is by no means an exclusively Croatian instrument, just as the *gusle* is not exclusively Serbian; their strong ethnic associations are in each case side-effects of the conflict.

17 These questions have already been treated in detail in Chapters 5 and 6.

18 Wallace himself predicts that ethnic differences will not merely become less important but will *vanish* in the future, with the acceptance of cultural variety being only a transitional stage in this direction (Wallace, 1999: 153).

References

Akbal, F., 1831 'Tarihinde osmanlı imparatorluğunda idarî taksimat ve nüfus', *TTKB*, 15 (1951), pp. 617–28.

Allen, W. E. D., *A History of the Georgian People*, (London: Kegan Paul, 1932).

Allworth, E., *The Modern Uzbeks: From the Fourteenth Century to the Present* (Stanford, CA: Hoover Institution Press, 1990).

Altstadt, A., *The Azerbaijani Turks* (Stanford, CA: Hoover Institution Press, 1992).

Altstadt, A., 'Decolonization in Azerbaijan', in D. V. Schwarz and R. Panossian (eds), *Nationalism and History. The Politics of Nation-Building in Post-Soviet Armenia, Azerbaijan and Georgia* (Toronto: University of Toronto Press, 1994), pp. 95–125.

Anassian, H. S., 'Une mise au point relative à l'Albanie Caucasienne (Aluank')', *Revue des Études Armeniennes, Nouvelle Série*, VI, (1969), pp. 299–330.

Anderson, B., *Imagined Communities: Reflections on the Origin and Spread of Nationalism*, rev. edn (London: Verso, 1991).

Angelov, V., 'Politikata na BKP po makedonskiya văpros (juli 1948–1956)', *Istoricheski Pregled*, 52, 5 (1996), pp. 83–107.

Anzulovic, B., *Heavenly Serbia: From Myth to Genocide* (London: Hurst and Co., 1999).

Armstrong, J., *Nations Before Nationalism* (Chapel Hill, NC: University of North Carolina Press, 1982).

Atkepe, M. M., 'Kosowa, Kosovo', *EI2*, vol. 5 (Leiden: E. J. Brill, 1986), pp. 275–7.

Auty, R., 'Czech', in Schenker and Stankiewicz, *Slavic Literary Languages* (1980), pp. 163–82.

Aves, J., *Georgia: From Chaos to Stability* (London: Royal Institute of International Affairs, 1996).

Balaian, Z., *Mezhdu Adom i Raem. Karabakhskie Etiudy* (Moscow: Akademiia, 1995).

Baldauf, I., 'The Making of the Uzbek Nation', *CMRS*, 32, 1 (Jan–Mar. 1991), pp. 79–96.

Banac, I., *The National Question in Yugoslavia* (Ithaca, NY: Cornell University Press, 1984).

Banac, I. (1992a) 'The Fearful Asymmetry of War: The Causes and Consequences of Yugoslavia's Demise', *Daedalus*, 121, 2 (Spring 1992), pp. 141–74.

Banac, I. (1992b) 'Yugoslavia', *American Historical Review*, 97, 4 (October 1992), pp. 1084–104.

Banks, M., *Ethnicity: Anthropological Constructions* (London: Routledge, 1996).

Barac, A., *A History of Yugoslav Literature* (Ann Arbor, MI: University of Michigan Press, 1976).

Barany, Z., 'Living on the Edge: The East European Roma in Postcommunist Politics and Societies', *SR*, 53, 2 (1994), pp. 321–44.

Barany, Z. 'Grim Realities in Eastern Europe', *Transition*, I, 4 (29 March 1995), pp. 3–8.

Bartak, K., 'Moscou dans le bourbier Caucasien', *MD* (April 1993), pp. 16–17.

Barth, F., 'Introduction', in F. Barth (ed.), *Ethnic Groups and Boundaries: The Social Organization of Culture Difference* (Oslo: Universitetsforlaget, 1969), pp. 9–38.

Barthold, W. and G. Hazai, 'Kazak', *EI2*, vol. 4 (Leyden: E. J. Brill, 1978), pp. 848–9.

Bartl, P., *Die Albanischen Muslime zur zeit der nationalen Unabhängigkeitsbewegung (1878–1912)* (Wiesbaden: Otto Harrassowitz, 1968).

Bartl, P., 'Die Mirditen', *Münchner Zeitschrift für Balkankunde*, I (1978), pp. 27–69.

Bartlett, R., *The Making of Europe. Conquest, Colonization and Cultural Change 950–1350* (London: Allen Lane, 1993).

Bartoš, J. and J. Gagnaire, *Grammaire de la Langue Slovaque* (Paris: Institut des Études Slaves, 1972).

Bartoš, J. and M. Trapl, *Československo 1918–1938. Fakty, materiály, reálie* (Olomouc: Interpress, 1994).

Bates, D., 'The Ethnic Turks', *Turkish Review of Balkan Studies*, 1 (1993), pp. 193–203.

Bauer, A., A. Kappeler and B. Roth (eds), *Die Nationalitäten des Russischen Reichs in der Volkszählung von 1897*, vol. 2 (Stuttgart: Franz Steiner Verlag, 1991).

Bax, M., 'Warlords, Priests and the Politics of Ethnic Cleansing: A Case Study from Rural Bosnia-Hercegovina', *ERS*, 23, 1 (January 2000), pp. 16–36.

Bazin, A., 'La Question des Sudètes: un poids dans les relations Germano-Tchèque aujourd'hui', *l'Autre Europe*, 34–35 (1997), pp. 118–39.

Bebler, A., 'Yugoslavia's Variety of Communist Federalism', *CPCS*, 26, 1 (1993), pp. 72–86.

Beissinger, M., 'Nationalist Violence and the State', *Comparative Politics*, 30, 4 (July 1998), pp. 401–22.

Bennigsen, A., 'Islamic or Local Consciousness among Soviet Nationalities?', in E. Allworth (ed.), *Soviet Nationality Problems* (New York: Columbia University Press, 1971), pp. 168–82.

Beradze, G. G. and G. A. Apakidze (eds) *Po Povodu Iskazheniia Gruzino-Abkhazskikh Vzaimootnoshenii (Otvet avtoram "Abkhazskago pis'ma")* (Tbilisi: Metsniereba, 1991).

Berolowitch, W., 'Entre Marxisme et Ethnicité: l'anthropologie russe selon Ernest Gellner', *Genèses*, 33 (Dec.1998), pp. 128–37.

Bibikova, O., 'Dreyf v storony samostoiatel'nosti', *Vostok*, 6 (1993), pp. 85–90.

Birch, A. H., *Nationalism and National Integration* (Boston: Unwin Hyman, 1989).

Blanc, A., *L'économie des Balkans* (Paris: Presses Universitaires de France, 1977).

Bobrovnikov, V., 'The Islamic Revival and the National Question in Post-Soviet Dagestan', *Religion, State and Society*, 24, 2/3 (1996), pp. 233–8.

Boeckh, K., *Von den Balkankriegen zum Ersten Weltkrieg: Kleinstaatenpolitik und ethnische Selbstbestimmung auf dem Balkan* (Munich: R. Oldenbourg Verlag, 1996).

Bojtár, E., *Foreword to the Past. A Cultural History of the Baltic People* (Budapest: Central European University Press, 1997).

Bonifačić, R. 'Regional and National Aspects of *Tamburica* tradition: The Case of the *Zlatni Dukati* Neotraditional Ensemble', in Pettan, *Music, Politics and War* (1998) pp. 131–49.

Borneman, J., *Settling Accounts: Studies in Violence, Justice and Accountability in Post-Socialist Europe* (Princeton, NJ: Princeton University Press, 1997).

Borneman, J., *Subversions of International Order: Studies in the Political Anthropology of Culture* (Albany, NY: State University of New York Press, 1998).

Bosworth, C. E., 'Al-Kabk', *EI2*, vol. 4 (Leiden: E. J. Brill, 1978), pp. 341–50.

Botev, N.,'Where East Meets West: Ethnic Intermarriage in Former Yugoslavia, 1962–1989', *American Sociological Review*, 59 (June 1994), pp. 461–80.

Bougarel, X., 'The Emergence of a Pan-Islamist Trend in Bosnia-Herzegovina', *Islamic Studies*, 36, 2/3 (1990), pp. 533–50.

Bougarel, X., *Bosnie: Anatomie d'un conflit* (Paris: La Découverte, 1996).

Boyd, C. G., 'Making Bosnia Work', *FA*, 77, 1 (1998), pp. 42–55.

Brass, P. R., *The Politics of India since Independence* (Cambridge University Press, 1990).

Bremmer, I. and R. Taras (eds), *Nations and Politics in the Soviet Successor States* (Cambridge University Press, 1993).

Bremmer, I. and R. Taras (eds), *New States, New Politics: Building the Post-Soviet Nations* (Cambridge University Press, 1997).

Bremmer, I. and C. Welt, 'The Trouble with Democracy in Kazakhstan', *CAS*, 15, 2 (1996), pp. 179–99.

Breton, A., 'The Economics of Nationalism', *Journal of Political Economy*, 72, 4 (1964), pp. 376–86.

Bringa, T., *Being Muslim the Bosnian Way. Identity and Community in a Central Bosnian Village* (Princeton, NJ: Princeton University Press, 1995).

Bromlei, Iu. V., I. S. Gurvich, V. I. Kozlev, L. N. Terent'eva and K. V. Chistov (eds), *Sovremennye Etnicheskie Protsessy v SSSR* (Moscow: Izdatel'stvo Nauka, 1975).

Broughton, S., M. Ellingham and R. Trillo (eds), *World Music. Volume I: Africa, Europe and the Middle East. The Rough Guide*, 2nd edn (London: Rough Guides., 1999).

Brubaker, R., *Nationalism Reframed: Nationhood and the National Question in the New Europe* (Cambridge University Press, 1996).

Budding, A. H., 'Yugoslavs into Serbs: Serbian National Identity 1961–1971', *NP*, 25, 3 (1997), pp. 407–26.

Bugajski, J., *Ethnic Politics in Eastern Europe. A Guide to Nationality Policies, Organizations and Parties* (Armonk, NY: M. E. Sharpe, 1994).

Buniiatov, Z., *Azerbaidzhan v VII–IX vv.* (Baku: Izdatel'stvo Akademii Nauk Azerbaidzhanskoi SSR, 1965).

Burg, S. L. and P. S. Shoup, *The War in Bosnia-Herzegovina. Ethnic Conflict and International Intervention* (Armonk, NY: M. E. Sharpe, 1999).

Burton, K.,'Balkan Beats', in S. Broughton, M. Ellingham, D. Muddyman and R. Trillo (eds), *World Music. The Rough Guide*, 1st edn (London: Penguin, 1994), pp. 83–94.

Büscher, K., 'Separatismus in Transnistrien. Die PMR zwischen Russland und Moldova', *OE*, 46, 9 (1996), pp. 860–75.

Bushkov, V. I. and D. V. Mikul'skii, *Anatomiia Grazhdanskoi Voiny v Tadzhikistane (Etnosotsial'nye protsessy i politicheskaia bor'ba 1992–96)*, 2nd edn (Moscow: Institut Etnologii i Antropologii RAN, 1997).

Bútoru, M. and Z. Bútorová, 'Neznesitel'na l'ahkost' rozchodu', in R. Kipke and K. Vodička, *Rozloučení s Československem, Příčiny a dusledky Česko-Slovenského Rozchodu* (Prague: Interpress, 1993), pp. 119–50.

Byron, J. L., *Selection Among Alternates in Language Standardization. The Case of Albanian* (The Hague: Mouton, 1976).

Cabanes, B., 'Les Albanais d'Albanie, une identité blessée', *Esprit*, 265 (July 2000), pp. 23–31.

Carr, E. H., *Socialism in One Country 1924–1926*, vol. 3, pt 1 (London: Macmillan, 1964).

Carrère d'Encausse, H., *The Great Challenge: Nationalities and the Bolshevik State, 1917–1930* (New York: Holmes and Meier, 1992).

Chazan, N., 'Ethnicity in Economic Crisis', in D. L. Thompson and D. Ronen (eds), *Ethnicity Politics and Development* (Boulder, CO: Westview Press, 1986).

Chervonnaya, S., *Conflict in the Caucasus: Georgia, Abkhazia and the Russian Shadow* (Glastonbury: Gothic Image Publications, 1994).

Chichlo, B., 'Histoire de la Formation des Territoires Autonomes chez les peuples Turco-Mongols de Sibérie', *CMRS*, 28, 3/4 (Jul–Dec 1987), pp. 361–402.

Chirot, D. (ed.), *The Origins of Backwardness in Eastern Europe* (Berkeley, CA: University of California Press, 1989).

Chorbajian, L., P. Donabedian and C. Mutafian, *The Caucasian Knot. The History and Geo-Politics of Nagorno-Karabagh* (London: Zed Books, 1994).

Cigar, N., *Genocide in Bosnia: The Policy of Ethnic Cleansing* (College Station, TX: Texas A & M University Press, 1995).

Cohen, L. J., *Broken Bonds: Yugoslavia's Disintegration and Balkan Politics in Transition*, 2nd edn (Boulder, CO: Westview Press, 1995).

Cohen, L. J., 'Kosovo: Nobody's Country', *Current History*, 99, 635 (March 2000), pp. 117–23.

Cohen, L. and P. Warwick, *Political Cohesion in a Fragile Mosaic: The Yugoslav Experience* (Boulder, CO: Westview Press, 1983).

Čolović, I., *Bordell der Krieger. Folklore, Politik und Krieg* (Osnabrück: Fibre Verlag, 1994).

Čolović, I., 'Football, Hooligans and War', in N. Popov (ed.), *The Road to War in Serbia. Trauma and Catharsis* (Budapest: Central European History Press, 2000), pp. 372–96.

Comrie, B., *Languages of the Soviet Union* (Cambridge University Press, 1981).

Creed, G. W., 'The Politics of Agriculture in Bulgaria', *SR*, 54, 4 (Winter 1995), pp. 843–68.

Crowe, D. M., *A History of the Gypsies of Eastern Europe and Russia* (London: I. B. Tauris, 1995).

Crowther, W., 'Moldova: Caught between Nation and Empire', in Bremmer and Taras, *New States* (1997), pp. 316–49.

Curipeschitz, B., *Itinerarium der Botschaftsreise des Josef von Lamberg und Niclas Jurischitz durch Bosnien, Serbien, Bulgarien nach Konstantinopel 1530*, ed. E. Lamberg-Schwarzenberg (Innsbruck: Verlag der Wagner'schen Universitätsbuchhandlung, 1910).

Cvijić, J., *La Péninsule balkanique. Géographie humaine* (Paris: Librairie Armand Colin, 1918).

Dallago, B. and M. Uvalić, 'Distributive Consequences of Nationalism: The Case of Former Yugoslavia', *E-AS*, 50, 1 (1998), pp. 71–90.

Danforth, L., *The Macedonian Conflict: Ethnic Nationalism in a Transnational World* (Princeton, NJ: Princeton University Press, 1995).

Danforth, L. M.,'Claims to Macedonian Identity', *Anthropology Today*, 9, 4 (August 1993), pp. 1–10.

Daničić, D. (ed.), *Rječnik Hrvatskoga ili Srpskoga Jezika* (Zagreb: Tisak Dioničke Tiskare, 1880–2).

Dartchiachvili D. and C. Urjewicz, 'L'Adjarie, Carrefour de Civilisations et d'Empires', *CEMOTI*, 27 (Jan.–June 1999), pp. 263–83.

Daudov, A. Kh., *Gorskaia ASSR. Ocherki Sotsial'no-ekonomicheskoi Istorii* (St. Petersburg: Izdatel'stvo S-Petersburgskogo Universiteta, 1997).

Deny, J., 'Ottoman Armenia', *EI2*, vol. 1 (Leiden: E. J. Brill, 1960), pp. 640–1.

Deutsch, K. W., 'The Trend of European Nationalism', in J. A. Fishman (ed.), *Readings in the Sociology of Language* (The Hague: Mouton, 1968), pp. 598–606.

De Vos, G., 'Ethnic Pluralism: Conflict and Accommodation', in Romanucci-Ross and De Vos, *Ethnic Identity* (1995), pp. 15–47.

de Zayas, A.-M., *A Terrible Revenge. The Ethnic Cleansing of the East European Germans 1944–1950* (New York: St. Martin's Press, 1993).

Dimitrijević, V., 'Ethnonationalism and the Constitutions: The Apotheosis of the Nation-state', *Journal of Area Studies*, 3 (1993), pp. 50–6.

Dinić, M., 'The Balkans, 1018–1499', in J. M. Hussey (ed.), *The Cambridge Medieval History*, vol. 4, pt 1 (Cambridge University Press, 1966), ch. 12, pp. 519–65.

Dixon, S., 'The Russians and the Russian Question', in G. Smith (ed.), *The Nationalities Question in the Post-Soviet States*, 2nd edn (London: Longman, 1996), pp: 47–74.

Djilas, A, *The Contested Country. Yugoslav Unity and Communist Revolution 1919–1953* (Cambridge, MA: Harvard University Press, 1991).

Djordjevic, J., 'The Creation of the 1974 Constitution of the SFRY', in R. A. Goldwin and A. Kaufman (eds), *Constitution Makers on Constitution Making: The Experience of Eight Nations* (Washington, DC: American Enterprise Institute, 1988), pp. 184–209.

Dragadze, T., 'Interview with Neimat Panakhov', *Central Asian and Caucasus Chronicle*, 8, 5 (October 1989), pp. 1–3.

Drakulić, S., *How We Survived Communism and Even Laughed* (London: Vintage, 1993).

Dreifelds, J., *Latvia in Transition* (Cambridge University Press, 1996).

Drettas, G., 'L'Albanais national – du choix politique au choix linguistique', in I. Fodor and C. Hagège (eds), *Language Reform. History and Future*, vol. 4 (Hamburg: Helmut Buske Verlag, 1989).

Drezov, K., 'Macedonian Identity', in J. Pettifer (ed.), *The New Macedonian Question* (London: Macmillan, 1999), pp. 47–59.

Dudwick, N., 'The Case of the Caucasian Albanians: Ethnohistory and Ethnic Politics', *CMRS*, 31, 2–3 (1990), pp. 377–84.

Duijzings, G., 'The Making of Egyptians in Kosovo and Macedonia', in C. Govers (ed.), *The Politics of Ethnic Consciousness* (London: Macmillan, 1997), pp. 194–222.

Duijzings, G., *Religion and the Politics of Identity in Kosovo* (London: C. Hurst & Co., 2000).

Du Nay, A., *The Early History of the Rumanian Language* (Lake Bluff, IL: Jupiter Press, 1977).

Duncan, P. J. S., 'Ukraine and the Ukrainians', in G. Smith (ed.), *The Nationalities Question*, 2nd edn (1996), pp. 188–209.

Dunlop, J. B., *The Rise of Russia and the Fall of the Soviet Empire* (Princeton, NJ: Princeton University Press, 1993).

Dunn, O.,'Diskussion', *Zeitschrift für Ethnologie*, 121, 1 (1996), pp. 53–5.

Durandin, C., 'Occidentalistes et nationalistes en europe centrale et orientale: de la guerre froide à la guerre chaude', *l'autre Europe*, 28–29 (1994), pp. 105–14.

Durham, M. E., *The Burden of the Balkans* (London: Edward Arnold, 1905).

Durham, E., *High Albania* (London: Virago, 1985).

Džaja, S. M., *Bosnia-Herzegowina in der österreichisch-ungarischen Epoche (1878–1918). Die Intelligentsia zwischen Traditionen and Ideologien* (Munich: Oldenbourg Verlag, 1994).

Edmunds, T., 'Power and Powerlessness in Kazakh Society', *CAS*, 17, 3 (Sept. 1998), pp. 463–70.

Eisener, R., *Auf den Spuren des tadschikischen Nationalismus. Aus Texte and Dokumenten zur Tadschikischen SSR* (Berlin: Verlag Das Akademische Buch, 1991).

Eisener, R., 'Zum Bürgerkrieg in Tadschikistan. Einige aktuelle and historische Dimensionen der Konflikte', *OE*, 44, 8 (Aug. 1994), pp. 776–90.

Eller, J. D., *From Culture to Ethnicity to Conflict: An Anthropological Perspective on International Ethnic Conflict* (Ann Arbor, MI: University of Michigan Press, 1999).

Eminov, A., *Turkish and Other Muslim Minorities in Bulgaria* (London: Hurst and Co., 1997).

Eriksen, T. H., *Ethnicity and Nationalism: Anthropological Perspectives* (London: Pluto Press, 1993).

Esenova, S., 'Tribalism and Identity in Contemporary Circumstances: The Case of Kazakhstan', *CAS*, 17, 3 (Sept. I998), pp. 443–62.

Evans, G., 'Ethnic Schism and Consolidation of Post-Communist Democracy', *CPCS*, 31, 1 (Mar. 1998), pp. 57–74.

Fane, D., 'Moldova: Breaking Loose from Moscow', in Bremmer and Taras, *Nations and Politics* (1993), pp. 121–56.

Fishman, J. A., (ed.) *Readings in the Sociology of Language* (The Hague: Mouton, 1968).

Forsyth, J., *A History of the Peoples of Siberia. Russia's North Asian Colony 1581–1990* (Cambridge University Press, 1992).

Fowkes, B., *The Disintegration of the Soviet Union* (London: Macmillan, 1997).

Franolić, B.,'The Development of Literary Croatian and Serbian', in I. Fodor and C. Hagege (eds), *Language Reform. History and Future*, vol. 2 (Hamburg: Helmut Buske Verlag, 1983), pp. 85–112.

Friedman, F., *The Bosnian Muslims. Denial of a Nation* (Boulder, CO: Westview Press, 1996).

Friedman, V. A., 'Linguistics, Nationalism and Literary Languages: A Balkan Perspective', in P. C. Bjarkman and V. Raskin (eds), *The Real-World Linguist: Linguistic Applications in the 1980s* (Norwood, NJ: Ablex Publishing Corporation, 1986), pp. 287–305.

Friedman, V. A., 'The Romani Language in the Republic of Macedonia', *Acta Linguistica Hungarica*, 46, 3–4 (1999), pp. 317–39.

Friedman, V. A., 'The Modern Macedonian Standard Language and its Relation to Modern Macedonian Identity', in V. Roudometof (ed.), *The Macedonian Question: Culture, Historiography, Politics* (New York: Columbia University Press, 2000), pp. 173–206.

Frye, R. N., *The Golden Age of Persia. The Arabs in the East* (London: Weidenfeld & Nicolson, 1975).

Fuller, E., 'Trial of "Separatists"', *CAM*, 4 (2000), pp. 29–30.

Gabanyi, A.-U., 'Rumäniens neue Regierung Ciorbea: Bilanz nach 200 Tagen', *SOE*, 46, 7–8 (1997), pp. 341–72.

Gallagher, T., *Romania After Ceausescu. The Politics of Intolerance* (Edinburgh: Edinburgh University Press, 1995).

Gallagher, T., 'Nationalism and the Romanian Opposition', *Transition*, 2, 1 (12 January 1996), pp. 30–7.

Galoian, G. A. and K. S. Khudaverdian (eds), *Nagornyi Karabakh. Istoricheskaia Spravka* (Erevan: Izdatel'stvo A. N. Armianskoi SSR, 1988).

Gangloff, S., 'L'emancipation Politique des Gagouzes, Turcophones Chrétiens de Moldavie', *CEMOTI*, 23 (Jan.–June 1997), pp. 230–58.

Gantskaia, O. A., 'Problemy Men'shinstv v Gosudarstvennoi Politike Pol'shi (1945–1997gg.)', *EO*, 1 (2000), pp. 88–99.

Garb, P., 'Ethnicity, Alliance Building and the Limited Spread of Ethnic Conflict in the Caucasus', in D. A. Lake and D. Rothchild (eds), *The International Spread of Ethnic Conflict* (Princeton, NJ: Princeton University Press, 1998), pp. 185–99.

Gavazzi, M., 'Die kulturgeographische Gliederung Südosteuropas', *Südostforschungen*, 15, (1956), pp. 5–21.

Geiss, P. G., *Nationenwerdung in Mittelasien* (Frankfurt-am-Main: Peter Lang, 1995).

Gellner, E., *Thought and Change* (London: Weidenfeld & Nicolson, 1964).

Geyer, D., 'Der Nationalstaat im postkommunistischen Osteuropa', *OE*, 48, 7 (1998), pp. 652–710.

Gilberg, T., *Nationalism and Communism in Romania. The Rise and Fall of Ceausescu's Personal Dictatorship* (Boulder, CO: Westview Press, 1990).

Gilliland, M. K., 'Nationalism and Ethnogenesis in the Former Yugoslavia', in Romanucci-Ross and DeVos, *Ethnic Identity* (1995), pp. 197–221.

Gleason, G., *Federalism and Nationalism in the USSR* (Boulder, CO: Westview Press, 1991).

Goethe, J. W. von, 'Noten und Abhandlungen zu besserem Verständnis des West-Östlichen Divans' in *Sämtliche Werke*, Band 11. 1.2., ed. K. Richter (Munich: Carl Hanser Verlag, 1998), pp. 129–282.

Golden, P. B., 'The Turkic Peoples and Caucasia', in R. G. Suny (ed.), *Transcaucasia Nationalism and Social Change Essays in the History of Armenia, Azerbaijan, and Georgia*, rev ed. (Ann Arbor, MI: University of Michigan Press, 1996), pp. 45–67.

Goldstein, I., *Croatia. A History* (London: Hurst & Co., 1999).

Goltz, T., 'Letter from Eurasia: The Hidden Russian Hand', *Foreign Policy*, 92 (Fall 1993), pp. 92–116.

Goody, J., 'Bitter Icons', *New Left Review*, new series, 7(Jan.–Feb. 2001), pp. 5–15.

Grant, J., 'Decolonization by Default: Independence in Soviet Central Asia', *CAS*, 13, 1(1994), pp. 51–9.

Graus, F., 'Die Entstehung der mittelalterlichen Staaten in Mitteleuropa', *Historica* (Prague) 10 (1965).

Grbic´, J., 'Searching for the Familiar, Facing the Foreign', *Narodna Umjetnost*, 34,1(1997), pp. 7–23.

Greenberg, J. H., *Language in the Americas* (Stanford, CA: Stanford University Press, 1987)

Grimm, G., 'Ethnographic Maps of the Kosova Region from 1730–1913', in A. Pipa and S. Repishti (eds), *Studies on Kosova* (New York: Columbia University Press, 1984), pp. 41–53.

Grmek, M., M. Gjidara and N. Šimac (eds), *Le Nettoyage Ethnique, Documents historiques sur une idéologie serbe* (Paris: Fayard, 1993).

Grothusen, K. D., 'Städtewesen and nationale Emanzipation in Südosteuropa', in K. D. Grothusen (ed), *Ethnogenese und Staatbildung in Südosteuropa* (Göttingen: Vandenhoeck & Rupprecht, 1974), pp. 72–92.

Guindon, H., *Quebec Society: Tradition, Modernity and Nationhood* (Toronto: University of Toronto Press, 1988).

Gumppenberg, M. C. von, 'Elitenwandel in Kazakhstan', *OE*, 49, 3 (1999), pp. 256–71.

Gunst, P., 'Agrarian Systems of Central and Eastern Europe', in Chirot, *Origins of Backwardness* (1989), pp. 53–91.

Gurr, T. R., 'Ethnic Warfare on the Wane', *FA*. 79,3 (2000), pp. 52–64.

Gusher, A., 'Rossiia-Gruziia. Utrachennoe Doverie', *Aziia i Afrika Segodnaia*, 6, 515 (2000), pp. 2–8.

Guthier, S. L., 'The Belorussians: National Identification and Assimilation 1897–1970. Part 2', *Soviet Studies*, 29, 2 (April 1977), pp. 270–83.

Guthier, S.L., 'The Popular Basis of Ukrainian Nationalism in 1917', *SR*, 38, 1 (March 1979), p. 46.

Haarmann, H., *Language and Ethnicity. A View of Basic Ecological Relations* (Berlin: Mouton de Gruyter, 1986).

Hall, B., *The Imposibble Country. A Journey Through the Last Days of Yugoslavia* (London: Secker & Warburg, 1994).

Hall, D. and D. Danta, 'The Balkans: Perceptions and Realities', in D. Hall and D. Danta (eds), *Reconstructing the Balkans. A Geography of the New Southeast Europe* (Chichester: John Wiley, 1996) pp. 3–13.

Hammel, E.A., 'Demography and the Origins of the Yugoslav Civil War', *Anthropology Today*, 9,1(1993), pp. 4–9

Hammond, N. G. L., *Migration and Invasion in Greece and Adjacent Areas* (Park Ridge, NJ: Noyes Press, 1976)

Hann, C. E., 'Postsocialist Nationalism: Rediscovering the Past in Southeast Poland', *SR*, 57,4(Winter 1998), pp. 840–63.

Hann C. M., 'Ethnic Cleansing in Eastern Europe: Poles and Ukrainians besides the Curzon Line', *Nations and Nationalism*, 2 (1996), pp. 389–406.

Harrell, S., 'Languages Defining Ethnicity in Southwest China', in Romanucci-Ross and De Vos, *Ethnic Identity* (1995), pp. 97–114.

Hart, L. K., 'Culture, Civilization and Demarcation at the North Western Borders of Greece', *American Ethnologist*, 26, 1 (February 1999), pp. 196–22.

Haumant, E., *La Formation de la Yougoslavie* (Paris: Éditions Bossard, 1930).

Hayden, R. M., 'Constitutional Nationalism in the Formerly Yugoslav Republics', *SR*, 51,4 (Winter 1992), pp. 654–73.

Hayden, R. M., 'The Use of National Stereotypes', in A. Gerrits and N. Adler (eds), *Vampires Unstaked* (North-Holland, 1995), pp. 207–22.

Hayden, R.M., 'Imagine Communities and Real Victims: Self-determination and Ethnic Cleansing in Yugoslavia', *American Ethnologist*, 23, 4 (Nov. 1996), pp. 783–801.

Hechter, M., *Containing Nationalism* (Oxford University Press, 2000).

Heinemann-Grüder, A., 'Integration durch Asymmetrie', *OE*, 48, 7 (1998).

Heinemann-Grüder, A., '1st Separatismus Unvermeidlich? Ein Rücklick auf Ethnizität und Föderalismus im Tschetschenien Konflikt', *OE*, 49, 2 (1999), pp. 160–74.

Heleniak, T. (1997a) 'The Changing Nationality Composition of the Central Asian and Transcaucasian States', *P-SGE*, 38, 6 (1997), pp. 357–78.

Heleniak, T. (1997b) 'Internal Migration in Russia during the Economic Transition', *P-SGE*, 38,2 (1997) pp. 81–104.

Herzfeld, M., *Ours Once More: Ideology and the Making of Modern Modern Greece* (Austiar University of Texas Press, 1982)

Hewitt, G., 'Abkhazia, Georgia and the Circassians', *CAS*, 18,4 (1999), pp. 463–89.

Hewsen, R., 'Ethnohistory and the Armenian Influence on the Caucasian Albanians', in T. Samuelian (ed.), *Classical Armenian Culture* (Armenian Texts and Studies, 4) (Chico, CA: Scholars Press 1982) pp. 27–40.

Hickok, M. R., *Ottoman Military Administration in Eighteenth Century Bosnia* (Leiden: E.J. Brill, 1997).

Hinrichs, U. (ed.), *Handbuch der Südosteuropa-Linguistik* (Wiesbaden: Harrassowitz Verlag, 1999).

Hitchins, K., *The Rumanian National Movement in Transylvania. 1780–1849* (Cambridge, MA: Harvard University Press, 1969).

Hobsbawm, E., 'Ethnicity and Nationalism in Europe Today', *Anthropology Today*, 8, 1(1992), pp. 3–8.

Hodnett, G., *Leadership in the Soviet National Republics: A Quantitative Study of Recruitment Policy* (Oakville, Ontario: Mosaic Press, 1978).

Hoensch, J. K., *Studia Slovaca. Studien zur geschichte der Slowaken und der Slowakei*, Veröffentlichungen des Collegium Carolinum, Band 93 (Munich: R. Oldenbourgh Verlag, 2000).

Hoffman, E. W., *The Balkans in Transition* (Princeton, NJ: Van Nostrand, 1963).

Holubychny, V., 'Spatial Efficiency in the Soviet Economy', in V. N. Bandera and Z. L. Melnik (eds), *The Soviet Economy in Regional Perspective* (New York: Praeger, 1973), pp. 1–43.

Holy, L., *The Little Czech and the Great Czech Nation. National Identity and the Post-communist Transition* (Cambridge University Press, 1996).

Hopf, C., *Sprachnationalismus in Serbien und Griechenland* (Wiesbaden: Harrassowitz Verlag, 1997).

Hösch, E., *The Balkans, A Short History from Greek Times to the Present Day* (London: Faber & Faber, 1972).

Hösch, E., 'Kulturgrenzen in Südosteuropa', *SOE*, 47, 12 (1998), pp. 601–23.

Hosking, G., *Russia: People and Empire 1552–1917* (London: Fontana Press, 1998).

Houle, R., 'Russes et non Russes dans la direction des institutions politiques et economiques en URSS', *CMRS*, 38, 3(1997), pp. 347–66.

Hrabak, B., 'Stočarsko-voljničko društvo Crne Gore u XVI veku', *Istorijski Zapisi*, 60 (1987), pp. 41–68.

Hroch, M., *Social Preconditions of National Revival in Europe* (Cambridge University Press, 1985).

Hukanović, R., *The Tenth Circle of Hell: A Memoir of Life in the Death Camps of Bosnia* (New York: Basic Books, 1996).

Huskey, E., 'Kyrgyzstan: The Politics of Demographic and Economic Frustration', in Bremmer and Taras, *New States* (1997), pp. 654–80.

Hussey, J. M. (ed.), *The Cambridge Medieval History*, vol. 4, pt 1 (Cambridge University Press, 1966).

Inalcık, H., 'Remarks on an Essay on the Economical Situation of Turkey', *TTKB*, 15(1951), pp. 85–90.

Inalcık, H., 'Rumeli', *E12*, vol. 8 (Leiden: E. J. Brill 1995), pp. 607–11.

Ivanova, Iu. V., 'Etnicheskie Protsessy na zapade balkanskogo poluostrova', *EO*, 5, (1999), pp. 80–97.

Izetbegović, A., *Islamska deklaraciia* (Sarajevo: Bosna, 1990).

Jackson, M. R., 'Changes in Ethnic Populations of Southeastern Europe: Holocaust, Migration and Assimilation', in R. Schönfeld (ed.), *Nationalitätenprobleme in Südosteuropa* (Munich: R. Oldenbourg Verlag, 1987), pp. 73–104.

Jelavich, C., *South Slav Nationalism. Textbooks and Yugoslav Union before 1914* (Columbus, OQ: Ohio State University Press, 1990).

Jelavich, C., 'Milenko M. Vukičević: Fom Serbianism to Yugoslavism', in D. Deletant and H. Hanak (eds), *Historians as Nation-Builders: Central and South-East Europe* (London: Macmillan, 1988), pp. 106–123.

Jelavich, C. and B. Jelavich, *The Establishment of the Balkan National States, 1804–1920.* (Seattle, Wash.: University of Washington Press, 1977).

Jenkins, R., 'Nations and Nationhood. Towards More Open Models', *Nations and Nationalism*, I, 3 (1995), pp. 369–90.

Jones, S. F., 'Georgia: A failed Democratic Transition', in Bremmer and Taras, *Nations and Politics* (1993), pp. 288–310.

Jones, S. F., 'Georgia: The Trauma of Statehood', in Bremmer and Taras, *New State* (1997), pp. 505–46.

Juchler, J., *Osteuropa im Umbruch: Politische, wirtschaftliche und gesellschaftliche Entwicklungen 1989–1993. Gesamüberblick und Fallstudien* (Zürich: Seismo Verlag, 1994).

Judah, T., 'Kosovo's Road to War', *Survival*, 41, 2 (Summer 1999), pp. 5–18.

Judah, T., *Kosovo, War and Revenge* (New Haven, CT: Yale University Press, 2000).

Kaiser, R. J., 'Ethnic Demography and Inter-state Relations in Central Asia', in R. Szporluk (ed.), *National Identity and Ethnicity in Russia and the New States of Eurasia* (Armonk, N.Y.: M. E. Sharpe, 1994), pp. 230–65.

Kaplan, R. D., *Balkan Ghosts. A Journey through History* (New York: St. Martin's Press, 1993)

Kaplan, R. D., *The Ends of the Earth. A Journey at the Dawn of the 21st Century* (London: Macmillan, 1996).

Karakasidou, A., *Fields of Wheat, Hills of Blood. Passages to Nationhood in Greek Macedonia 1870–1990* (Chicago: University of Chicago Press, 1997).

Karcz, J. F., 'Reflections on the Economics of Nationalism and Communism in Eastern Europe', *East European Quarterly*, 5, 2 (1971), pp. 232–59.

Karpat, K. H., 'The Balkan National State and Nationalism: Image and Reality', *Islamic Studies*, 36 2/3 (1997), pp. 329–60.

Kaufman, S. J., 'Spiraling to Ethnic War: Elites, Masses and Moscow in Moldova's Civil War', in M. F. Brown *et al.* (eds), *Nationalism and Ethnic Conflict. An International Security Reader* (Cambridge: MA: MIT Press, 1997), pp. 169–99.

Kedourie, E., *Nationalism* (London: Hutchinson, 1960).

Kiaupa, Z., J. Kiaupiene and A. Kuncevičius, *The History of Lithuania before 1725* (Vilnius: Lithuanian Institute of History, 2000).

Kideckel, D. A., *The Solitude of Collectivism. Romanian Villagers to the Revolution and Beyond* (Ithaca NY: New York Cornell University Press, 1993).

King, R. R., *Minorities under Communism. Nationalities as a Source of Tension among Balkan Communist States* (Cambridge, MA: Harvard University Press, 1973).

Kirch, M. and A. Kirch, 'Ethnic Relations: Estonians and Non-Estonians', *NP*, 23, 1 (Spring 1995), pp. 43–59.

Kirschbaum, J. M., *Slovakia: Nation at the Crossroads of Europe* (New York: Robert Speller, 1960).

Kirschbaum, J. M., *A History of Slovakia: The Struggle for Survival* (London: Macmillan, 1995).

Kitromilides, P. M., 'Imagined Communities and the Origins of the National Question in the Balkans', *European History Quarterly*, 9, 2 (1989). pp. 149–92.

Kitromilides, P. M., *Enlightenment, Nationalism, Orthodoxy: Studies in the Culture and Political Thought of South-Eastern Europe* (Aldershot: Variorum, 1994).

Knight, A., *Beria. Stalin's First Lieutenant* (Princeton: Princeton University Press, 1993).

Kofos, E., *Nationalism and Communism in Macedonia* (Thessaloniki: Institute for Balkan Studies, 1964).

Kolstø, P., 'Anticipating Demographic Superiority. Kazakh Thinking on Integration and Nation-Building', *E-AS*, 50, 1, (1998), pp. 51–69.

Kolstø, P., A. Edemsky and N. Kalashnikova, 'The Dniester Conflict: Between Irredentism and Separation', *E-AS*, 45, 6 (1993), pp. 973–1000.

Kolstø, P. and A. Malgin, 'The Transnistrian Republic: A Case of Politicised Regionalism', *NP*, 26, 1 (1998) pp. 103–27.

Koneski, B., 'Macedonian', in Schenker and Stankiewicz, *Slavic Literary Languages* (1980), pp. 53–63.

Konstantinou, Y., 'Strategies for Sustaining a Vulnerable Identity: The Case of the Bulgarian Pomaks', in H. Poulton and S. Taji-Farouki (eds) *Muslim Identity and the Balkan State* (London: Hurst and Co., 1997), pp. 33–53.

Koroteyeva, V. and E. Makarova, 'The Assertion of Uzbek National Identity: Nativization or State-building Process?', T. Atabaki and J.O.'Kane (eds), *Post-Soviet Central Asia* (London: I. B. Tauris, 1998), pp. 137–43.

Kraster, I., 'Back to Basic in Bulgaria', *Transition*, 3, 4, 7 (7 March 1997),

Krawchenko, B., *Social Change and National Consciousness in Twentieth Century Ukraine* (London, 1985).

Kremenchiev, B. A., *Bulgarian and Macedonian Folk Music* (Berkeley, CA: University of California Press, 1956).

Kruus, H., *Histoire de l'Estonie* (Paris: Payot, 1935).

Kubicek, P., 'Authoritarianism in Central Asia', *Third World Quarterly*, 19, 1 (1998), pp. 29–44.

Kubicek, P., 'What Happened to the Nationalists in Ukraine?', *Nationalism and Ethnic Politics*, 5, 1 (1999), pp. 29–45.

Kuran, T., 'Ethnic Dissimulation', in R. B. Lake and D. Rothchild (eds), *The International Spread of Ethnic Conflict* (Princeton, NJ: Princeton University Press, 1998), pp. 35–60.

Laber, J., 'Bosnia. Questions about Rape', *The New York Review of Books* (25 March, 1993), pp. 3–6.

Laitin, D. D., *Identity in Formulation: The Russian-speaking Population in the Near Abroad* (Ithaca, NY: Cornell University Press, 1998).

Lampe, J. R., 'Redefining Balkan Backwardness', in Chirot, *Origins of Backwardness*, (1989), pp. 177–209.

Lampe, J. R., *Yugoslavia as History. Twice there was a Country* (Cambridge University Press, 1996).

Lederer, I. J., 'Nationalism and the Yugoslavs', in P. F. Sugar and I. J. Lederer (eds), *Nationalism in Eastern Europe* (Seattle, Wash.: University of Washington Press, 1969), pp. 396–438.

Leeper, N. E., 'Ossetians', *EI2*, vol. 8 (Leiden: E. J. Brill, 1995), pp. 179–80.

Leff, C. S., *National Conflict in Czechoslovakia. The Making and Remaking of a State* (Princeton, NJ: Princeton University Press, 1988).

Leff, C. S., 'Democratization and Disintegration in Multinational States: The Breakup of the Communist Federations', *World Politics*, 51, 2 (Jan. 1999), pp. 205–35.

Lezhava, G. P., *Mezhdu Gruziei i Rossiei* (Moscow: Institute Etnologii i Antropologii RAN, 1997).

Lieven, A., *Chechnya.Tombstone of Russian Power* (New Haven, CT: University Press, 1998).

Ling, J., *A History of European Folk Music* (Rochester, NY: University of Yale Rochester Press, 1997).

Lipkin, S., *Dekada* (New York: Chalidze Publications, 1983).

Liu, G., 'Ethnic Harmony and Conflict in Central Asia', in Zhang and Azizian, *Ethnic Challenges* (1998) pp. 73–92.

Lockwood, W., *Eurorean Moslems : Economy and Ethnicity in Western Bosnia* (New York: Academic Press, 1975).

Lockwood, W., 'Living Legacy of the Ottoman Empire: the Serbo-Croatian Speaking Muslims of Bosnia-Hercegovina', in A. Ascher, T. Halasi-Kun and B. K. Király (eds), *The Mutual Effects of the Islamic and Judeo-Christian Worlds: The East European Pattern* (Brooklyn College Press, 1978), pp. 209–25.

Loit , A., 'Die Nationalen Bewegungen im Baltikum während des 19 Jahrhunderts in vergleichender Perspektive', in A. Loit (ed.), *National Movements in the Baltic Countries during the 19th Century* (Acta Universitatis Stockholmensis. Studia Baltica Stockhomensia, 2)(Stockholm, 1985), pp. 59–77.

Longuet-Marx, F., 'La Tchétchénie', *Esprit*, 260 (Jan 2000), pp. 6–14.

Lyon, J. M. B., 'Will Bosnia Survive Dayton?', *Current History*, 99, 635 (March 2000), pp. 110–16.

Macartney, C. A., *Hungary: A Short History* (Edinburgh: Edinburgh University Press, 1962).

MacKenzie, D., 'The Background: Yugoslavia since 1964', in G. W. Simmonds (ed.), *Nationalism in the USSR and Eastern Europe* (Detroit, 1977), pp. 446–56.

Magid, A., *Private Lives/Public Surfaces* (Boulder, CO: Columbia University Press, 1991).

Magocsi, P. R., *Historical Atlas of East Central Europe* (Seattle, Wash.: University of Washington Press, 1993).

Magocsi, P. R., 'Une Nouvellé Nationalite Slave: les Ruthènes de l'Europe du Centre-Est', *Revue des Études Slaves*, 69, 3 (1997), pp. 417–28.

Malcolm, N., *Bosnia, A Short History* (London: Macmillan, 1994).

Malcolm, N., *Kosovo, A Short History* (London: Macmillan, 1998).

Manutscharjan, A., 'Lewon Ter-Petrosjan', *Orient. Deutsche Zeitschrift für Politik und Wirtschaft des Orient*, 39, 3 (Sept. 1998), pp. 377–84.

Marples, D. R., *Belarus: A Denationalized Nation* (Amsterdam: Harwood Academic Publishers, 1999).

Martin, T. (1998a) 'Origins of Soviet Ethnic Cleansing', *JMH*, 70 (Dec. 1998), pp. 813–61.

Martin, T. (1998b) 'The Russification of the RSFSR', *CMRS*, 39, 1–2 (1998), pp. 99–118.

Martin, T. D., 'An Affirmative Action Empire. Ethnicity and the Soviet State, 1923–1938', Ph.D. dissertation, University of Chicago (1996), 2 vols.

Martiny, A., 'Das Verhältnis von Politik und Geschichtsschreibung in der Historiographie der sowjetischen Nationalitäten', *Jahrbücher für die Geschichte Osteurogas*, 27 (1979), pp. 238–72.

Masaryk, T. G., *Slovanské problémy* (Prague: Státni nakladatelstvi, 1928).

Mayo, P., 'Belorussian', in B. Comrie and G. C. Corbett (eds), *The Slavonic Languages* (London: Routledge, 1993), pp. 887–946.

Meininger, T. A., *The Formation of a Nationalist Bulgarian Intelligentsia, 1835–1878* (New York: Garland Publishing, 1987).

Melčić, D., 'Der Jugoslawismus und sein Ende', in D. Melčić (ed.) *Der Jugoslawien-Krieg. Handbuch zu Vorgeschichte, Verlauf und Konsequenzen.* (Opladen: Westdeuthscher Verlag, 1999), ch. 14, pp. 208–226.

Meshcheriakov, V., 'Armeniia. Zalozhnitsa chuzhoi geopolitiki?', *Aziia i Afrika Segodnaia*, 8, 517 (2000), pp. 2–9.

Meštrović, S. G., *Habits of the Balkan Heart: Social Character and the Fall of Communism* (College Station, TX: Texas A & M University Press, 1993).

Miller, J. L., 'Cadres Policy in Nationality Areas', *Soviet Studies*, 29 (1977), pp. 3–36.

Millet, Y., 'Continuité et Discontinuité: cas du Tchèque', in I-Fodor and C. Hagège (eds) *Language Reform. History and Future*, vol. 2 (Hamburg: Helmut Buske Verlag, 1983), pp. 479–504.

Milosz, C., 'Vilnius, Lithuania: An Ethnic Agglomerate', in Romanucci-Ross and De Vos, *Ethnic Identity* (1995) pp. 249–63.

Moacanin, N., 'Les Croates et l'empire Ottoman. Quelques reflexions sur leurs rapports', *RIMM*, 66(1992–4), pp. l35–8.

Moser, C. A., *A History of Bulgarian Literature, 865–1944* (The Hague: Mouton, 1972).

Motyl A. J., 'After Empire: Competing Discourses and Inter-State Conflict in Post-Imperial Eastern Europe', in B. R. Rubin and J. Snyder (eds), *Post-Soviet Political Order: Conflict and State Building* (London: Routledge, 1998), pp. 14–33.

Mouradian, C., 'Problémes linguistiques et culturels en Arménie depuis Stalin: résistance nationale ou intégration sovie´tique?', *Slovo* (Paris), 5(1984), pp. 111–3.

Mucha, J., 'The Problem of the Cultural Dilemma of Ethnic Minorities in Poland', in B. Baila and A. Sterbling (eds), *Ethnicity, Nation, Culture. Central and East European Perspectives* (Hamburg: Verlag Dr. R. Krämer, 1998), pp. 165–77.

Muiznieks, N., 'Latvia: Restoring a State, Rebuilding a Nation', in Bremmer and Taras, *New States* (1997), pp. 376–403.

Mutafian, C., 'Karabagh in the Twentieth Century', in Chorbajian *et al.*, *The Caucasian Knot* (1994), pp. 109–70.

Nagel, J., 'Constructing Ethnicity: Creating and Recreating Ethnic Identity and Culture', *Social Problems*, 41, 1 (Feb 1994), pp. 152–76.

Najcevska, M., E. Simoska and N. Gaber, 'Muslims, State and Society in the Republic of Macedonia: The View from Within', in G. Nonneman, T. Niblock and B. Szajkowski (eds), *Muslim Communities in the New Europe* (London: Ithaca Press, 1996), pp. 75–97.

Neuburger, M. (1997a) 'Bulgarian Nationalism and the Re-dressing of Muslim Women 1878–1989', *NP*, 25, (1 Mar. 1997) pp. 169–83.

Neuburger, M. (1997b) 'Bulgaro-Turkish Encounters and the Re-imaging of the Bulgarian Nation 1878–1995', *East European Quarterly*, 31, 1 (Mar. 1997), pp. 1–20.

Nichanian, M., *Ages et Usages de la Langue Arménienne* (Paris: Editions Entente, 1989).

Njegoš, P. P., *Gorski Vijenac*, (Belgrade: Jugoslovenska knjiga, 1947).

Olcott, M. B., 'Central Asia's Catapult to Independence', *Foreign Affairs*, 71, 3 (Summer 1992), pp. 108–30.

O'Loughlin, J., V. Kolossov and A. Tchepalyga, 'National Construction, Territorial Separation and Post-Soviet Geopolitics in the Transdniestr Moldovan Republic', *P-SGE*, 9, 6 (1998), pp. 332–58.

Ormrod, J., 'The North Caucasus: Confederation in Conflict', in Bremmer and Taras, *New States* (1997), pp. 96–131.

Ozgan, K., 'Abkhazia – Problems and the Path to their Resolution', in O. Høiris and S. M. Yürükel (eds), *Contrasts and Solutions in the Caucasus* (Aarhus: Aarhus University Press, 1998), pp. 184–9.

Paillarès, M., *L'Imbroglio Macédonien* (Paris: P.-V. Stock, 1907).

Pavković, A., 'The Serb National Idea: A Revival, 1986–1992', *Slavonic and East European Review*, 72, 3 (1994), pp. 449–55.

Payne, J., 'Tajikistan and the Tajiks', in G. Smith, *The Nationalities Question* (1996), pp. 367–84.

Pennington, A. and P. Levi (with introduction and notes by S. Koljević), *Marko the Prince: Serbo-Croat Heroic Songs* (London: Duckworth, 1984).

Peroutka, F., *Budování Statu*, vol. 1 (first published 1933) (Prague: Lidové noviny, 1991).

Petrović, R., 'The National Composition of the Yugoslav Population', *Yugoslav Survey*, 1 (1992), pp. 3–24.

Pettai, V. and M. Kreuzer, 'Party Politics in the Baltic States: Social Bases and International Context', *EEPS*, 13, 1 (Winter 1999), pp. 148–89.

Pettan, S., 'Music, Politics and War in Croatia in the 1990s: An Introduction', in S. Pettan (ed.) *Music, Politics and War: Views from Croatia* (Zagreb: Institute of Ethnology and Folklore Research, 1998), pp. 9–27.

Piirimäe, H., 'The Use of the Estonian Language during the Swedish Rule', in A. Loit and H. Piirimäe (eds), *Die Schwedischen Ostseeprovinzen Estland und Livland im 16–18. Jahrhundert* (Uppsala: Textgruppen i Uppsala AB, 1993), pp. 367–82.

Pinson, M., 'The Muslims of Bosnia-Hercegovina under Austro-Hungarian rule, 1878–1918', in M. Pinson (ed.), *The Muslims of Bosnia-Hercegovina* (Cambridge, MA: Harvard University Press, 1994), pp. 84–128.

Popov, N. (ed.), *The Road to War in Serbia. Trauma and Catharsis* (Budapest: Central European History Press, 2000).

Port, M. van de, *Gypsies, Wars and Other Instances of the Wild: Civilization and its Discontents in a Serbian Town* (Amsterdam: Amsterdam University Press, 1998).

Povrzanović, M., 'The Imposed and the Imagined as Encountered by Croatian War Ethnographers', *Current Anthropology*, 41, 2 (Apr. 2000), pp. 151–62.

Pražák, A., *Češi a Slováci: literárně dějepisné poznámky k československému poměru* (Prague: Státní nakladatelství, 1929).

Prazauskas, A., 'Ethnopolitical Issues in Central Asia', in Zhang and Azizian, *Ethnic Challenges* (1998), pp. 50–69.

Qosja, R., *La Question Albanaise* (Paris: Fayard, 1995).

Radić, R., 'The Church and the "Serbian Question"', in Popov, *The Road to War in Serbia* (2000), pp. 247–73.

Radvanyi, J. and N. Berontchachvili, 'L'Adjarie, atout et point sensible de la Géorgie', *CEMOTI*, 27 (Jan–June 1999), pp. 229–39.

Ramer, A. M., P. A. Michalove, K. S. Baertsch and K. L. Adams, 'Exploring the Nostratic Hypothesis', in J. C. Salmons and B. D. Joseph (eds), *Nostratic: Sifting the Evidence* (Amsterdam: John Benjamin, 1993), pp. 61–84.

Ramet, S. P., 'Shake, Rattle and Self-Management: Making the Scene in Yugoslavia', in S. P. Ramet (ed.), *Rocking the State: Rock Music and Politics in Eastern Europe and Russia* (Boulder, CO: Westview Press, 1994), pp. 103–40.

Raun, T. U., *Estonia and the Estonians* (Stanford, CA: Hoover Institution Press, 1987).

Raun, U., 'Estonia: Independence Redefined', in Bremmer and Taras, *New States* (1997), pp. 404–33.

Redžić, E., 'Kállays Bosnische Politik. Kállays These über die "Bosnische Nation"', *Österreichische Osthefte*, 7 (1965), pp. 367–79.

Reuter, J., 'Serbien and Kosovo. Das Ende eines Mythos', *SOE*, 48, 11–12 (1999), pp. 629–45.

Reynolds, S., *Kingdoms and Communities in Western Europe 900–1300* (Oxford University Press, 1992).

Riasanovsky, N. V., *Nicholas I and Official Nationality* (Berkeley, CA: University of California Press, 1959).

Riasanovsky, N. V., *A History of Russia*, 6th edn (Oxford University Press, 2000).

Ridgway, J., 'Preface', in J. Udovički and J. Ridgway (eds), *Burn This House. The Making and Unmaking of Yugoslavia* (Durham, NC: Durham University Press, 1997), pp. ix.

Rodinson, M., *Cult, Ghetto and State* (London: Al Saqi Books, 1983).

Rohde, D., 'Kosovo Seething', *Foreign Affairs*, 79, 3 (May–June 2000), pp. 65–79.

Romanucci-Ross, L. and G. De Vos (eds), *Ethnic Identity. Creation, Conflict and Accommodation* (London: Sage, 1995).

Roosens, E. E., *Creating Ethnicity: The Process of Ethnogenesis* (London: Sage, 1989).

Rothberg, G. E, *The Austrian Military Border in Croatia, 1522–1747* (Urbana, IL: University of Illinois Press, 1960).

Rothschild, J., *East Central Europe between the Two World Wars* (Seattle, Wash.: University of Washington Press, 1974).

Roucek, J. S., *Central Eastern Europe* (New York: Prentice-Hall, 1946).

Roy, O., *The New Central Asia: The Creation of Nations* (London: I. B. Tauris, 2000).

Rudolph, R. L., 'Reflections on Economic Nationalism in Eastern Europe 1945–1989', in V. Heuberger, O. Kolar, A. Suppan and E. Vyslonzi1 (eds), *Nationen, Nationalitäten, Minderheiten. Probleme des Nationalismus, 1945–1990* (Vienna: Verlag für Geschichte und Politik, 1994), pp. 55–76.

Samary, C., 'L'opposition Serbe au piège de la reconstruction', *MD* (Feb. 2000), p. 8.

Sarkisyanz, E., *Geschichte der orientalischen Völker Russlands bis 1917. Eine Ergänzung zur ostslawischen Geschichte Russlands* (Munich: R. Oldenbourg, 1961).

Schaller, H.-W. (ed.), *Sprache und Politik: die Balkansprachen in Vergangenheit and Gegenwart*, Südosteuropa Jahrbuch 27 (Munich: Südosteuropa-Gesellschaft, 1996).

Schaller, H. -W, 'Die Lehnwortbeziehungen der Sprache in Südosteuropa', in Hinrichs, *Handbuch der Südosteuropa-Linguistik* (1999), pp. 463–85.

Schenker, A. M. and E. Stankiewicz (eds), *The Slavic Literary Languages: Formation and Development* (New Haven, CT.: Yale Commission on International and Area Studies, 1980).

Schmaus, A., 'Volks- and Hochkultur in Südosteuropa', in *Gesammelte Slawistische und Balkanologische Abhandlungen. Teil II* (Munich: Dr. Dr. Rudolf Trofenik, 1973), pp. 291–302.

Schmidt, F. and P. Moore, 'Die Albaner im ehemaligen Jugoslawien als Sicherheitsfaktor', in G. Seewann (ed.), *Minderheiten als Konfliktpotential in Ostmittel- und Südosteuropa* (Munich: R. Oldenbourg Verlag, 1995), pp. 70–139.

Schmidt-Neke, M., 'Makedoniens Albaner: Konfliktpotential oder Stabilisierungsfaktor?', *SOE*, 48, 3–4 (1999), pp. 191–212.

Schoeberlein-Engel, J., 'The Prospects for Uzbek National Identity', *CAM*, 2 (1996), pp. 12–20.

Sekelj, L., *Yugoslavia: The Process of Disintegration* (New York: Columbia University Press, 1993).

Sekelj, L., 'Parties and Elections in the Federal Republic of Yugoslavia', *E-AS*, 52, 1 (2000), pp. 57–73.

Sells, M. A., *The Bridge Betrayed: Religion and Genocide in Bosnia* (Berkeley, CA: University of California Press, 1996).

Senn, A. E., 'Lithuania: Rights and Responsibilities of Independence', in Bremmer and Taras, *New States* (1997), pp. 353–69.

Serrano, S., 'Les Azéris de Géorgie: quelles perspectives d'intégration?', *CEMOTI*, 28 (Jun.–Dec. 1999), pp. 231–51.

Seton-Watson, R.W., *Slovakia Then and Now* (London: Allen & Unwin, 1931).

Shackleton, M. R., *Europe, a Regional Geography* (London: Longmans, 1954).

Sharlet, R., 'Russian Constitutional Crisis: Law and Politics under Yel'tsin', *Post-Soviet Affairs*, 9, 4 (Oct.–Dec. 1993), pp. 314–36.

Shnirelman, V. A., *Who Gets the Past? Competition for Ancestors Among Non-Russian Intellectuals* (Washington, DC: Johns Hopkins University Press, 1996).

Simon, G., *Nationalism and Policy towards the Nationalities in the Soviet Union* (Boulder, CO: Westview Press, 1991).

Slezkine, Yu., 'The U.S.S.R. as a Communal Apartment, or How a Socialist State Promoted Ethnic Particularism', *SR*, 53, 2 (1994), pp. 414–52.

Slider, D., 'Crisis and Response in Soviet Nationality Policy: the Case of Abkhazia', *CAS*, 4, 4 (1985), pp. 51–68.

Smith, A. D., *The Ethnic Revival* (Cambridge University Press, 1981).

Smith, A. D., *Ethnic Origins of Nations* (Oxford University Press, 1986).

Smith, A. D., *National Identity* (London: Penguin Books, 1991).

Smith, G., 'The Soviet State and Nationalities Policy', in G. Smith (ed.), *The Nationalities Question in the Post-Soviet States*, 2nd edn (Longman, 1996), pp. 2–22.

Smith, J., *The Bolsheviks and the National Question, 1917–23* (London: Macmillan, 1999).

Smolii, V. A. (ed.), *Istoriia Ukrainy* (Kiev: Alternatyvy, 1997).

Socor, V., 'Why Moldova Does Not Back Re-unification', *RFE/RLRR*, 1, 5 (1992), pp. 27–33.

Soucek, S., *A History of Inner Asia* (Cambridge University Press, 2000).

Srubar, I., 'Ethnicity and Social Space', in B. Balla and A. Sterbling (eds), *Ethnicity, Nation, Culture, Central and East European Perspectives* (Hamburg: Verlag Dr. R. Krämer, 1998), pp. 47–63.

Stalin, I. V., *Sochineniia*, vol. 4 (Moscow: Gosizpollit, 1947).

Stalin, J., 'Marxism and the National and Colonial Question', in *Works*, vol. 2 (1907–13) (Moscow: Foreign Languages Publishing House, 1953).

Starchenkov, G. and M. Makhkamov, 'Tadzhikskaia Tragediia: Final ili Antrakt?', *Aziia i Afrika Segodnaia*, 11, 437 (1993), pp. 26–30.

Stavrianos, L. S., *The Balkans Since 1453* (New York: Holt, Rinehart & Winston, 1958).

Stoianov, V., *Turskoto Naselenie văv Bălgaria mezhdu poliusite na etnicheskata politika* (Sofia: Lik, 1998).

Stojanović, D.,' The Traumatic Circle of the Serbian Opposition', in Popov, *Road to War* (2000), pp. 449–78.

Subtelny, O., *Ukraine. A History*, 2nd edn (Toronto: University of Toronto Press, 1994).

Sugar, P. F., *Southeastern Europe under Ottoman Rule, 1354–1804* (Seattle, Wash.: University of Washington Press, 1977).

Sumbatzade, A. S., *Azerbaidzhantsy – etnogenez i formirovanie naroda* (Baku: Elm, 1990).

Sundhaussen, H., 'Nationenbildung and Nationalismus im Donau-Balkan-Raum', *Forschungen zur osteuropäischen Geschichte*, 48 (1993), pp. 233–58.

Suny, R. G., *Looking Toward Ararat. Armenia in Modern History* (Bloomington, Ind.: Indiana University Press, 1993).

Suny, R. G. *The Making of the Georgian Nation*, 2nd edn (Bloomington, Ind.: Indiana University Press, 1994).

Suny, R. G., 'Nationalism and Social Class in the Russian Revolution: The Cases of Baku and Tiflis', in Suny, R. G. (ed.), *Transcaucasia Nationalism and Social Change. Essays in the History of Armenia, Azerbaijan, and Georgia*, revd edn (Ann Arbor, MI: University of Michigan Press, 1996), pp. 241–60.

Suny, R. G., 'Provisional Stabilities', *International Security*, 24, 3 (1999–2000), pp. 139–78.

Šušak, B., 'An Alternative to War', in Popov, *Road to War* (2000), pp. 479–508.

Swietochowski, T., *Russian Azerbaijan 1905–1920: The Shaping of National Identity in a Muslim Community* (Cambridge University Press, 1985).

Swietochowski, T., 'Russia's Transcaucasian Policies and Azerbaijan: Ethnic Conflict and Regional Unity', in M. Buttino (ed.), *In a Collapsing Empire. Underdevelopment, Ethnic Conflicts and Nationalisms in the Soviet Union*, Annali Feltrinelli, vol. 28 (Milan: Feltrinelli, 1993), pp. 189–96.

Swietochowski, T., 'National Consciousness and Political Orientations in Azerbaijan, 1905–1920', in Suny (ed.), *Transcaucasia* (1996), pp. 218–23.

Szarka, L., 'Geschichte der Slowaken und des multinationalen ungarischen Staates im Spiegel aktueller ungarischer Schulbücher', *SOE*, 46, 9–10 (1997), pp. 511–27.

Tanner, M., 'Illyrianism and the Croatian Quest for Statehood', *Daedalus*, 126, 3 (Summer 1997), pp. 47–62.

Thomas, R., *Serbia under Milošević: Politics in the 1990s* (London: Hurst, 1999).

Thompson, M., *Forging War: The Media in Serbia, Croatia and Bosnia-Hercegovina* (London: Article 19, International Centre Against Censorship, 1994).

Thomson, R. W., 'The Origins of Caucasian Civilization: The Christian Component', in Suny (ed.) *Transcaucasia* (1996), pp. 25–43.

Tillett, L., *The Great Friendship: Soviet Historians on the Non-Russian Nationalities* (Chapel Hill, NC: University of North Carolina Press, 1969).

Todorov, N., *The Balkan City 1500–1900* (Seattle, Wash.: University of Washington Press, 1983).

Toumanoff, C., 'Iberia on the Eve of Bagratid Rule: An Enquiry into the Political History of Eastern Georgia between the VIth and the IXth Century', *Le Muséon*, 65 (1952), pp. 199–258.

Toumanoff, C., 'Introduction to Christian Caucasian History', *Traditio*, 15 (1959), pp. 1–106.

Toumanoff, C., *Studies in Christian Caucasian History* (Washington, DC: Georgetown University Press, 1963).

Toumanoff, C., 'Armenia and Georgia', in Hussey (ed.), *Cambridge Medieval History*, (1966), ch. 14, pp. 593–637.

Třeštík, D., 'Moderne Nation, Hochmittelalterliche Politische Nation', in A. Bues and R. Rexheuser (eds), *Mittelalterliche Nationes – Neuzeitliche Nationen. Probleme der Nationenwerdung in Europa* (Wiesbaden: Harrassowitz Verlag, 1995), pp. 161–81.

Troebst, S., 'Makedonische Antworten auf die "Makedonische Frage" 1944–1992: Nationalismus, Republiksgründung, Nation-Building', *SOE*, 41, 7/8 (1992), pp. 423–42.

Troebst, S., 'Autonomiebewegungen im Osteuropa der Nach "Wende"-Zeit. Mähren-Schlesien, Subkarpaten-Rus' und Gagausenland', *OE*, 49, 6 (1999), pp. 597–615.

Trofimova, A. G., 'Razvitie Literatury i Iskusstva', in V. K. Gardanov (ed.), *Kul'tura i Byt Narodov Severnogo Kavkaza (1917–1967gg)* (Moscow: Izdatel'stvo Nauka, 1968), pp. 303–28.

Trubetskoi, N. N., 'Proposition 17', in *Actes du Premier Congrès International des Linguistes à la Haye, du 10–15 April 1928* (Leiden: A. W. Sijthoff's Uitgevers-maatschappij N.V., 1930), pp. 17–18.

Tscherwonnaja, S., 'Der Ossetisch-Inguschische Konflikt II', *OE*, 45, 9 (1995), pp. 825–9.

Tscherwonnaja, S., Die Karatschaier und Balkaren im Nordkaukasu – Konflikte und ungelöste Probleme', *Orient*, 41, 1 (2000), pp. 83–111.

Udovički, J. and J. Ridgway (eds), *Burn This House. The Making and Unmaking of Yugoslavia* (Durham, NC: Durham University Press, 1997).

Ugrešić, D., *The Culture of Lies. Antipolitical Essays* (London: Phoenix House, 1998).

Uvalić, M., 'Disintegration of Yugoslavia', *CEET*, 5, 3 (1993), pp. 273–93.

Vakar, N. P., *Belorussia: The Making of a Nation: A Case Study* (Cambridge, MA: Harvard University Press, 1956).

Vardys, V. S. and J. B. Sedaitis, *Lithuania: The Rebel Nation* (Boulder, CO: Westview Press, 1997).

Varshney, A., 'Postmodernism, Civic Engagement and Ethnic Conflict', in *Comparative Politics*, 30, 1 (Oct. 1997), pp. 1–20.

Vateishvili, D. L., *Russkaia Obshchestvennaia Mysl' i Pechat' na Kavkaze v pervoi treti XIX veka* (Moscow: Izdatel'stvo "Nauka", 1973).

Veljanovski, R., 'Turning the Electronic Media Around', in Popov, *Road to War*, (2000), pp. 565–86.

Verdery, K., *Transylvanian Villagers* (Berkeley, CA: University of California Press, 1983).

Verdery, K., *National Ideology under Socialism. Identity and Cultural Politics in Ceausescu's Romania* (Berkeley, CA.: University of California Press, 1991).

Verdery, K. (1993a) 'Ethnic relations, economies of shortage and the transition in Eastern Europe', in C. M. Hann (ed), *Socialism: Ideals, Ideologies and Local Practice*, ASA Monographs 31 (London: Routledge, 1993).

Verdery, K. (1993b) 'Nationalism and National Sentiment in Post-Communist Romania', *SR*, 52, 2 (1993), pp. 179–203.

Verdery, K. (1993c) 'Whither "Nation" and "Nationalism"?', *Daedalus*, 122, 3 (1993), pp. 37–45.

Verdery, K, 'Ethnicity, Nationalism, and State-making', in Vermeulen and Govers, *Anthropology of Ethnicity* (1996), pp. 33–58.

Vermeulen, H. and C. Govers (eds), *The Anthropology of Ethnicity* (The Hague: Martinus Nijhoff, 1996).

Vickers, M., *The Albanians. A Modern History* (London: I. B. Tauris, 1995).

Vickers, M., *Between Serb and Albanian. A History of Kosovo* (London: Hurst & Co., 1998).

Volkan, V., *Bloodlines. From Ethnic Terrorism* (Boulder, CO: Westview Press, 1997).

Volkova, N. G. and L. I. Lavrov, 'Sovremennye etnicheskie protsessy', in V. K. Gardanov (ed.), *Kul'tura i Byt Narodov Severnogo Kavkaza (1917–1967gg)* (Moscow: Nauka, 1968), pp. 329–46.

Vryonis, S., Jr, 'Religious Changes and Patterns in the Balkans, 14th–16th Centuries', in H. Birnbaum and S. Vryonis, Jr, (eds) *Aspects of the Balkans: Continuity and Change* (The Hague: Mouton, 1972), pp. 151–76.

Vuckovic, G., *Ethnic Cleavage and Conflict: The Sources of National Cohesion and Disintegration. The Case of Yugoslavia* (Aldershot: Ashgate, 1997).

Vujović, S., 'An Uneasy View of the City', in Popov, *Road to War* (2000), pp. 123–45.

Wachtel, A. B., *Making a Nation, Breaking a Nation. Literature and Cultural Politics in Yugoslavia* (Stanford, CA: Stanford University Press, 1998).

Wagley, E. and M. Harris, *Six Case Studies: Minorities in the New World* (New York: Columbia University Press, 1964).

Wallace, W. L., *The Future of Ethnicity, Race and Nationality* (Westport, CT: Praeger, 1999).

Wallis, B. C., *Europe*, vol. 1 (London: Edward Stanford, 1924).

Wardhaugh, R., *Investigating Language. Central Problems in Linguistics* (Oxford: Basil Blackwell, 1993).

Ware, R. B. and E. Kisriev, 'The Islamic Factor in Dagestan', *CAS*, 19, 2 (Jun. 2000), pp. 235–52.

Ware, R. B. and E. Kisriev, 'Ethnic Parity and Democratic Pluralism in Dagestan: A Consociational Approach', *E-AS*, 53, 1 (Jan. 2001), pp. 105–32.

Werner, K. F., 'Les Nations et le sentiment national dans l'Europe médiévale', *Revue Historique*, 244 (1970), pp. 285–304.

West, R., *Black Lamb and Grey Falcon*, vol. 1 (Edinburgh: Canongate Press, 1993).

Whitelam, K. H., *The Invention of Ancient Israel* (London: Routledge, 1996).

Wiet, É., 'Mémoire sur le Pachalik de Prisrend', *Bulletin de la Société de Géographie*, 5th series, vol. 12 (October 1866), pp. 273–89.

Wilkinson, H. R., *Maps and Politics* (Liverpool: Liverpool University Press, 1951).

Willemsen, H. and S. Troebst, 'Transformationskurs Gehalten', *OE*, 3, 51 (2001), pp. 299–315.

Williams, R. M., Jr, 'Sociology of Ethnic Conflicts: Comparative International Perspectives', *Annual Review of Sociology* 20 (1994), pp. 49–80.

Wilson, A., *Ukrainian Nationalism in the 1990s. A Minority Faith* (Cambridge University Press, 1997).

Wittkowsky, A., 'Der Nationalstaat als Rentenquelle. Determinante der ukrainischen Politik', *Internationale Politik und Gesellschaft*, 2 (1999), pp. 150–61.

Wixman, R., *Language Aspects of Ethnic Patterns and Processes in the North Caucasus* (Chicago, IL: University of Chicago, 1980).

Wolff, L., *Inventing Eastern Europe: The Map of Civilization on the Mind of the Enlightenment* (Stanford, CA: Stanford University Press, 1994).

Woodward, S., *Balkan Tragedy: Chaos and Dissolution after the Cold War* (Washington, DC: The Brookings Institution, 1995).

Žanić, I., *Prevarena povijest. Guslarska estrada, kult hajduka i rat u Hrvatskoj j Bosnii-Hercegovini 1990–1995* (Zagreb: Durieux, 1998).

Zaprudnik, J., *Belarus: At a Crossroads in History* (Boulder, CO: Westview Press,1999).

Zhang, Y. and R. Azizian (eds), *Ethnic Challenges Beyond Borders: Central Asian Conundrums* (London: Macmillan, 1998).

Zimmerman, W., 'Is Ukraine a Political Community?' *CPCS*, 31, 1 (Mar. 1998), pp. 43–55.

Zverev, A., 'Etnicheskie Konflikty na Kavkaze 1986–1994', in B. Coppieters (ed.), *Spornye Granitsy na Kavkaze* (Moscow: Izdatel'stvo Ves' Mir, 1996), pp. 10–76.

Index